HOCKEY'S QUIET REVOLUTIONARY
CLARE DRAKE
THE COACHES' COACH

DEREK DRAGER

Library and Archives Canada Cataloguing in Publication

Drager, Derek, 1954-
Clare Drake, the coaches' coach : hockey's quiet revolutionary / Derek Drager.

Co-published by: Corporate Identity Inc.
and the Faculty of Physical Education & Recreation, University of Alberta
Includes bibliographical references and index.
ISBN 978-0-919035-30-0 (leather bound).–ISBN 978-0-919035-32-4 (bound). –
ISBN 978-0-919035-34-8 (pbk.)

1. Drake, Clare, 1928- 2. Golden Bears (Hockey team) – History.
3. University of Alberta – Sports – History. 4. University of Alberta –
Hockey – Biography. 5. Hockey coaches – Alberta – Biography.
6. Hockey coaches – Canada – Biography. I. University of Alberta. Faculty
of Physical Education and Recreation. II. Title.

GV848.5.D65D74 2007   796.962092   C2007-905076-X

Copyright ©2007 Derek Drager
All rights reserved.
No part of this publication may be produced, stored in a retrieval system or transmitted in any form or by any means, electronic, mechanical, photocopying, recording, or otherwise, without prior permission from the copyright owners.

Designed by Richard Pape
Edited by Katherine Koller
Printed and bound by Friesens in Altona, Manitoba, Canada

CONTENTS

Foreword – *vii*

Introduction – *viii*

Chapter One – *Whose Game is it Anyway?* – *2*

Chapter Two – *"Play up! play up! and play the game!"* – *18*

Chapter Three – *Firsts: The Russians, A Scouting Report, A National Title* – *40*

Chapter Four – *A Man Ahead of His Time* – *72*

Chapter Five – *The Russians... Again!* – *114*

Chapter Six – *"The man's fingerprints are all over the game"* – *140*

Chapter Seven – *Clare Drake on Coaching* – *170*

Acknowledgements – *192*

Index – *196*

*For Clare and Dolly
and
Jack and Joan
and
All the Golden Bears*

Foreword

I never played for Clare Drake. I never coached for him or against him. But I've spent over a quarter of a century watching him, listening to him and learning from him. I'm proud to call him a mentor, and I know I'm not the only one in my profession who feels this away about him. There are many other head and assistant coaches in the NHL who feel the way I do, and many more again coaching in minor pro, university and junior.

Some of them are his ex-players or worked on staffs he headed, quite a few coached against him, and by now, maybe the majority are from the second or even third generation – guys, and women, in coaching who learned from someone who learned from Clare. I'd even guess there are a lot of coaches using concepts they learned through Canada's National Coaching Certification Program who aren't aware of one of the main sources of it all. Indirectly, they've been mentored by Clare as well.

The point is, all of us in this profession, no matter what level we work at, owe Clare a huge vote of thanks. I might even go so far as to say he's a big reason that those of us who love hockey, who love to teach the game, build teams and see young people succeed, can even call ourselves professionals. He was among the very first to apply professional standards to coaching in our game. He helped define the game. His innovative, analytical brain helped turn hockey from shinny into the organized, patterned-yet-still-creative sport we see today.

And it wasn't just his mind that exerted such great influence; it was his heart too. He started sharing what he knew and what he'd learned through his own observation and experience. He did this in a time when nobody else would even think of doing it. He did it humbly, respectfully and consistently over many years, so that others started doing it as well and after a while we had a coaching fraternity in Canada that turned into a coaching certification program that turned into a whole system of teaching and developing coaches. Not only did he help start all this with his values around learning and teaching and sharing knowledge, but he coached young men through tumultuous decades of social change in our culture. All the while he stayed true to his values – teamwork, loyalty, discipline, collaboration, integrity, respect – and soldiered on, instilling them in young people while everything changed around him.

I've always been intrigued by the question of how and why Clare was able to achieve what he did. He's never cared much about getting credit, and except from those of us within the coaching profession, he hasn't really received the credit he deserves. So I'm excited that the whole story's finally been told. This book is long overdue and it should be a good read for hockey fans everywhere. Because it's the story of how one man worked quietly and faithfully for half a century to change a game now embraced by millions around the world.

Ken Hitchcock
Columbus, Ohio
March / 2007

Introduction

I met Clare Drake and Sir Douglas Bader on the same day. It was the first time I'd spoken to either man; one I would never see again, the other would have a profound impact on my life. It was during the summer of 1976… July, I think; I remember the day as cool, windy and grey. The occasion was the Canadian Paralympic Games, hosted by the University of Alberta, staged at the campus track and field oval immediately to the west of what was then called Varsity Arena. Bader was there because, as a double amputee, he was one of the world's most famous "handicapped" people. The term "persons with disabilities" had not yet been invented.

Sir Douglas Bader was one of the great Allied heroes of World War II. I'd read his story in *Reach for the Sky*, an inspirational, yet true, tale of airborne derring-do that could scarce have been dreamed up by the most imaginative writer of fiction. Bader had scored a heroic hat trick with me during my hopeful, middle-class adolescence: he had lost both legs during the 1930s, yet still managed to fly a Spitfire to glory during the Battle of Britain; he was shot down and escaped his burning aircraft by unbuckling his wooden legs, leaving them in the plane and parachuting to safety; and, to top it all, he convinced his German captors to allow the Red Cross to airlift him a new pair of legs, then promptly escaped on them. Whatta guy!

I'd walked over to the U of A track from my on-campus apartment hoping to see Bader because I'd heard he would be there. In those days, there was no security or accreditation at public events like this; besides, paralympic sports were still way beyond the pale of public interest and awareness. So into the athletics grounds I wandered and there, off to the side from a small knot of onlookers, stood my hero. He wore a blue blazer, grey slacks, white shirt and yellow ascot, looking like an older version of the man in the pictures of his book. He looked very British, much like my uncles, whom I knew to be kind and interesting gentlemen, if somewhat reserved.

But when I approached and blurted out my sense of honor and privilege at meeting him, spoke of my long-time familiarity with and admiration for his exploits, I got virtually nothing in response. There was no warm glint in the eye with fatherly pat on back nor proffered encouragement to become my own man; not even stammered thanks with shy smile; nothing but a hesitant handshake and an incommunicative grunt. He was, indeed, British, to the very core! In retrospect, I realize I had probably embarrassed him. I also learned later from other sources that some knew him to be not all that nice a guy. But at the time, I could only walk away struggling with conflicting feelings, mature enough to understand that I had no right to expect anything from the man, yet still childish enough to be disappointed. My hero had legs of wood and feet of clay.

I took the next few moments to be amazed by some of the athletes performing on the track and in the field. I was especially impressed by Arnie Boldt, a one-legged high jumper from Saskatoon who reached greater heights as a monoped than all but the most gifted bipedal athletes. And as I watched, who should come ambling along but another, if slightly lesser, light from my boyhood pantheon of heroes… Clare Drake.

I had watched Drake's U of A Golden Bears since the mid-1960s. My Dad had taken me to see them as well as Edmonton's more famous junior team, the Oil Kings. I'd seen several of the legendary, blood-spattered games between the two squads, including the 1972 fixture, the very last one in the series where Drake's Bears had pounded (both physically and on the score board) a talent-laden Kings lineup that sent many of its members on to the pros.

Varsity Arena was invariably jam-packed in the sixties, in those days when people supported amateur hockey enthusiastically. The NHL was far, far away, and only accessible via the TV once a week on Saturday nights. It was usually noisy in Varsity Arena, with a brass band somehow creating a more exciting atmosphere than the loudest arena sound systems pumping hockey rock nowadays. It helped that the fans were there to watch hockey, rather than "experience an entertainment spectacle." They fed off the natural energy generated by the game, and the game, in turn, fed off them.

And there amidst the hoopla, apparently untouched by it all but seemingly in control of everything, stood Clare Drake. Oil Kings coaches came and went; even Toe Blake and Punch Imlach eventually stepped down from the Canadiens and Leafs benches. But there stood Clare Drake, year in and year out. As a high school kid I'd check the university hockey standings in the *Edmonton Journal* sports section and it seemed his team was always on top. I'd heard about their national championship in 1964 and read about their second one in the spring of 1968, my last year of junior high. And wait a minute, he coached football, too! The mighty football Bears won the national title in the fall of 1967, masterminded by Clare Drake in his ball cap with the big letters "GB" on the front. How could anybody be smart enough to coach one group of Bears to the national championship in the fall and then take some more Bears back down east in the spring and win another national championship in another sport? And one of them was my sport... my passion.

I'd loved playing minor hockey as a kid, and as a U of A student I was a devoted Bears fan, attending every home game and a few on the road, too, against the insufferable University of Calgary Dinosaurs in their little bandbox of an arena where the fans poured beer over our players both on the ice and on the bench. Throughout my undergraduate years, year after year, home and away, win or lose (but mostly win), Clare Drake stood on the Bears bench, in control. He always looked dapper, dressed far better than most coaches in those days, but never flashily. From afar, from the stands, he was a small, neatly turned out man, with fine facial features that in repose suggested intelligence and decency to me. I'd seen him smile during television interviews and noticed how his face changed, lighting up with warmth and friendliness. My mother, in her own pleasant way, had referred to him as "that nice looking man from the university."

Clare Drake was at the Canadian Paralympic Games that summer day of 1976 not as a celebrity, but as a genuinely interested observer. He has always cared about the broad spectrum of sport and those who partake in it. In watching disabled athletes he was merely being true to form, as he has remained throughout the years with his interest and competence in a number of sports beyond hockey. So that's what Clare Drake was doing that summer afternoon in 1976, simply checking out some more athletes.

And having been blown off by my "big hero," I decided to approach that "nice man" whom I admired in a less fantastical fashion. I had an agenda as I walked up to him; for several months I'd thought about applying to be the volunteer student manager/trainer of the Bears hockey team because I knew there was a vacancy for the 1976-77 season. I didn't know how to begin this process but here in front of me was the man himself, so in the spirit of *carpe diem* I stuck out my hand, told him my name and said, "I'd like to be your manager this year." I gave him a very brief verbal résumé of why I thought I was qualified, but there was no friendly smile in response, not even a firm handshake. He did take my hand rather unenthusiastically, while coolly looking me up and down and hesitantly replying something like, "We'll see." Nothing else was forthcoming; he wasn't going to throw me a bone. Daunted but nonetheless persistent, I asked him when he would know who his manager would be and he answered evasively. I finally got him to agree that I could come and see him in his office the following week and discuss the idea some more.

Once again I walked away confused and disappointed. I wasn't having a great day. Sir Douglas Bader had wanted me to leave him alone and Clare Drake didn't seem at all to be the nice man I'd imagined him to be. I was wrong on one count: it turned out to be one of the greatest days of my life, in the sense that it was one of the most momentous. But I was probably right that Sir Douglas Bader really did just want to be left alone and Clare Drake wasn't the "nice" man I'd thought he was. Not that he was mean, or anything close to it, but "nice" wasn't the first (or second or even third) word one would use to describe him.

What I came to learn from Clare Drake went far beyond "nice." I discovered him to be, above all, a fine man. I had already completed an undergraduate degree by the time I met him and was one year into a master's program. But my real education began the day I met the coach of the Golden Bears. It was the day I began to shuck my boyhood fantasies about heroes and commence the long and painful process toward becoming an adult. Clare Drake helped kickstart me on that journey and was one of the principal teachers of lessons that have carried me through life since that summer day in 1976.

Over the years, after my time as a Golden Bear, I remained involved with the community of men Clare Drake influenced, whose lives he touched, through the team alumni association. For almost a quarter of a century, the Golden Bear alumni have maintained a weekly ritual called "Friday night hockey," a post-work scrimmage at what is now known as Clare Drake Arena. It's just a bunch of old friends, with a few "black aces" from the current Bears mixed in, getting together for some shinny; nothing to prove, nothing on the line, just good old-fashioned fun and a "coupla cold ones" in the dressing room afterward. The between-shift conversations on the bench can range widely, from friendly banter about on-ice exploits, to work, to family, etc. In one such chat during the early 1990s, my former teammate John Devaney and I were musing on Coach Drake's incredible career – especially that he had accomplished so much and yet been given so little credit by the hockey world at large – when "Jed" looked at me pointedly and said, "Yeah, someone should write a book about him."

Thus was planted a seed that took about ten years to germinate. It needed much pondering and equivocating on my part; a lot of "watering" in the form of exhortations from my wife Teresa, whose appraisal of my writing chops gave me the confidence to start; and finally, a galvanizing conversation with Ken Hitchcock, who confirmed my suspicion that Drake was indeed an unsung coaching colossus whose influence extended far beyond the university context wherein he toiled for most of his career. Oh yes… it also needed the support and cooperation of the man himself, which proved the most difficult element to put in place. When I phoned Clare to ask for his blessing and involvement in this project, he was about as enthusiastic as the first day we met. His immediate response was, "Why would anybody want to read a book about me?" It took a fair bit of coaxing, several years of on-and-off reminiscing and interviewing and eventually some gentle pressure from his friends and colleagues for Coach to put away his reservations and overcome his inherent diffidence at talking about himself. The rest, as they say, is history. See for yourself.

Derek Drager
Edmonton, Alberta
February / 2007

CHAPTER ONE

Whose Game is it Anyway?

An it's hard to admit but
I guess even if we
beat the Russkies
they did teach us a little
about our game
"Coach II," *More! All Star Poet,* Stephen Scriver

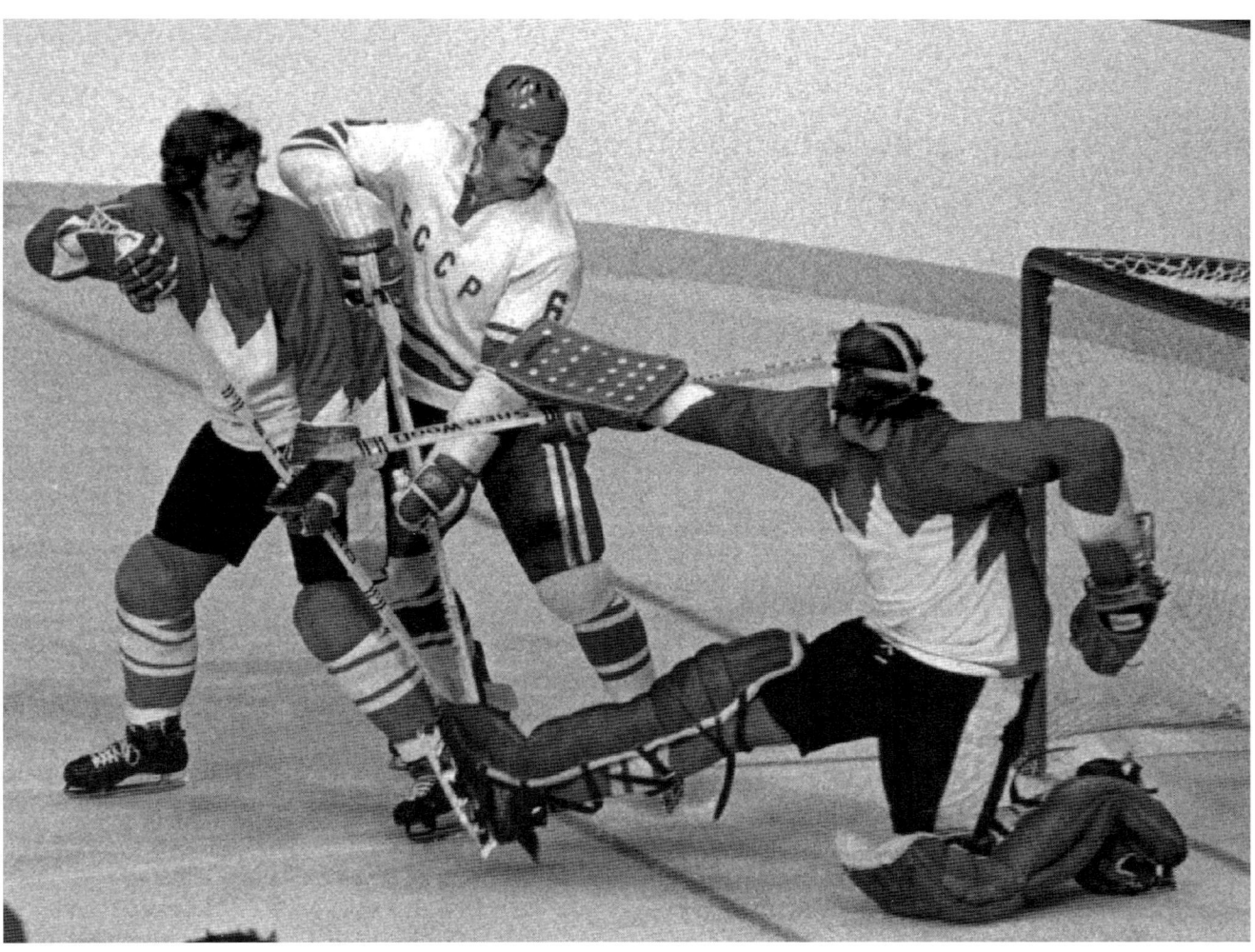
Summit Series hero. Ken Dryden saves a goal and Canada's honor against Russian great Valery Vasiliev, September 1972.

Paul Henderson scored the goal of his life, the goal of Canada's life, on September 28, 1972. Most Canadians born before 1965 can remember where they were on that glorious day. They can remember Foster Hewitt's reedy voice crying out in exultation with only thirty-four seconds left in the final game of the greatest hockey series ever played. "Here's another shot, right in front, they scooore! Henderson has scored for Canada!"

And indeed, all of Canada erupted in a mighty paroxysm of joy. The nation had ridden an emotional roller coaster since the Canada-Soviet Summit Series began on September 2 in Montreal. After surviving the stomach-churning ups and downs of expectation, disappointment, shock, anger and renewed, flickering hope, the national mood peaked out on the bliss meter at the dramatic conclusion of Game Eight on the 28th.

Among the many millions of celebrants — an estimated three quarters of the population were tuned in on radio or TV — was a hockey coach in Edmonton. Had the historic match been played in Canada, instead of Moscow's strange and stark Luzhniki Ice Palace, game time would have been early evening — an occasion for the company of friends, and perhaps, a couple of rum and cokes. Because it was a morning telecast, he watched the grainy satellite picture quietly in the comfort of his living room, alone with his good wife and fellow lover of the game. A faithful Canadian, this hockey man was excited by the victory, but he hadn't been on the same roller coaster ride as his compatriots over the preceding three weeks. He hadn't fallen prey to the naïve predictions sweeping the country prior to the series, and he wasn't at all surprised by the Soviet Union's fast, skilled and canny brand of hockey. He'd had more than an inkling that Canada's road to victory would be a long, hard slog. For, unlike most Canadians, fans and NHL insiders alike, this man was well acquainted with the Russians and knew pretty much what to expect. He was the coach of the University of Alberta Golden Bears – Clare Drake.

Had anybody asked him during the pre-Summit hype, Clare Drake would have sounded a note of caution as Canada's experts bragged up on our team of NHL stars. He had learned from his own recent exposure to a dominant Russian squad featuring some of the same players who would give Team Canada so much trouble. Clare Drake didn't go on record with his opinions because no one sought them and, if they had, he would have stated them hesitantly, respectfully, because that's always been his way.

But nobody asked Clare Drake. He was a university hockey coach, an outsider to the elite world of NHL hockey, far removed from the bright lights of The Show. Ditto for several of Drake's colleagues in the Canadian Interuniversity Athletic Union (now the CIS, Canadian Interuniversity Sport) – Tom Watt of the University of Toronto, George Kingston of the University of Calgary and Bob Hindmarch of UBC – each of whom also knew the Russians. As Team Canada goaltender Ken Dryden suggested in a 2006 conversation, it would have taken a fundamental shift in paradigms for the world's supreme hockey league, with the game's biggest names, to look outside its own frame of reference as it prepared to meet the upstart hockey aliens from the Soviet Union.

The men of the CIAU came from a different paradigm though, one that by September 1972 had afforded them deep understanding and a healthy respect for Russian hockey. Drake had first encountered the burgeoning Soviet powerhouse at the 1955 world championships in Germany, where he'd spent the season coaching Düsseldorf of the German *Landesliga*. Because he was in the right place at the right time, he'd been asked to scout the Russians for Canada's legendary Penticton Vees. The captain and star of the 1955 Soviet National Team was Vsevolod Bobrov, who got plenty of face time on Canadian TV seventeen years later as head coach of the Summit Series squad. And in 1965, Drake got reacquainted with the Soviets when he was the playing coach on Canada's representatives to the Ahearne Cup, an international tournament in Sweden.

It was also during the sixties that Bob Hindmarch got to know the Russians. He'd been with Canada's amateur Olympic Team at the 1964 games in Innsbruck, Austria, and followed that by inviting the renowned Anatoly Tarasov — the father of Soviet hockey — to Vancouver to demonstrate Russian practice methods at UBC. Tom Watt first met the Russians in 1968 at the Winter Universiade (world student games) in Innsbruck. As Canada's hockey representatives at the games, his University of Toronto Blues won a bronze medal against "student" teams (comprised of de facto professionals) from behind the Iron Curtain, losing to Czechoslovakia and tying the USSR.

At the next Winter Universiade at Lake Placid, New York, in February 1972, Drake and Watt took on the Russians together, respectively as head coach and general manager. Together, they led Canada's first Student National Team to a silver medal, losing to another so-called student squad from the Soviet Union. The big line for the Soviets? Vyacheslav Anisin, Yuri Lebedev and Alexander Bodunov, who became the blossoming young stars on the Russian Summit Series Team that September. And the coach of this student group was the impassive Boris Kulagin — later dubbed "Chuckles" by Canadian media wags — who served as Bobrov's assistant on the Summit Series Team and then masterminded Soviet victories against NHL teams during the mid-seventies.

The summer prior to Drake and Watt's Lake Placid adventure, the University of Calgary's George Kingston had done the unthinkable in that Cold War era — he'd taken his family to Moscow for three weeks, where he met with Soviet hockey officials to observe their off-season training program and learn about their entire state-sponsored approach to sport. Off-season training was a notion that wouldn't make its way into the NHL for years to come.

This small group of university coaches held insights into Russian hockey that could have saved Team Canada and its fans considerable angst. But the reality of hockey's pecking order in 1972 excluded the university guys from the equation. Their wealth of knowledge would have served Team Canada's braintrust, but heedless, the NHL's best stumbled blindly and overconfidently into this greatest of hockey wars. Canadians had been clamoring for a chance to pitch "our best against theirs" for years. Yet when all the negotiating and political manoeuvring finally produced this first-ever clash of titans on ice, our professionals weren't prepared.

Who could blame them, given the nation's fit of overexuberance as the series drew near? In his homage to Canada entitled (tongue-in-cheek) *Why I Hate Canadians*, author-patriot Will Ferguson truly criticizes his homeland in only one chapter, "The Cold War on Ice." Here he describes the Canuckle-headed smugness before the Summit Series: "The Canadians were confident to the point of being insufferable. The scouting reports had all but laughed at the Russian players... Alan Eagleson, [a key series organizer, then boss of the NHL players' union and now a convicted criminal] never one to put pressure on his boys, said that anything short of a complete sweep of the series by Team Canada would be a national disgrace."

Eagleson pretty much spoke for the entire country. Commenting on pre-series hysteria just three months after the fact, Jack Ludwig wrote in *Maclean's*, "we wanted a series between the USSR and a team of NHL stars not to prove anything to ourselves. Our convictions required no proofs. We wanted that contest only as a means of teaching the usurpers what hockey was really all about." Looking back from thirty-four years later, Ken Dryden explained in his thoughtful way: "the assumption was that the NHL professionals were the greatest stars in the game and that if anyone had to prepare for this series and adjust, it would be the Russians." He added that, given the common understandings of the time, this was not an unreasonable assumption. Reasonable or not, Canadians anticipated a thorough drubbing of these Soviet pretenders to hockey's throne, whom we saw as "sneaky Communists" for their use of professionals to dominate the ostensibly amateur competitions at the Olympics and world championships. Once they faced our own professionals instead of the game but outmatched amateurs we'd been sending to the Olympics, they'd learn who the true masters of hockey were. It was our game; we were better at it than anyone else simply because we were Canadian. It was in our DNA, for Pete's sake!

So Canada's NHL celebrities readied themselves accordingly. In keeping with the long-standing tradition of those times, they didn't train at all during the summer and were content to play themselves into shape the way they always had. In Jack Ludwig's *Maclean's* column, his wry reference to Canada's all-too-brief training camp noted the "familiar kibitz-loaf-spurt style [of working out] that goes with being an NHLer." In truth, Team Canada was a poorly conditioned, disorganized collection of all-stars with little sense of cohesion and even less understanding of their challengers. The Russians, on the other hand, were trained to razor sharpness, precision-honed to play their complex, patterned team game. As several of their people had told George Kingston in the summer of '71, they were counting on the fact that, should they ever play the NHL stars, they would have superior knowledge of their opponents and enjoy a sizeable edge in fitness.

This Russian wisdom proved prescient during the first four games – all played on this side of the Atlantic – and Canada reeled, gob-smacked. The Summit Series meant far more than hockey to most Canadians. It was a monumental battle between cultures, ideologies and hemispheres. International awareness and understanding, two of the more promising characteristics of today's global village, were in noticeably less supply during the 1970s. Back in that simpler time, there were good guys and bad guys, and nobody needed a scorecard to tell the difference. It was all spelled out clearly – the bad guys were the helmeted, wooden-faced Russians, endlessly and almost perversely circling back and back with the puck, passing and passing and waiting and waiting until suddenly and appallingly it was in Canada's net. Ken Brown, in his seminal Canadian play *Life After Hockey*, fittingly called the smooth-skating Soviets "those dark infidels in red."

Our own bare-headed, emotions-on-their-sleeves NHL heroes stood in stark contrast: big Phil Esposito, the "garbage collector"; plucky Yvan Cournoyer, the "Roadrunner"; bald, toothless Gary Bergman; hirsute, toothless Bobby Clarke; big, powerful striders like Serge Savard and the Mahovlich brothers; lanky Ken Dryden, the enigmatic young goalie; and tough guys J.P. Parise and Wayne Cashman, Canadian tenacity personified.

But our heroes, tenacity notwithstanding, couldn't handle the calculated Russian attack. They opened with a 7–3 loss to the Reds in Montreal. In post-game interviews, Team Canada head coach Harry Sinden was asked if he was surprised at the level of Russian play. "I'm stunned!" he replied candidly. A 4–1 Canadian rally in Toronto was no turn-around, but instead led to a tie in Winnipeg and a disturbing 5–3 loss on September 8 in Vancouver. By then, we were starting to get the idea that the guys in the CCCP jerseys were pretty darned good. The broadcast team of Foster Hewitt and Brian Conacher sang the Russians' praises during that game. Conacher remarked repeatedly on their skating prowess and exclaimed that their puck pursuit was "absolutely fantastic." Hewitt admitted that the Russian passing and puck control was "making the Canadians a bit dizzy at times."

The Vancouver fans booed mercilessly, especially as the weary, dejected Canadians left the ice. For those who witnessed it, who can forget the image of Phil Esposito, standing at the end of the rink during his post-game interview with Johnny Esaw? Rivers of sweat pouring down his face, hair matted to his brow, shoulders slumped, Espo was the picture of demoralized exhaustion. "Jesus," he said (using language never heard on TV then), "I'm really… all of us guys are really disheartened… We're doing the best we can."

Disheartened they may have been, but the Canadians didn't quit, and their best turned out to be enough. All perspiration and dash and swagger, they fought and clawed their way back into the series once it moved overseas. The NHLers came together once they'd left home and the intensity of their demanding fans. Ten more days of conditioning and exhibition play in Sweden set them up for the fabled comeback in Moscow – a close, hard-fought loss in Game Five and then three straight wins. In that apocalyptic eighth game, they crashed the Soviet net in waves, sweat-soaked long hair flying over swashbuckling sideburns, hearts pumping with every ounce of courage and grit they could muster for each other and their Canada. And when Paul Henderson, who had also nailed the winner late in Game Seven, bashed in that miraculous, last-second rebound past the inscrutable Vladislav Tretiak, he erased the fear and pain of an entire nation. Instead, there was profound, soul-lifting relief, and a shout of elation that echoed from coast to coast throughout the True North Strong and Free.

Jim Coleman, the dean of Canadian sportswriters, opened his post-series column by breezily teasing his readers: "I don't know what the heck you were worrying about." Twenty-five years later, James Deacon wrote a retrospective on the series for *Maclean's* magazine in which he called the victory "therapy for the national psyche." The Russians had a different take on it all. Anatoly Tarasov was the former coach of the Soviet National Team and architect of the "Big Red Machine" that dominated international hockey from the late 1950s through the 1970s. Of the '72 series he said, "The Canadians battled with the ferocity of a cornered animal. They believed the stories of their hockey superiority, which were not quite correct. Our players were better conditioned physically and stronger in skills than the Canadian professionals. But we could not match them in heart and desire."

While Canada celebrated at the end of that magnificent September, Clare Drake continued to follow the same seasonal cycle that had shaped his life since the late 1950s. For the University of Alberta Golden Bears, 1972's fall training camp marked the beginning of their fourteenth year under Drake's tutelage. In the previous thirteen campaigns, he'd won ten conference championships and two Canadian Interuniversity Athletic Union hockey titles. He'd become a hometown hero and a venerated leader among university coaches. Five years earlier, he'd elevated his stature to colossal proportions within the Canadian varsity coaching fraternity by winning two different national championships, one in football and one in hockey, during the same university year. His achievements of the 1967–68 season prompted *Edmonton Journal* sports columnist Wayne Overland to compare him to American college coaching luminaries like Bear Bryant.

And yet, despite all his international experience and his university championships, Drake was well under the NHL's radar in 1972, and even that of the upstart World Hockey Association, though the new league had a team in Edmonton. He continued to blend in – un-Bryant like – with the university community to which he belonged. He would park his unpretentious Ford LTD in the Stadium Parkade on 89 Avenue, walk half a block to his small office in the Physical Education Building, teach the coaching courses that were part of his duties as an associate professor in the Faculty of Physical Education, and run the Golden Bears' late afternoon practices in the modest, 2,800-seat facility known then as Varsity Arena.

With the exception of a brief and ill-starred foray into the pro limelight in 1975 – the somewhat jaundiced light of the WHA's Edmonton Oilers – Drake would toil on in the obscurity of the CIAU for almost two more decades. Yet eventually, big league hockey would come to Clare Drake. Eventually the insiders would invite the outsider to share his knowledge. Eventually they would listen and change, and they would recognize him as a hockey revolutionary.

During the years that Drake labored away at the U of A, the NHL went through a period of almost untrammeled growth, some of it with adverse effects on Canada's game. In 1972, the big league was synonymous with Canadian hockey. While the NHL had already engineered three expansions into the United States and grown to sixteen teams, it was still fundamentally a Canadian institution. Virtually all its general managers, coaches and players were Canadians and its authoritarian president was that crusty old lawyer from Edmonton, Clarence Campbell. When it came to hockey, there was no differentiating between the black and white shield with the three consonants running aslant and up, and the red and white flag with the big maple leaf in the middle. As Jack Ludwig analyzed Canada's miraculous September comeback for *Maclean's*, he used the terms "NHL" and "Team Canada" interchangeably. He also reported his discoveries about the Soviet approach to sport while in Moscow: systematic, academic and scientific – so different from our own. He wondered if we hadn't been "deluding ourselves and hoaxing our hockey players" and he called for a revolution in Canadian hockey. This revolution, he suggested,

> should turn its attention to helping boys who want to play hockey build the muscles and the skills needed to play hockey the best. The NHL will have to rethink its training camp programs: the NHL will have to get itself some coaches and people who want to coach in hockey will have to use their imaginations, and their intelligence, and open hockey up to new possibilities. Unless that happens this great Moscow triumph could only be a final epitaph: it would make a mockery of Team Canada's achievement if the final word on Canadian hockey became: *Their greatest victory was also their last.*

Ludwig wasn't the only Canadian asking for a revolution; his was just one of the more eloquent voices giving call. And a revolution did indeed come, but not in answer to the alarm he and other enlightened Canadians were sounding. The pro hockey revolution of the 1970s was about something altogether different and, other than a five-month stint with the Edmonton Oilers in 1975–76, it didn't involve Clare Drake.

The apparatchiks of this hockey revolution were less concerned with the game than with the money to be made from it. Thanks to NHL expansion and the rise of the WHA, the top tier of North American pro hockey had swollen from six teams to thirty-three between 1967 and 1975. Instead of developing better coaches, new training methods, and new systems for developing young players, the leaders of professional hockey in North America were mesmerized with market growth and bidding for stars in the war between the rival leagues.

In 1979, the NHL swallowed the remains of the WHA, incorporating its four surviving teams, which included the Edmonton Oilers and a teenaged Wayne Gretzky. Pro hockey's continuing expansion demanded a larger player pool, and the NHL looked south to the USA: in the 1960s, the American players in the league could be counted on one hand, but as the decade turned, the first National Collegiate Athletic Association draft picks began to trickle in and over the ensuing twenty years that trickle became a constant flow.

Around the same time, the NHL began its transmutation into the most truly international league in North American pro sport. The Detroit Red Wings were among the earliest pioneers, importing Swedish defenceman Thommie Bergman in 1972. But it was the WHA's Winnipeg Jets that took European scouting to another level, bringing in the Swedish troika of Anders Hedberg, Ulf Nilsson and Lars-Eric Sjoberg in 1974. From that time on, both leagues saw an increasing stream of Swedes, Finns and Czechs. After 1989, with the dismantling of the Iron Curtain, the floodgates opened and ever since, the NHL has featured a medley of nationalities and a plethora of Russian stars. Those Russians we so loved to hate in 1972 have now become fan favourites in NHL cities like Fort Lauderdale, Tampa, Nashville and Atlanta. As Canadians basked in their self-congratulatory glow in 1972, who among them could have foreseen the players and the places of the twenty-first century NHL?

Through all these upheavals, one fact became abundantly clear: whether the fans approved of the European influx or railed against it like Don Cherry, Canada's beloved hockey curmudgeon; whether they sided with players or management over the revenue and salary issues that shut down the 2004-05 season; whether they cared about Thrashers, or Lightning, or Ducks; it was no longer possible to think of the NHL as a Canadian institution. Now, nobody can conflate the NHL and Team Canada, as everyone did in 1972.

Ironically, as the NHL grew and changed, Canadian hockey began to shape its own identity separate from that of the league it spawned. We'd always had our own international presence in the game, distinct from our elite professional league. But historically, we'd been represented by amateurs, not the cream of the NHL who carried our colors in '72. Canadian amateur club teams had worn the maple leaf for decades at the Winter Olympics and world championships and, with few exceptions, had produced golden results. As the Soviet sports machine came to prominence in the 1950s and 1960s, however, top amateur club teams could no longer deliver the victories Canadians had come to expect. By 1972, Canada hadn't won an Olympic gold medal in twenty years, since Edmonton's Waterloo Mercurys had returned triumphant from Oslo; it would be another thirty years before a Canadian would ascend a podium to accept Olympic hockey gold. By 1972, it had been eleven years since Canada's last world championship gold, won by the Trail Smoke Eaters. Another twenty-two would pass before we reclaimed gold at the world championships.

Canada's international efforts in the 1960s were guided by Father David Bauer, the Catholic priest with hockey as his calling. His brother Bobby had played on the Boston Bruins' famed "Kraut line" in the 1940s and coached the Kitchener-Waterloo Dutchmen to Olympic bronze in 1956 and silver in 1960. David had played for and coached the St. Michael's Majors junior team in Toronto, helping lead them to a Memorial Cup in 1961. In 1963, while serving at St. Mark's College at the University of British Columbia, Father Bauer convinced the Canadian Amateur Hockey Association to fund a true Canadian National Team. For the next seven years, these dedicated amateurs would live together, practice together and bleed Canadian red and white together. They represented Canada at two Winter Olympics (1964, 1968) and four world championships (1965, 1966, 1967, 1969), with Father Bauer as their head coach or general manager. The "Nats" battled the Soviet de facto professionals bravely, eking out two Olympic bronze medals (their 1964 bronze was finally officially recognized in 2005), with two fourth-place finishes and two bronzes to show for their world championship efforts. But they failed to meet Canada's golden standards and so were disbanded after 1969. In the 1970s, Canada stopped sending teams to the Olympics and the Worlds and during that shining month in 1972, the NHL became Canada's international face.

The quality of hockey in the Summit Series, combined with its reaffirmation of our "innate hockey superiority" after a decade of frustration, left Canadians with a taste for more. Seeking to capitalize on this fervor, the parvenu WHA negotiated a return engagement with the Russians in 1974. Using former NHL stars like Gordie Howe, Bobby Hull, Frank Mahovlich and '72 hero Paul Henderson, the WHA donned the maple leaf and launched another version of Team Canada in an attempt to reprise the splendor of two years earlier. It was a disaster. In eight games split between Canada and Moscow, the shambolic, out-of-shape Canadians could only muster one victory and three ties against the ever-prepared Soviets. The lessons of '72 went unheeded, and this time guts and determination weren't enough.

Hockey Canada, established by the federal government in 1969 as the official agency for international hockey, had been an organizing partner in the Summit Series. But after '72, the NHL wanted more control over how and when it played the Russians – its players had to be in mid-season form, and play solely in league buildings under the dictates of its own rule book. So the NHL struck out on its own, seeking marketing opportunities in the rivalry with our Cold War enemies. It resorted to capitalism's most effective weapon against communism – cold hard cash – to entice the Soviets into a long run of club-versus-club matches, all played in North America. One of the earliest of these was the legendary 3-3 tie on New Year's Eve, 1975, between Moscow's Central Red Army squad and the Montreal Canadiens, considered by many to be singly the greatest game of hockey ever played.

Between 1975–76 and 1988–89, Soviet club teams would cross the Atlantic continuously, lured by American dollars to play a total of fifty-six games against NHL clubs. The Soviets won thirty-four of those contests and tied three, against nineteen losses. They posted this record of dominance on long, exhausting road trips that took them far from home to play in front of hostile crowds on ice surfaces much smaller than their own.

Of far greater import than these club exhibitions were the major tournaments that Hockey Canada and the NHL co-promoted as a substitute for our professional involvement in the Olympics and world championships. The first of these was the Canada Cup, which took place in September 1976. Five countries participated – Canada, the USA, Czechoslovakia, the Soviet Union and Sweden – and Canada drew from both the NHL and WHA to ice its best team to that date in international

"The Catholic priest with hockey as his calling." Father David Bauer, founder and first coach of Canada's Olympic Team (seen here in his role as general manager of the 1980 squad).

competition: Bobby Orr, Serge Savard, Larry Robinson, Bobby Hull, Phil Esposito, Guy Lafleur, Marcel Dionne... the roster reads like a Hall of Fame who's who. The Russians sniffed dismissively at the tournament, maintaining they cared more about the Olympics and the Worlds than this trumped-up North American invention. They sent a competent team, but not their best. Among the notable absentees from the Soviet line-up was the dazzling Valery Kharlamov, one of the great Russian stars of '72 and dominator of the fabled New Year's Eve game in the Montreal; he'd been badly injured in a car accident. Canada beat the Soviets 3–1 in the round robin and dispatched defending World Champion Czechoslovakia two games to none in the best-of-three final.

Speaking for many observers, *MacLean's* senior editor Michael Posner cited Canada's cream puff schedule, the small North American ice surfaces and an undermanned Russian squad as reasons to not celebrate the tournament victory too loudly. "Of all the conclusions now being drawn from last month's Canada Cup," he wrote, "the least persuasive is that Canada once again reigns supreme in hockey. Anybody naïve enough to believe that [Canada's stars] have rescued the great Canadian game from all those barbarous imitators in Europe deserves a week in Murmansk with Alan Eagleson."

Posner's words proved prophetic. The next instalment of "our best versus theirs" came in 1979. This time, "our best" included more than just Canadians. The NHL put together an all-star team that included all the Canadian greats of the time (Denis Potvin, Mike Bossy, Bryan Trottier, Steve Shutt, Lafleur, Robinson *et al*) plus Swedish stars Borje Salming, Anders Hedberg and Ulf Nilsson. Staged in New York's Madison Square Garden and billed as the "Series of the Century," Challenge Cup '79 was a best-of-three affair intended to showcase the frozen game in the media capital of the world. New York and the heavily-courted American TV market yawned.

The Soviets, suffering from jet lag, took a game and a half to get untracked. After losing the first game 4–2 and facing a two-goal deficit in the second, they exploded for nine unanswered goals in the final five periods of the series. They won the second game 5–4 and crushed the pride of the NHL 6–0 in the third. Confusing a pro hockey league with a nation, American hockey writer E.M. Swift said in *Sports Illustrated*, "In hockey, Canada is now No. 2." Soviet team captain Boris Mikhailov, to Canadians perhaps the nastiest Russian hockey villain of all time, indulged in what might be the first recorded instance of Communist trash talk. "Soviets: one," he smirked, "Kanadski: two."

Canadian writer Hal Quinn declared fatalistically: "the NHL myth disintegrated and the crown travelled 5,000 miles to the east, probably never to return." Even NHL insiders attested to Soviet brilliance. Hall of Famer Jean Beliveau said, "They have shown us that hockey is a game of speed and we have never had a team as fast as theirs. We must regroup and examine what we have lost."

Beliveau's sage advice went unheeded and Canada suffered further humiliation at the hands of the Russians in the 1981 Canada Cup. Canada cruised through the six-nation round robin (Finland had joined the original five from '76) with a team that included young stars Wayne Gretzky and Ray Bourque. The Russians also brought youngsters, names that would eventually be seen on NHL rosters: the KLM line of Vladimir Krutov, Igor Larionov and Sergey Makarov, with Alexei Kasatonov and Viacheslav Fetisov on defence. Their coach was Viktor Tikhonov, the man who would come to be the most despised of all Soviet bench bosses – by Russians and Canadians alike.

Canada's 7–3 defeat of the Soviets during the round robin promised big things for the rematch in the tournament final; surely this was a sign that the hockey planets had returned to their proper alignment after the devastating loss of '79. But when the two bitter rivals took the ice at the Montreal Forum, the team wearing the CCCP logo was different from the one that played in the first encounter. Oh, the players were the same, but they had somehow transformed into an inexorable machine that annihilated Canada 8–1, our worst-ever beating. There was speculation that Tikhonov had coached his squad to play possum in the round robin match, but there was no doubt that Canada had reached the nadir of its long, storied history in international hockey. While the business of hockey flourished and expanded ever onward towards the bright, lucrative lights of the American marketplace, Canada's game – the keystone of our national identity – languished.

Twenty-five years later, Canada has emerged from those dark depths to take what we believe to be our rightful place as leaders in a restructured hockey world. Despite a seventh-place stumble at the 2006 Turin Olympics, Canadian hockey teams are respected – even feared – not for the brutality of the old days, but for their ability to balance speed and finesse with enthusiasm and toughness. Canadian hockey is still known for its passion, but our teams now play with skill and discipline to rival anyone. And they never sit back.

It was a long, arduous road to recovery, with the first signs of Canada's return to glory coming at the world junior championships. Our teams took seven gold medals between 1990 and 1997; from 1999 to 2004, we were in the money every year but had some tough luck in medal semi-finals and finals. By 2005, Canada's juniors were back in form, going undefeated through the entire tournament and clobbering Russia 6–1 in the final. They delivered an encore performance in 2006, with an almost identical result against the same opponent, and rang up the hat trick in 2007, beating the Russians 4–2 to bring home the gold from Leksand, Sweden.

During the 1990s, Canada also returned to top form at the world men's hockey championships. George Kingston, that same CIAU adventurer who journeyed behind the Iron Curtain during the Cold War, coached a team of Canadian pros to world championship gold in 1994, breaking a forty-two-year drought. While we Canadians have never taken the world championships too seriously (their annual spring schedule doesn't allow us to send our best possible lineup), we've enjoyed our twenty-first century successes at the tournament – gold medals in 2003 and 2004, and a silver in 2005.

We have to give the Czechs and the Swedes credit for their own recent triumphs, which make them legitimate co-claimants with Canada to the title of "world's best hockey nation." The Czechs won Olympic gold at Nagano in 1998, followed by three straight world championships (1999, 2000, 2001) and the 2005 crown. And how 'bout those Swedes? For so long considered the underachievers of the hockey world, they finally met the expectations created by their talented player pool, winning both Olympic and world championship gold in 2006.

The Swedes also pulled off a huge upset in women's hockey at the 2006 Olympics, knocking out the heavily favored Americans to challenge Canada for gold. The women's game was almost unheard of back in 1972, but is now a growing part of Canada's hockey identity. We own the world of women's hockey, except for occasional interference from the Americans. Between 1990, when the first women's world championships were held, and 2003, Canada won not only every gold medal, but every game at this best-on-best tournament. The Americans finally caught us at the 2005 Worlds, winning their first gold in an overtime shoot-out. Canada also lost to the USA in the gold medal match at the first Olympic women's hockey tournament in Nagano in 1998, but came back four years later to best the

A Drake disciple at the top. Ken Hitchcock, Stanley Cup winning head coach of the Dallas Stars, 1999.

Americans heroically in front of their rabid fans in Salt Lake City. And in 2006, we won Olympic gold again, this time beating the startling Swedes.

Canada: Olympic Hockey Champions. Those words hadn't been spoken at all, no matter the gender, between 1952 and 2002. Yet on the same Salt Lake City ice surface where our women won their first gold, the Canadian men finally ended a half-century long Olympic drought. Granted, the nemesis was no longer the Russians, but rather the Americans, who had infiltrated our game since the 1970s. But Canadian hearts swelled with pride no less as our boys sang out the words to "O Canada" on American soil, in front of a thoroughly beaten American team, following the 5-2 gold medal victory.

Emotions in Edmonton ran high. After all, it was an Edmonton team – the Waterloo Mercurys (named after a sponsoring city Ford dealership) – that had won Canada's last Olympic gold medal. Several members of that club, old men now but still heroes in their home town, had been flown to Utah and given their fifteen minutes of national fame in an interview with Hockey Night in Canada's Ron MacLean. The memories of Oslo 1952 were celebrated in anticipation, and then affirmation, of the glorious conquest in Utah.

There were other Edmonton connections with the 2002 squad – included on the Canadian roster were Edmonton Oilers Ryan Smyth and Eric Brewer, and the Calgary Flames' Jarome Iginla, an Edmonton product whose play drew rave reviews. There was also the fabled loonie, now in the Hockey Hall of Fame, surreptitiously planted by Edmonton icemaker Trent Evans. He'd been added to the American crew at the Salt Lake City "E Center" for his expertise and took it upon himself to bury our beloved one-dollar coin at center ice as a Canadian good luck charm.

And perhaps most important of all, there was Ken Hitchcock, another Edmontonian born and bred. He was an associate coach of the Canadian team at Salt Lake City, playing a valuable role among the team's leadership cadre: executive director Wayne Gretzky and his assistant Kevin Lowe, director of player personnel Steve Tambellini, head coach Pat Quinn and associate coaches Wayne Fleming and Jacques Martin. Gretzky's and Lowe's strong Edmonton ties were also a matter of record, but Hitchcock has been the most outspoken about his hometown as a career incubator, and about the guiding influence of one fellow Edmontonian, in particular.

On March 22, 2005, three years after the illustrious victory in Salt Lake City, Ken Hitchcock came home for a visit, welcomed with open, affectionate arms by old friends, colleagues and fans. He's a local boy made good, and most hockey people in Edmonton know his story of steady progress up the coaching ranks: first, the suburban Sherwood Park midget AAA team; then, the Kamloops Blazers of the Western Hockey League, two WHL coach of the year awards, Canadian major junior coach of the year and a Memorial Cup appearance; a gold medal as assistant coach of Canada's 1987 World Junior Champions; then onto the American Hockey League and finally to the big time in 1995, where he turned the Dallas Stars into a contender and won the 1999 Stanley Cup. After a stint with the Philadelphia Flyers, this highly respected and influential bench master was hired in 2006 by the Columbus Blue Jackets. Hitchcock is one of a growing number of career coaches in the NHL, a relatively new breed of professionals who never played the game at the highest level but are nonetheless capturing head positions in a league traditionally coached by former players.

"Countercultural… revolutionary." Clare Drake in his seventies.

Ken Hitchcock was in Edmonton on that March evening in 2005 for two reasons: one, because he had the time to make the trip from Philadelphia thanks to the NHL lockout; and two, because he'd been invited to speak at the coaches' forum for the CIS (formerly CIAU) Hockey Nationals, hosted by the University of Alberta. Part of an expert panel that included NHL colleagues such as Craig MacTavish, Bill Moores and Craig Simpson of the Oilers and Perry Pearn of the New York Rangers, the then-Flyers coach took the floor last. While the previous speakers were all given due respect, "Hitch" was the guy the audience was really there to hear. He stood at the front of a 250-seat lecture hall on the U of A campus, packed to overflowing with city folk of all ages and both genders. They were mostly coaches, managers and interested parents connected with teams in Edmonton's minor hockey system, one of Canada's largest and best organized. They hung on Hitchcock's every word, not just because he's one of the biggest stars in the coaching firmament, but also because he's an engaging, entertaining man. He opened with a joke that expressed his frustration about the lockout and got a big laugh, explaining that the Flyers were making him do public relations jobs to earn his salary, such as playing judge at a chicken wing eating contest. Hitch summarized the contest rules in one line: "Ya heave, ya leave!"

Then he gave a fascinating account of how the Olympic team coaching staff managed the challenging conditions at the Salt Lake City tournament. He described the intense media pressure, the frustrating security procedures, the difficulty of organizing practice times and the cramped living conditions in the Olympic dorm. He even got into the coaches' rooming arrangements, and to gales of laughter, bemoaned a certain colleague's tendency to pass gas.

Hitchcock is a media person's dream, a walking, talking collection of quips, one-liners and sound bites. He can also offer thoughtful analysis, and in this case gave great insights on how the team succeeded at this high-stress tournament, with all of Canada expecting nothing but gold. He pointed to the team policy, instigated by Wayne Gretzky, of choosing only the fastest, most skilled Canadians available, rather than trying to fill a "ghost roster" of shooters, passers, checkers and other role players. He talked about the coaches' focus on team energy levels and how crucial it was to make sure their players were properly rested.

Finally, after an enthraling twenty minutes with the microphone, he concluded by thanking the forum organizers for inviting him. One of them was Bill Moores, the former head coach of the U of A Golden Bears who had graduated to the NHL. Another was Wilf Brooks, long-time friend of Hitch's and owner of United Cycle, the Edmonton sporting goods store where Hitchcock worked before he got paid for coaching hockey. Then, he turned to the face the silver-haired gentleman watching quietly and intently from the side.

It had been thirty-three years since this same quiet watcher scrutinized the Canadians and the Russians in Summit Series '72; thirty-three years of wins and losses, failures and successes, in Europe, the Canadian university ranks, the WHA, the Olympics and the NHL. The old coach had chipped in his own comments as a panel member on that March evening and many of the listeners even knew a little about him. They knew that his name was on the arena just across campus, and that he used to coach the Golden Bears, and that he won a lot. A few of his former players were in the crowd that night, and most of these men could even cite some of his numbers and achievements – wins, championships, an Olympic head coaching job and assistant positions in the NHL. But not many, even of this group, could have explained exactly why Hitchcock turned to the old coach last and said, "And thanks most of all to Clare. None of us would be here without him. We all copy him. We're all better for it."

Hitchcock had paid tribute to Clare Drake on other occasions. One was just a few months earlier in Philadelphia, during the third month of the lockout. He told a caller from Edmonton how he'd been filling time by dropping in on amateur hockey practices in the Philadelphia area – sometimes to help out, sometimes just to watch because he lives and breathes hockey and needed a fix. He saw all the same on-ice activity that he'd see at a kids practice in any Canadian town: youngsters skating elaborate patterns around orange traffic cones, coaches with sticks and whistles, different drills unfolding on different parts of the ice with small groups of players. He noted the familiarity of it all, and particularly the terminology the coaches used. Harkening back to his early days as a midget and junior coach, he said "these coaches were barking all the same stuff" at their players that he began to use in western Canada in the early 1980s, that he and many of his peers now use in the modern NHL.

When asked how this "stuff" had migrated from Alberta and B.C. in the 1980s to the NHL and Pennsylvania in the first decade of the twenty-first century, Hitchcock explained that Hockey USA had adopted Hockey Canada's coaching certification materials for use in their own hockey coaching system. He credited a group of men for the foundational work of conceiving these ideas and creating these materials, but he singled out one man as the leader, the originator, the first innovator, the driver behind it all: Clare Drake. He spoke of Drake reverently, describing him as countercultural, a man who'd gone into "dangerous" areas, a revolutionary. In fact, said Hitchcock, "the man's fingerprints are all over the game."

CHAPTER TWO

"Play up! play up! and play the game!"

This they all with a joyful mind
Bear through life like a torch in flame,
And falling fling to the host behind –
"Play up! play up! and play the game!"
"Vitaï Lampada," Sir Henry Newbolt

"The punch in the Thunderbird attack." Drake as a UBC forward, 1948 - 51.

The Drake gravitas. "Coach" on the bench during the 70s as his players knew him; intense concentration, eyes all-seeing, jaw set.

Clare Drake is a small man. Perhaps 5' 7" now in his advanced years, at best 5' 8" and 151 pounds in his playing days, he is neat, tidy-looking and compact of frame, with fine features that light up completely when he smiles. During his coaching career, his bright, open smile was reserved mainly for friends and family, and bestowed upon his players only intermittently. They usually saw his face set with intensity; sometimes this conveyed stern disapproval but mostly it revealed deep concentration on the task at hand – excellence. Not a man given to emotional outbursts, Clare Drake's face nonetheless betrayed clearly what he was feeling as a coach. When displeased, there was a telling rigidity to his jaw and steely glint in his eye that could chill the most recalcitrant of his players.

When satisfied with their efforts (and their efforts were always more important to him than wins and losses), his expression would open up to deliver encouragement, although he usually set his brilliant smile aside for team bonding times away from the ice. Drake's old friend and colleague Dr. Murray Smith, a consulting sport psychologist and professor emeritus at the University of Alberta, described him in a 1987 academic paper on coaching philosophy:

> To say that he is predominantly rational (that is he relies on analysis and reason) does not mean he is unemotional. He is intent and frequently shows intense emotion. But his emotionality, like that of Hugh Campbell, five-time Grey Cup winning coach of the Edmonton Eskimos, and Tom Landry of the Dallas Cowboys, is virtually either always positive (that is encouraging and rewarding), or directed at events, and not directed punishingly at players.

Now in his seventies, the Drake smile appears more readily and the old intensity, while still noticeable when he's concentrating on some hockey matter, is not the constant it used to be. He is one of those fortunate people who happen to both look, and be, intelligent. Like most true individuals and those who lead rather than follow, he is also a man with his own easily identifiable personal characteristics. His walk, for example: the smart, crisp steps of a "little guy" athlete, shortened now by two hip replacements; his habit of standing slightly canted to one side, head cocked a little, unconsciously hitching at the waist of his pants with tucked-in elbows; the thoughtful scratching of the back of his head as he ponders a question posed; and the distinctive style of pointing, usually to a position on the ice at practice, with arm half extended, thumb up, index finger and pinkie almost straight out, and the remaining two digits curled inward toward his palm.

Generations of his players made good-natured fun of these and other mannerisms at team skit nights; the many impressions of him are part of Golden Bear lore and exaggerated in the retelling at alumni gatherings. Clare Drake has always been a dynamic individual whose forceful presence demands attention. His players learned to listen to him carefully, at times warily, or else hopefully, in anticipation of his approval and the powerful, motivating effect it carried. But while dynamic, he is also by nature an observer, a quiet watcher. So within the team environment, Drake was both the observer and the observed, the nexus, the center of much attention within the small community of the team and its alumni.

To be the nexus is a fundamental characteristic of most successful leaders; however, quietude is an anomaly in the genetic makeup of most coaches. Most coaches, hockey coaches in particular, are anything but quiet. Many are screamers and ranters, or at the very least, stentorian. Drake was different though. In a profession where screaming and ranting have long been the norm, he used measured tones and carefully considered language, he was a thoughtful communicator and watcher. And although like any coach he was watched in turn by his players and mimicked in the way of locker room culture, unlike most others he came to be mimicked on another level and for other reasons by other people. It wasn't his mannerisms they copied, it was his ideas. And it wasn't just a few doing the copying, or dozens, or hundreds – Clare Drake came to be copied by thousands, eventually in many parts of the world.

In his 2002 bestseller *The Tipping Point*, Malcolm Gladwell analyzes the phenomenon of sweeping social or market change, when an idea takes root in society and is adopted by enough people that it becomes massively popular. He talks about things like fashion trends, transformations such as the rise of the anti-smoking movement, or as he puts it, "any number of mysterious changes that mark everyday life." According to Gladwell, these changes are a form of social epidemic and spread "just the way viruses do."

One critical factor that drives this kind of epidemic is something he calls "the Law of the Few." The "Few" are the messengers or harbingers of change, the "virus spreaders" who create the epidemic. The Few consist of certain basic types of people, whom Gladwell labels "Connectors, Mavens and Salesmen."

Maven is a Yiddish word that means "expert" in colloquial American. However, in addition to capitalizing the M, Gladwell adds his own more precise meaning to the definition of maven for the sake of his argument. For Gladwell, mavens aren't just accumulators of knowledge, they are socially motivated to share their knowledge out of a genuine desire to help others. He calls mavens "information brokers" who share and trade what they know. They are the "data banks" who provide the message carried by, or driving, the social epidemic. Perhaps most important, says Gladwell, to be a maven is "to be a teacher. But it is also, even more emphatically, to be a student." Makes you wonder if the guy had a picture of Clare Drake on his desk when he came up with his definition for maven. The old coach would never claim to be one, and with his small-town Saskatchewan roots he's about as Yiddish as Gordie Howe, but in the strictest Gladwellian meaning of the term, Clare Drake is the quintessential maven.

Many call him mentor, most notably Ken Hitchcock and his NHL peers Mike Babcock, Tom Renney and Andy Murray. Others who do so include former head NHL coaches Dave King and George Kingston (now an NHL assistant), current NHL assistants like Bill Moores, Perry Pearn and Mike Johnston, as well as many Canadian university and junior coaches. And yet, if you ask Drake about his own mentors, he will throw most of those same names right back at you, in addition to others from whom he has learned during his career.

Of course, there are those who were senior to him when he was a callow youth, men like his father, CJ Drake, and young Clare's coach at the University of British Columbia, NHL Hall-of-Famer Frank Frederickson. But Drake is pointed in his conviction that he has learned from virtually everyone he himself has taught. A Gladwellian maven to the very core of his being, Clare Drake is a true knowledge gatherer. He's just as interested in what he can learn from someone as he is in what he can teach that person. He's a teacher and a student both. This is what Ken Hitchcock meant during his lockout-bound conversation with his Edmonton caller when he archly referred to Drake's ventures into "dangerous areas" and his groundbreaking, countercultural behavior. He was talking about Drake's commitment to sharing information, to divulging his own secrets to his fellow coaches in a game and at a time when this was just not done. There are still coaches in North American pro sports who swear by this dictum: if you've figured out a way to beat your opponent, then you keep that knowledge locked up tighter than the skin on Joan Rivers's cheekbones. Find your edge and just win, baby! If this philosophy is still alive among the schools of thought embraced by twenty-first century coaches, in the 1950s it was the only one. Nobody, **nobody**, told his competitors what made him a winner.

Clare Drake started the movement that changed all that, which is why Hitchcock calls him the "grandfather of the sharing of information." Murray Smith explains the difference between Drake and his fellow hockey coaches of the 1950s: "They were hard-nosed, single-purpose guys" who held to "a real ethic of keeping your own secrets." Drake, on the other hand, was "naturally an open sort of person." Smith goes on: "He's an astute observer and has always been more interested in learning than advancing his own career."

One of Drake's former Golden Bears, Dale Henwood, fashioned a career for himself as a coach and athletic administrator based on things he learned from the maven; he's now president of the Canadian Sport Centre Calgary, which includes that city's National Coaching Institute among its programs. Henwood leads an organization whose mission is the strategic support of Canadian Olympic athletes in a variety of disciplines. He knows high performance sport; he knows elite coaching. Henwood uses the same descriptors as other Drake analysts – "sharing knowledge, learning" – as he extols the man's enduring commitment to building his profession. Henwood remarks on Drake's ceaseless search for "a better way to teach the game, to help you understand it."

Dave Adolph is the head coach of the University of Saskatchewan Huskies (who have resided near the top of the CIS rankings throughout his tenure) and a leader among a new generation of professional coaches in Canadian hockey. Adolph is voluble in his appreciation for Clare Drake as a key influence in his own development. He echoes the others' views, having been a beneficiary of many Drake presentations at coaching seminars staged by Hockey Canada: "I can give you a list of guys at coaching clinics who can't wait to show you how much they know. Clare has never claimed to be an expert. When he presents, he's not bragging about what he knows, he's just sharing what he's learned."

In the eyes of his friends and colleagues, if not his own, Clare Drake is undeniably a maven. His wealth of knowledge, and his willingness to share it, have gained him great respect among today's coaching cognoscenti. But these qualities alone may not have been enough to make him a Gladwellian maven, one of "the Few" who created a "Tipping Point" for our Canadian game. Perhaps it's the humility that Dave Adolph refers to – in combination with Drake's drive to observe, learn and share – that enabled Drake to exert such a powerful influence. In an arena where ego, power and the "just win, baby" ethos are the hard currency of success, this man who cares more about the game than his own "props" became one of its greatest agents of change; he became a Canadian hockey revolutionary.

In their book *The Power of Ethical Management*, organizational theorists Ken Blanchard and Norman Vincent Peale coined the kind of catchphrase that experts of their ilk are known for: "People with humility don't think less of themselves, they think about themselves less." Clare Drake is the kind of man who only talks about his accomplishments when pressed. And when he does, he never utters the word "I." Drake doesn't use the hoary old "there's-no-I-in-team" cliché, he just lives it. If you can get the coach telling stories about seasons past, games or championships won and lost, new tactics or systems devised, he always says "we," never, ever "I." By "we" he can mean his wife Dolly, whom he constantly lauds for her support, or any of the myriad of assistant coaches, co-coaches and other hockey collaborators with whom he has touched minds through his long career. Spend hours and hours in conversation with this man, and the only time you'll hear him say "I" is when he talks about the mistakes he's made. Mistakes: these he'll discuss at his own volition and without equivocation. This is true humility, this is the down-to-earth sense of self that makes Drake a poster boy for the values espoused by Blanchard and Peale.

Clare Drake's credo is: "It's amazing what can be accomplished when nobody cares who gets the credit." This is the mantra of the "team first" cult he established at the University of Alberta decades ago. That cult's adherents continue worshipfully to this day, the Drake mantra painted in bold strokes high on the Golden Bears dressing room wall for all who hang their skates there to see and internalize. Even in this matter Drake takes no credit, citing the source of this mantra as his inspiration. That source? Another foundational coach, another old sage of high principle and true humility – John Wooden, legendary leader of UCLA's basketball Bruins from the 1950s to the 1970s.

It is no small coincidence that Ken Hitchcock calls his mentor the "John Wooden of Canadian hockey." Like Wooden, Drake posted a coaching record of dominance and excellence almost unmatched in his game. He won 697 of the 1030 games he coached in the CIAU, an exceedingly healthy career winning percentage of .695. When he retired from the University of Alberta in 1989 he held the North American record for wins by any coach of amateur hockey at any level. He won seventeen Canada West conference championships and six CIAU national championships. He was conference coach of the year three times and twice named CIAU coach of the year. He spent two full-time seasons in the NHL as an assistant coach with Winnipeg, and parts of other seasons consulting with San Jose, Dallas, Vancouver, Calgary and Edmonton. He coached numerous amateur teams that represented Canada internationally, most notably winning gold at the 1981 Winter Universiade, gold at the 1984 Spengler Cup, bronze at the 1987 Winter Universiade and leading Canada to a heartbreaking sixth place at the 1980 Winter Olympics. He holds two undergraduate degrees (Physical Education from UBC and Education from the U of A), a Master of Science from the University of Washington and an honorary Doctor of Laws from the U of A, where he is a professor emeritus in the Faculty of Physical Education. He's a member of the Yorkton (Saskatchewan) Sports Hall of Fame, the Edmonton Sports Hall of Fame, the Alberta Sports Hall of Fame and the Canadian Sports Hall of Fame. The latest feather in his cap came in 2006, when he was given the Geoff Gowan Award by the Coaching Association of Canada to honor his lifetime contribution to coaching development.

Like Wooden, Clare Drake has also influenced an entire generation of coaches in his sport. Dale Henwood calls him "an icon, in a class of one." He says that Drake's influence on his profession goes beyond hockey, that he's "an impressive standard bearer for coaches in all sports." "He's widely revered in our business," says Ken Hitchcock, "and as highly as he's thought of in Canada, he's just as revered in Europe."

Many Canadian hockey fans might wonder how this could be, given that Clare Drake never played in the NHL, never won a Stanley Cup and never held a head coaching position in the world's best league. In spite of all his travels and travails through fifty years in the world of hockey, Clare Drake spent most of his career labeled as a university coach, the same guy nobody had bothered to ask about the Russians in 1972, the same guy who sat quietly on the side at the 2005 CIS forum while the NHL coaches held the spotlight.

Hitchcock searches for an explanation: "There's always a feeling in our coaching community that there's a higher sense of purpose than winning and losing." He then speaks for his brothers in the coaching fraternity, the NHL professionals against whom he competes, the Canadian coaches who guided our return to Olympic glory, the coaches at all levels throughout Canada, North America and other parts of the world, and for any Canadian who loves our game and suffered with it through the dark years. Ken Hitchcock speaks of Clare Drake's faithfulness in sharing his knowledge to improve the game, his lifelong commitment to excellence and the influence he exerted that brought such profound results:

> This is a man who dedicated his life to teaching. We want to know how he did that, why he did that, how he was able to continue his thirst and quest for knowledge, we want to know what drove him to do that.

Ken Hitchcock wants to hear the story that should intrigue every Canadian lover of hockey – what made Clare Drake a revolutionary, how did he become "dangerous," how did Clare Drake's fingerprints get all over the game?

It started in Yorkton, Saskatchewan. Born there on October 9, 1928, Clare James Drake was the only child of Clarence Josiah and Grace Drake. Except for the fact that he had no siblings, his was the most ordinary and typical of twentieth century upbringings – sports, friends, school and more sports – in a typical western Canadian farming community. Located in southeastern Saskatchewan, Yorkton had been settled by homesteaders only forty-odd years prior to Drake's birth and had grown slowly to reach city status of 10,000 souls in the same year as his arrival. Five years into our new century, it has barely doubled in size.

His father was a teacher and principal of Burke School, a two-story brick edifice that opened in April 1921. Located on Yorkton's Second Avenue North, it served the city as an educational wellspring until 1973. Drake's mother, Grace, was a family-oriented woman, content to set a well-prepared table for her small clan and play a keen game of bridge. This, in contrast to her husband, who was one of Yorkton's leading citizens. Drake the elder, called CJ, was known and respected not just because of his position as a senior educator, but also by dint of his personal character and the lasting impact he had on the local young people.

CJ Drake was a pillar of the community in the best sense of the word. He ran the school, taught in the classroom, coached men, boys and girls in hockey, baseball and softball, was a member of the Lions Club, a church elder and, for a short while, a city alderman. His son and daughter-in-law hold him in fond memory, as does Vern Pachal, one of CJ's former students and players. Pachal remembers old Mr. Drake's generosity in buying bundles of hockey sticks to give to Yorkton's Depression-era kids, of which he was one.

In 1956, when CJ Drake died unexpectedly from an asthma attack at the age of sixty-two, a saddened community lamented the passing of this "beloved school teacher and sportsman extraordinary." His obituarist lauded him for his "teaching prowess… his love for youth and his stout heart" and his eulogist, a local minister, said he was "more than a guide and mentor – he was a friend." Drake senior was also an exceptional coach in his own right. He nurtured the blossoming hockey careers of Yorkton stars like Pachal, his own son Clare and 1950s NHL stalwarts Eddie Litzenberger and Metro Prystai. He coached Yorkton's senior men's softball team to the first Saskatchewan provincial championship in 1940. But his most celebrated coaching feat was in girls' softball, where he led Burke School's teams to a .950 winning percentage from 1925 to 1956. Yorktonians drew comparisons between CJ Drake and

Percy Page, the renowned master coach of the Edmonton Grads high school girls' basketball team, world beaters for decades on end.

When he retired from coaching in 1956, CJ would express feelings and use words that must have had a formative effect on his son's retirement announcement thirty-three years later. He told the *Yorkton Enterprise*, "I love the game, I think I could still carry on and to quit now is like having my right arm cut off. But a man should make way for others and that's the only reason I've decided to call it a day." In 1989, Clare Drake spoke calmly to a gathering of colleagues, media and alumni at the University of Alberta Butterdome, saying that while he still enjoyed the challenge of coaching the Golden Bears, it was time for him to move on and make room for Bill Moores, who had served so long as his assistant, to take the reins at Alberta.

There are other, more significant parallels between father and son. Vern Pachal played youth baseball and hockey in Yorkton with young Clare Drake and Metro Prystai among his older teammates, all of them coached by Clare's dad. More than twenty years later, after two years as a high-scoring professional playing for Eddie Shore and the Springfield Indians of the American Hockey League, Pachal returned to the amateur ranks to star at the University of Alberta for Drake the younger. He recounts what it was like to play for the father: "He was solemn and funny. He was serious both in school and at the rink, always wanting you to do your best, but he could switch to a laugh in the same moment." He then reflects on his Golden Bear experience: "Clare was like him that way. He was solemn and conscientious, but he could laugh with the boys, too." Of course, Pachal is referring to the Drake *gravitas* and its natural relief mechanism, the warm and winning smile. Of the kinship between father and son, Pachal concludes: "I think Clare got a lot from him."

The son makes no bones about it, especially when it comes to values. He remembers his dad as a positive man who offered constant encouragement, not just to his own son but to all his students and players. At age seventy-eight, Clare can still recite the Burke School motto, which, if not chosen by his father the principal, was certainly expounded upon by him unremittingly: "Play up! play up! and play the game!" To young Clare, this meant "make sure you always give it your best." And as Pachal says, CJ exhorted his charges to aspire to this standard whether they were learning math, playing hockey or serving as a member of the community. Clare volunteers that he didn't always meet his dad's standards: "I liked to test the boundaries," he recalls of his youth, "and my dad gave me the strap at school a couple of times."

But when it came to Clare's life in sports, CJ's teachings imprinted deeply. "Play up! play up! and play the game!" meant respecting the game for its own sake, giving it everything you had, but always within the rules. It meant discipline, loyalty, honest effort, fairness; values that seem anachronistic in the modern sports world. When Clare Drake was a youngster, though, there were many examples of how to live by these values. It's no surprise that his boyhood hockey hero was Syl Apps, the great multi-sport athlete who starred in the 1930s and forties for the Toronto Maple Leafs. Apps represented Canada in the 1934 British Empire Games and the 1936 Olympics in pole vault. He was an elite football player and an NHL standout in his time. He won the Calder Trophy as the league's top rookie in 1937. He played ten seasons with the Leafs, garnering two all-star selections while captaining his team to four Stanley Cups. But it was his comportment, both on and off the ice, which made him a hero for young Clare.

Apps was equally respected for his exceptional hockey skills and his gentlemanly play, for which he won the Lady Byng Trophy in 1942. Considered one of the finest NHL leaders of his generation, he applied this character trait in all his endeavors. He left the Leafs in the prime of his career to volunteer for the Canadian Army during World War II, returning to take up his captaincy at war's end. He served in public life after his hockey career as a member of the Ontario legislature and cabinet minister in the 1960s and seventies. He was awarded the Order of Canada in 1977. One of the most telling stories about Syl Apps is from the 1942-43 season, when a broken leg caused him to miss half the schedule. Feeling that he wasn't earning his salary, he approached Leafs owner Conn Smythe and offered to return $1,000 of the meager $6,000 Smythe was paying him; to his credit, Smythe refused the offer. In Syl Apps, young Clare Drake could see the embodiment of the Burke School motto.

"Play up! play up! and play the game!" sounds kind of corny to twenty-first-century ears, the term "play up" carrying confusing connotations derived from the eternal question of pickup hockey: "who's gonna play up and who's gonna play back?" But to an educated, early twentieth-century mind leavened with classical English literature as CJ Drake's was, the Burke School motto would have had a familiar ring to it. It's the sort of language, evoking the kind of sentiment, that hearkens back to British public school culture of the Victorian era. It's redolent with the same meaning as the Duke of Wellington's famous statement in retrospect of his historic 1815 victory over Napoleon: "The battle of Waterloo was won on the playing fields of Eton." By this, Wellington suggested that the gentleman officers who led his army to glory against the French learned leadership and courage on the cricket and rugby pitches of the great British public schools – Eton, Rugby and Harrow – where the members of their class were educated.

This notion, that sport could be used to train young British gentlemen to lead and conquer on behalf of Queen and Empire, became a popular theme in nineteenth-century English literature. Thomas Hughes, author of the mid-century classic *Tom Brown's Schooldays*, was perhaps the most famous literary proponent of this idea; another was the late-Victorian poet and historian, Sir Henry Newbolt, who wrote "Vitaï Lampada" in 1897. This poem, about a British schoolboy cricketer who later in life rallied the troops during a bloody skirmish in some far-flung corner of the Empire, won both critical and popular acclaim in its time. Translated from the Latin, the title means "Torch of Life." Note the repeating last line of each stanza:

> There's a breathless hush in the Close to-night –
> Ten to make and the match to win –
> A bumping pitch and a blinding light,
> An hour to play and the last man in.
> And it's not for the sake of a ribboned coat,
> Or the selfish hope of a season's fame,
> But his Captain's hand on his shoulder smote
> "Play up! play up! and play the game!"
>
> The sand of the desert is sodden red, –
> Red with the wreck of a square that broke; –
> The Gatling's jammed and the Colonel dead,
> And the regiment blind with dust and smoke.

> The river of death has brimmed his banks,
> And England's far, and Honor a name,
> But the voice of a schoolboy rallies the ranks,
> "Play up! play up! and play the game!"
>
> This is the word that year by year
> While in her place the School is set
> Every one of her sons must hear,
> And none that hears it dare forget.
> This they all with a joyful mind
> Bear through life like a torch in flame,
> And falling fling to the host behind –
> "Play up! play up! and play the game!"

Through the poem's three stanzas you can see the progression from cricket pitch to battlefield to an ethos handed down through time, but the third stanza is the most interesting because of the recognizable hockey connection it carries. The lines "Bear through life like a torch in flame, And falling fling to the host behind" are strikingly similar to those in Canadian John McCrae's famous poem, "In Flanders Fields," written only eighteen years later: "To you from failing hands we throw the torch; be yours to hold it high." Many Canadian hockey fans know that these same words are on the dressing room wall of the Montreal Canadiens, underneath the pictures of the great Habs stars enshrined in the Hall of Fame.

For CJ Drake, there would have been an extra connection with Sir Henry Newbolt, in addition to his love of the last line of "Vitai Lampada." One of his small idiosyncrasies was that he liked being called the "Admiral." This alluded to his claim to be directly descended from the great Elizabethan adventurer, Sir Francis Drake. Newbolt had written another highly regarded poem entitled "Drake's Drum," celebrating the old seadog's defeat of the Spanish Armada and his epic role in British history.

Victorian notions of sports and leadership, heroic poetry, and the legacy of Sir Francis Drake all came together in the keen mind and generous heart of a prairie schoolmaster. CJ Drake turned "Play up! play up! and play the game!" into an exhortation that inspired and informed the lives of many young men and women. Metro Prystai, who won Stanley Cups with Ted Lindsay, Gordie Howe and the Red Wings dynasty of the 1950s, summed up CJ's contribution best when he said: "I owe so much to Mr. Drake… he had so much courage and gave us the fortitude we needed for the game on and off the ice."

One young woman whom CJ Drake influenced was Isabel "Dolly" Carlson. Although not his student, she learned lessons from old CJ because she and his son became life partners. An accomplished softballer from Preeceville, Saskatchewan, Dolly met Clare when she came in to Yorkton for high school. She was drawn to him because of his boyish good looks and a shared interest in sports. The two would become good friends by the time they finished high school and eventually marry in 1951; more than fifty years later they preside together over a close-knit family and remain boon companions.

A petite, bright-eyed woman with a warm personality and an easygoing, endearing way about her, Dolly Drake has been an integral part of her husband's career through its every turn. Clare rarely passes up an opportunity to thank her for her support or, in his own, oft-repeated words, "for her love, patience, guidance of our two daughters, and her sharing and understanding of the complexities of a coach's life."

Those complexities included waiting and working in Yorkton while young Clare pursued a hockey career. His first step was to the Regina Pats juniors, where he played the front half of the 1947-48 season under Murray Armstrong, who would move on to become the long-time and highly respected coach of the University of Denver Pioneers. He made a strong impression on Drake, who saw him as a thoughtful communicator and "way ahead of the curve." After Christmas, Armstrong sent Drake to the Medicine Hat Tigers, a team in its first year in the Western Canada Junior League and in need of players. Roy Bentley, a member of the illustrious sporting family from Delisle, Saskatchewan (his brothers Max and Doug, along with Bill Mosienko, made up the Black Hawks' famed Pony Line of the mid-1940s), was the coach of this fledgling team. And there was another great hockey name associated with the 1947-48 Tigers: Dick Warwick. Dick's older brothers Bill and Grant had both played for the New York Rangers in the early 1940s, and Grant was still with them when Clare Drake showed up in Medicine Hat.

The three Warwicks would form one of Canada's most famous lines, on one of its most heralded teams, when they united in Penticton in 1952. Together they would lead the Peach City's senior amateur team, the Vees, to the 1954 Allan Cup and the 1955 world hockey championship. Clare Drake couldn't know it at the time, but his arrival in Medicine Hat in early 1948 was to bear significant consequences for his own career and for Canadian hockey history. He and Dick Warwick were thrown together as teammates and became friends by choice.

Malcolm Gladwell's "Law of the Few" identifies three distinct personality types that drive social change – Connectors, Mavens and Salesmen. Drake the maven was still in the incubator, but he also fits into another of Gladwell's categories, and this facet of his character was already plainly evident. As Dick Warwick reminisces about Clare's appearance in the Hat, he starts with a hockey assessment, saying that Drake was a good player who was well received by the team and Coach Bentley. But then Warwick zeroes in on the salient features of Drake the person, maintaining that he "should have been in the diplomatic corps." In addition to being very intelligent, says Warwick, "that guy had all the panache and finesse you could ever want in a human being." There isn't a hint of sarcasm in Warwick's voice, nor the intimation of hyperbole; all a listener can hear is admiration for the man's old teammate and friend. Dick's older brother Bill would meet Clare a few years later in Germany. While not as eloquent as his younger sibling, Billy Warwick's portrayal of Drake is just as effective: "a helluva guy!" These labels describe the connector of Malcolm Gladwell's theories.

For Gladwell, connectors are those people, small in number yet great in influence, who have that "truly extraordinary knack of making friends and acquaintances." They differ from most others both in the quality of their friendships and the quantity of their acquaintances. They are **not** networkers, in the sense that they use relationships for gain, but are genuinely "gregarious and intensely social" people who intrinsically value interaction with their fellow human beings. Clare Drake is one of these people, and this aspect of his personality played a crucial role in his growth as a coach and, ultimately, in the revolutionary influence he had on the Canadian game. In 1948 though, it was simple serendipity that linked these two young men in Medicine Hat, the new arrival a born connector and nascent maven, the incumbent a member of one of Canadian hockey's Herculean families.

As an athlete, Drake was respected for his hustle, his quickness and his smarts. His play earned the admiration of teammates like Warwick and Vern Pachal, who recalls Drake's Yorkton nickname – "Busher" – as representative of his ebullient on-ice persona. The passion and intensity that would distinguish him as a coach showed early in his hockey development. But Drake himself was under no illusions, even at the tender age of nineteen. He had the good sense, perhaps imbued by his father the educator, to have a plan for his life that didn't depend on becoming a professional hockey player. Drake was a little guy, even by the smaller physical standards of his time, and skill, passion and intensity weren't always enough. He knew during his first year of junior that he wasn't going to make it to the big leagues, and was particularly appreciative of his Regina coach, Murray Armstrong, for being honest with him on this count. He knew his more practical career options included teaching, and perhaps coaching, to keep him connected with the sporting world that he so loved. For Clare Drake, one season of junior hockey was enough.

So in September 1948, Drake set foot on the beautiful Point Grey campus of the University of British Columbia. He chose UBC because at that time, it was one of only two universities in Canada to offer a degree in physical education. It offered Clare the chance to combine his love of sport with academic learning. It also brought him under the influence of Hall-of-Famer Frank Frederickson. By the time Drake encountered him at UBC, this great Canadian had lived a life of adventure and achievement not to be found in many a Hollywood script. Ironically, Drake, who worked as a professional coach well into his seventies, remembers Frederickson as being "elderly." In 1948, the part-time UBC coach was only fifty-three, but to the twenty-year-old Drake, he obviously looked somewhat aged.

Frank Frederickson was the son of Icelandic parents who immigrated to Winnipeg in the 1890s. Although he was born in Canada, he didn't learn to speak English until he was five, when his father built a backyard rink for him that attracted the neighborhood kids. He and other sons of Winnipeg's Icelandic community, facing discrimination as "rag-tag immigrant kids," banded together to form the Falcons hockey club. By 1915 Frederickson had gained a reputation as one of the best amateurs in Canada, captaining the Falcons and the University of Manitoba team as well. Together with a group of his Icelandic-Canadian teammates, he joined the army and was sent overseas in 1917 during the latter stages of World War I. Once they got to Europe, he and a pal decided they wanted to become fighter pilots and joined the Royal Flying Corps, serving a tour of duty in Egypt. While crossing the Mediterranean on his way back to England, his transport ship was torpedoed by a German submarine and Frederickson spent twelve hours floating on a life raft in his pajamas before being rescued.

Apparently unfazed, Frederickson returned to Winnipeg at war's end and helped reorganize the Falcons. Continuing to battle prejudice because of their fair hair and pale skin, the Scandinavians couldn't get games against the clubs of the established Winnipeg Hockey League and so started the Manitoba League with teams from outside the city. In 1919-20 they went on a remarkable run, sweeping their own league, defeating the Winnipeg League Champions and soundly beating the favored University of Toronto to win the Allan Cup. All of a sudden, the Winnipeg Falcons were Canada's Senior Champions and became the nation's representative at the first-ever Olympic hockey tournament in Antwerp, Belgium, in 1920. They beat the Czechs, the Americans and then thrashed Sweden 12-1 to win the gold medal. When Canada's 2004 World Cup and 2005 World Junior teams opened their respective tourneys in gold and black replica jerseys adorned with a red maple leaf, they were commemorating Frank Frederickson's Winnipeg Falcons and Canada's first Olympic hockey gold.

A true renaissance man, Frederickson was an accomplished musician in addition to being a hockey star and aviator. After Antwerp, he picked up his violin and earned a chair in the band at Winnipeg's posh Fort Garry Hotel. But the legendary Lester Patrick, founder of the Pacific Coast Hockey Association (an early rival league to the NHL) and later general manager and coach of the New York Rangers, tracked Frederickson down and talked him into turning pro with the Victoria Cougars of the PCHA. Within five short years, Frank Frederickson, Olympic gold medalist, had also won a PCHA scoring title and led the Cougars to the 1925 Stanley Cup championship. He moved to the NHL's Detroit Cougars in 1926 and ended his time in the league in 1931 as player-coach of the Pittsburgh Pirates. He was inducted into the NHL Hall of Fame in 1958.

When Clare Drake met him, Frank Frederickson was a Vancouver insurance underwriter who also happened to be in his fourth season as part-time coach of the UBC Thunderbirds. Drake saw him as a "different kind of guy," perhaps indicative of the man's wealth of experiences and talents, and later understood him to be "years ahead of his time." This same epithet would be applied to Drake himself in the decades to come. Frederickson was conspicuous for his "academic" approach; Drake respected him for his professional demeanor and his thoughtful, analytical way of teaching the game. One of his innovations, at least in Drake's mind, sprang from the difficulties Coach Frederickson faced in getting his team on the ice.

In 1948, there was just one available ice surface in Vancouver – the old Forum. The Kerrisdale Arena would open during Drake's stay at UBC but in '48, owing to booking pressure on the Forum and their own class schedules, the Thunderbirds could access only two ice times a week for practice. Using necessity as the mother of invention, Frederickson turned to on-campus lunch hour meetings to school his team in the tactics he wanted them to use. And in these meetings, distinctive for the time in their own right, he would take the rather unusual step of drawing plays and positional deployments on the blackboard. He would even go so far as to hand out mimeographed pages typed with the same instructions he'd written on the blackboard. Illustrated with a few hand-drawn diagrams, these primordial "playbooks" covered topics such as "Two Defence Parries Three Man Attack," the role of the goalkeeper and other defensive strategies for varying game situations.

To twenty-first-century eyes, the language in Frederickson's handouts appears antiquated, and the hockey principles he preached seem basic. But to players more than fifty years ago, this information was novel, explicit and pure gold in its value. And in some of Frederickson's teachings we can see the genesis of the Clare Drake way. For example, under the heading "Positions of Defending Forwards and Defencemen when Attacking Player has Puck in Corner of Defending Zone," Frederickson instructed the back side defenceman (the left D in his example), to watch the attacking center while stationed in front of the net. But the D-man was also ordered to "take an odd quick glance to see that the attacking left wing man doesn't beat both defending right defence man and defending right wing." Modern Drake disciples, master coaches like Dave King among them, remark on his time-honored and distinctive admonishment, most often directed to the back side D-man at net front, to "keep your head on a swivel"; this is surely a variation on taking an "odd quick glance." Of greatest portent, though, was a Fredericksonian scribble, handwritten and underlined like an important afterthought at the very end of one of his early handouts: "Positional play is of paramount importance." This was to become one of the underpinnings of Drake's winning philosophy.

Frank Frederickson's uniquely professorial approach to coaching wasn't the only thing that inspired

*"The smartest choice Drake ever made."
Clare and Dolly, nuptials, May 1951.*

Barnstorming at $200 a month. Drake played summer ball for the Kamsack (Saskatchewan) Cyclones in the 1940s, and here, with teammate Bob Stewart, for the Falher (Alberta) Pirates in the 1950s.

respect amongst Drake and the T-Birds. His values rubbed off as well, although in Drake he was already preaching to the converted. John Frederickson, in summing up his father, the great Canadian champion, said: "If we look at the heroes of modern-day hockey there is lots of glitz and glamor.... In the days when my father was playing that wasn't the case. They played together as a team.... They worked to win, and didn't talk about themselves as heroes." Frank Frederickson was one of those men who, rather than thinking less of himself, simply thought about himself less. He was a man of true humility who believed that the team came before the individual, and like CJ Drake, he modeled that trait for young Clare.

Frederickson built a team still considered one of the best ever at the University of British Columbia. Clare Drake's 1948 arrival at Point Grey coincided with that of four other prairie boys – Jack McFarlane (an ex-teammate of Dick Warwick's in Humboldt, Saskatchewan), Stu Bailey (Drake's future best man), Bob Lindsay and Ken Hodgert – and together this gang of flatlanders helped lift the Thunderbirds to heights they've reached only occasionally since then.

Thanks to Frederickson, the Thunderbirds had found a home in the high caliber British Columbia Senior A League against teams like the New Westminster Royals and the Nanaimo Clippers, who featured Drake's pal Dick Warwick in their lineup. For reasons financial and geographical, UBC hadn't participated in the Western Canada Intercollegiate Athletic Union formed by the distant schools east of the Rockies. The universities of Alberta, Manitoba and Saskatchewan had been competing for the Halpenny Trophy, emblematic of the WCIAU championship, since 1922. In 1950, the powerful Golden Bears of Alberta had "owned" the Halpenny for seventeen straight years and the WCIAU retired the old mug and gave it to the U of A in perpetuity. That same year, excited by his team's burgeoning prowess, UBC chancellor Eric Hamber challenged the University of Alberta to a head-to-head series that in UBC's eyes would determine true western Canadian university hockey supremacy.

The inaugural Hamber Cup was contested in Drake's second year with the T-Birds. By then, he and his linemates Stu Bailey and Bob Lindsay, along with ex-pro Bob Koch, were key producers. Drake was described by the campus paper, *Ubyssey*, as a "team man first" with "terrific fight and drive" and was praised for his passing, stickhandling and checking skills. The best-of-five series started in Edmonton, where the 'Birds shocked the confident Bears with 3-2 and 5-4 wins on January 10 and 11. Then there was a hiatus; the Bears continued the final Halpenny series with Saskatchewan and Manitoba while UBC took a trip south of the forty-ninth parallel. In a momentous pair of victories they defeated that year's American collegiate champions, Colorado College, 8-4 and 5-3; covering the series, the *Denver Clarion* credited Drake with putting "the punch in the Thunderbird attack." The T-Birds returned to Vancouver to resume Hamber hostilities on Monday, January 23, losing 3-2 in overtime to a tired Alberta team that had played Friday and Saturday night in Saskatoon and then traveled to the coast. The next night, the University of British Columbia hockey program completed its greatest accomplishment since its inception thirty-five years earlier. The T-Birds downed the exhausted Bears 7-2 to hoist the first Hamber Cup and lay legitimate claim, after beating both the American college and WCIAU champions, to being the best university team in western Canada and one of the best in North America for 1950.

This was a signal moment in UBC hockey history. The Thunderbirds wouldn't win the Hamber Cup again until 1963, when they were coached by Father Bauer and bolstered with players from his National Team program. In twenty-five years of competition for the old chancellor's silver cup, UBC would only win it four times. The first Hamber Cup Champions may have been UBC's finest hockey team ever;

such was the speculation upon their 2000 induction into the UBC Sports Hall of Fame.

The year 1950 was a big one for Clare Drake. Its early championship luster gave way to a fall reunion with his sweetheart. Dolly Carlson's business school training helped her parlay her job at the Yorkton Sears into an administrative position with the chain's downtown Vancouver store. Her move to the coast led to the smartest choice Drake ever made; at Christmas of that year he and Dolly were engaged. The following May, in 1951, he put his brand new and, for the time, exceedingly rare, Bachelor of Physical Education degree in his pocket, married his hometown girl and set off in search of a career. His first job application was for the position of recreation director in the south Okanagan town of Penticton. There, he could have played semi-pro summer baseball and worked in his chosen field, but the town gave the job to someone else. This false start was unremarkable except that, unbeknownst to him then, Drake was soon to play his part in propelling Penticton to the forefront of the world hockey stage.

With no other prospects on the horizon, the newlyweds returned to Yorkton, where Dolly could go back to work for Sears and Clare knew he could make "summer money" playing semi-pro ball for one of Saskatchewan's barnstorming tournament teams. He loved baseball and excelled at it, and his speed, slick infield skills and active bat would earn him $200 a month, a liveable sum in the summer of '51, touring with the Kamsack Cyclones. When the season ended and fall arrived, Drake found himself in Yorkton with no career in the works in spite of his education and the promise it held. He was married to an independent woman who knew how to earn her own living, but Dolly was now pregnant and there was no such thing as maternity leave in 1951. The young man with the plan was in limbo. So he just did what his father had taught him to do; he got involved.

Having attended high school at Yorkton Collegiate, Drake knew the gym teacher and football coach there and volunteered to help him run football practices. One day in early September as they were out on the practice field, the school principal, Russ Baldwin, came wandering by for a chat. Discovering that his former student was at loose ends, he asked him if he'd like to fill a teaching vacancy that had suddenly come up. This caught Clare a little by surprise, given that he hadn't been one of the principal's favorite students. Drake recalls having been summoned to Baldwin's office for several "discussions" while in high school. Looking back on his sometimes testy teenage relationships with adults like his dad and Baldwin, Drake likes to quote Mark Twain: "When I was a boy of fourteen... I could hardly stand to have [my dad] around. But when I got to be twenty-one, I was astonished at how much he had learned in seven years." Regardless of Drake's adolescent cockiness, Russ Baldwin obviously saw something he liked in the young grad and arranged for him to obtain a temporary teaching certificate. That piece of paper allowed Clare to teach in Saskatchewan for two years without an education degree, and so he did.

The Drakes' first child arrived during that winter, early in the New Year and, as Dolly laughingly notes, "exactly nine months and nineteen days after our wedding day." Except for daughter Debbie's birth, those two years in Yorkton passed uneventfully, with Clare teaching English and phys. ed., coaching basketball, football and track, playing hockey for the Yorkton Legionnaires intermediate team and barnstorming on the western Canadian baseball tournament circuit during the summers.

But two years of teaching in Yorkton moved Drake to make another momentous choice, perhaps his second smartest after marrying Dolly. Thinking it would be a good idea to hold permanent teaching qualifications, he decided to return to university to get his education degree. Connector that he was, Drake stayed in touch with many of the people he'd met along the way in his hockey travels. Bob

Lindsay, one of his prairie-based teammates at UBC, had headed back east of the Rockies to complete his schooling in the education faculty at the University of Alberta while playing for the Golden Bears. He was impressed with both his hockey and academic experience in Edmonton and encouraged Clare to enrol in the U of A's one-year, post-degree education diploma program. So Clare and Dolly did some soul searching and she agreed to stay in Yorkton, working and caring for their infant child while he went off to the not-so-big city to polish up his teaching chops. It was a life-altering decision, launching the twenty-five-year-old and his faithful supporter on an odyssey that would take them through half a century of adventure on ice.

When Clare Drake showed up in Edmonton in 1953, the city was on the brink of an economic boom driven by the big oil strike at nearby Leduc in 1947. Edmonton was a bustling little burgh of 183,000, the provincial capital and home to the province's only university. Founded in 1908, the University of Alberta was not yet fifty years old and with roughly 3,500 students, it lacked the size and prestige of Drake's alma mater in Vancouver or the even older and bigger schools of eastern Canada. Nonetheless, there was a sense of excitement and new growth on the campus, beautifully situated on the south bank of the North Saskatchewan River's panoramic valley. At the beginning of the decade, enrolment had dropped slightly after a late-forties surge that resulted from the return of World War II veterans. Now the student population was growing rapidly and so were the university's programs. The year before Drake's arrival, the U of A admitted its very first Ph.D. candidate, giving it the credibility of a full-fledged secondary institution with advanced graduate studies. Since 1947, new buildings had been springing up like daisies, among them grand structures housing the medical and agriculture schools, an imposing red brick edifice on the eastern edge of the campus called the Rutherford Library, and the spanking new Student Union Building.

One of the university's eventual flagship programs was just starting to come into its own. It hadn't become a degree-granting faculty yet, but the School of Physical Education, founded by Canada's great pioneer of physical education, Maury Van Vliet, was an aggressive, forward-thinking group of academics determined to carve out legitimacy and respect for physical education within the university landscape. An American ex-patriot, Dr. Van Vliet had already established himself as a fine multi-sport coach and educator at UBC, where he'd planted the seeds for that institution's degree program in physical education. In 1945 he took a position as the University of Alberta's first professor of physical education and began a thirty-year tenure as the founder and dean of Canada's most advanced physical education faculty. One of the fruits of Van Vliet's drive and leadership was an athletics program that featured powerhouse football, basketball and hockey teams. That Drake's Thunderbirds had beaten the Golden Bears three years earlier was an anomaly; the U of A's domination of western opponents on ice and gridiron was longstanding, and would only increase over the years under Van Vliet. Another Van Vliet distinctive was his firm commitment to the academic approach to sport; he wanted the varsity teams coached by on-campus faculty members, preferably from within his own small but growing staff complement. So in the same year that Drake moved to the banks of the North Saskatchewan, Dr. Van Vliet appointed Professor Donald Smith to coach the Golden Bears hockey team.

An outstanding athlete at the University of Toronto, Don Smith was a phys. ed. grad with the intellectual confidence to coach a sport in which he had little expertise. Many of his players — men like

Bear veteran Ron Donnelly, medical student Doug Ringrose and Drake himself – could tell Dr. Smith lacked hockey savoir-faire, but forgave him for it because of his sterling character, his concern for them as students and his ability to lead and motivate. "He didn't know a lot about hockey," says Drake, "but he sure could coach."

It's important to remember that the art of coaching hockey, at any level, wasn't well developed in the 1950s; men like Frank Frederickson and Murray Armstrong were few and far between. Clare's friend Murray Smith played varsity football at U of A in the late 1940s and filled in occasionally with the hockey Bears when their twelve-man roster (typical of those times) was depleted by injuries. He points out that a hockey coach's biggest job prior to the Drake era was to "open the gate for your players and make sure you didn't get your thumb caught in it when it slammed shut again." Don Smith's sparse hockey knowledge didn't impair his team's performance as much as his leadership helped it and, in Drake's only year as a Golden Bears skater, the team won the Hamber Cup and their second Hardy Cup. The latter chalice, named after the U of A's distinguished classics professor Dr. W.G. Hardy, had replaced the Halpenny Trophy in 1951 as the new prize awarded to the champions of the WCIAU.

The university hockey season was a short one in those days, with a few exhibition games against local senior teams, the five-game Hardy Cup series against Manitoba and Saskatchewan (the Bears were 3-2 in 1954) and the Hamber series against UBC (that year a two-game, total-point affair dominated by Alberta). Clare Drake was the Bears assistant captain and leading scorer in his single season. He and his mates played in the 1920s-vintage University Arena, an arch-ribbed building with a bowed roof located on what is now the parking lot of Edmonton's venerable south side concert hall, the Jubilee Auditorium. With its natural ice surface, the antiquated arena often couldn't host practices and games until well into December, and the varsity schedule usually didn't start until January. As with most old western Canadian rinks, the temperature inside could well be lower than it was outside, unless there was a wind blowing. No whiz on skates, Don Smith conducted his practices from the boards, giving general instructions and leaving his players to their work like a teacher at the blackboard giving out math problems.

Drake flourished in this academic environment. He was an education student but with his B.P.E he gravitated toward the physical education school and its people, and relished being part of a hockey tradition that already boasted a long string of championships. He was also stoked by the energy of a burgeoning city and its university and, as a connector, he delighted in the opportunities to meet new people. One of these new people was Murray Smith, equally a talented athlete and scholar. In the fall of 1953 Smith had just taken a teaching job at Strathcona High School on Edmonton's south side, a few blocks east of the university campus. In addition to his football and hockey prowess, Smith was an accredited swimming instructor and had spent the summer of '53 doing water safety training for the Red Cross along with a guy named Ken Hodgert. Hodgert was Drake's former Thunderbird teammate, and he became the link between the connector/coach-in-the-making and Smith, the future sport psychologist.

Murray Smith would join the staff of the U of A's phys. ed. school in 1958, going on to earn a doctorate in educational psychology and becoming a full professor and department chairman in physical education after it became a faculty in 1964. He would also serve as head coach of the Edmonton Huskies junior football team, the U of A swim team, and as head coach and assistant coach with the Golden Bears football team, including the Vanier Cup Champions of 1980. As a consulting psychologist he has worked with the Edmonton Oilers and the Winnipeg Jets of the NHL, the Kamloops Blazers and

A young, steely-eyed Murray Smith, The future sports psychologist and Drake mentor as he looked when Clare first met him in the 1950s.

Assistant captain and leading scorer. Drake's single season as a Golden Bear, 1953 - 54.

Old friends fifty years later. Murray Smith at right, and Frankie Morris (a CFL Hall-of-Famer and Drake football mentor), with Clare on the left.

Kelowna Rockets of the Western Hockey League and the Golden Bears hockey and basketball teams.

In 2004, Vancouver Canucks' assistant coach Mike Johnston and former NHL all-star Ryan Walter published *Simply the Best – Insights and Strategies from Great Hockey Coaches*. Clare Drake was one of the dozen coaches they profiled in this interview-based book, and when they asked Drake to name some of his own mentors, Murray Smith's name was prominent on his list. As a matter of fact, Drake calls Smith "my most influential mentor."

Clare honors his old friend for his wisdom and the many ideas he's borrowed from him to improve his own coaching. He confers the title of "deep thinker" on Smith, a special epithet in the Drake lexicon reserved for a chosen few. Near the end of Drake's interview with Johnston and Walter, he says: "Associate with positive, enthusiastic, and optimistic people if you can and eventually these will become your qualities." It's difficult to tell who influenced whom in this regard when it comes to the Drake/Smith friendship; Drake is all these things himself, but Murray Smith has the same bundle of qualities in a more extroverted and outspoken package. At eighty, Smith continues to exude vitality and good will, and is still a font of up-to-date knowledge about the mental aspects of individual and team performance in sport. In 2006, with his consulting practice still going strong, he was in his sixth year as team psychologist to the Kelowna Rockets, who won the Memorial Cup in 2004 and also qualified for the championship tourney in 2003 and 2005.

Murray Smith's extensive research, and clinical experience from his own career as a coach, added substance to Drake's innately healthy instincts as a motivator and leader of young men. Ken Hitchcock's admiration of Drake extends far beyond his ability to break down the game and teach it technically; Hitchcock says that one of Drake's other standout qualities is his ability to build teams. Drake cites Murray Smith as the source of many of his ideas in this highly sensitive part of the job. Thanks to their comparable intelligence and common interest in sport, Smith and Drake hit it off in 1953 and have remained good friends for over fifty-two years. Their mutual admiration and collaborative approach to work and life has paid huge dividends for both of them.

The close of the 1953-54 university session saw Clare Drake armed with a teaching certificate and ready to resume his pedagogical career. But fate intervened in the form of another connection, this one between two czars of the international hockey world. Dr. W. G. Hardy had joined the University of Alberta as a professor of classics in 1920 and coached the Golden Bears hockey team during its "prehistoric" era, in 1926-27. He was primarily known as an intellectual and academic colossus of the university community, serving twenty-six years as head of the Department of Classics until his retirement in 1964, and establishing an exceptional collection of antiquities that today bears his name. He was also the eponym of the trophy that WCIAU hockey teams vied for each season starting in 1951. His love of scholarship and sport were intertwined and, in his mind, not at all mutually exclusive. He once said to a U of A phys. ed. graduating class: "People always ask why I, a professor of classics, have such an interest in sport. I tell them, it is ***because*** I am a professor of classics that I am interested in sport." He then went on to explain the important role sport played in the history of ancient Greece and submitted that it should enjoy similar status in modern life.

Dr. Hardy's interest was in fact a passion, a passion that took him to great heights. From 1948 to 1951, he served as president of the International Ice Hockey Federation, the first North American to hold a position that until then had been the sole domain of Europeans. One of his international cronies was Dr. Gunther Sabetzki, who ran the provincial hockey association in Düsseldorf, Germany. As IIHF president from 1975 to 1994, Gunther Sabetzki would lead the global expansion of the game, but in 1954 he was just looking for a coach. He contacted George Hardy to inquire if he knew of a young Canadian with good hockey skills and the right attitude who could run the elite team in Düsseldorf. Hardy phoned Don Smith and asked him if any of his players fit the bill; Dr. Smith suggested Clare Drake's name and Dr. Hardy passed it back to Dr. Sabetzki – from doctor to doctor to doctor. Never in the history of hockey, a sport not known for its intellectuals, have so many Ph.D.s been involved in a transaction.

Clare Drake was presented with a rare and wonderful opportunity for any Canadian in the 1950s, a chance to earn a living abroad in the game that he loved. Again, Clare and Dolly conferred, but this time they agreed the family would stick together; nine months apart while Clare studied in Edmonton was enough. So in October 1954, Clare, Dolly and two-year-old Debbie took the train to Quebec City and boarded the *S.S. Arosa Star*, a refitted World War II troopship, for the trans-Atlantic trip to Germany. Inhabitants of today's global village can scarcely understand the extraordinary nature of the decision this young couple made. It was only nine years after the end of the Second World War. Europe was still digging itself out of the rubble and many in North America continued to think of Germany as an enemy country. What's more, people didn't travel internationally the way they do now, let alone relocate thousands of miles away from friends and family on a long-term basis. And this was long before the pipeline of Canadian hockey talent began to flow toward Europe. The Drakes were truly sailing off into uncharted waters, with their toddler in tow. Their open-mindedness was matched only by their sense of adventure. Talk about "positive, enthusiastic and optimistic."

At twenty-six, Clare Drake had come to the end of the line as an amateur hockey player and student athlete. His contract, worth 800 *Deutschmarks* a month, called for him to "teach the theoretical as well as practical training… according to a plan of training agreed upon with the DEG [the Düsseldorf ice hockey team]." It also stipulated that he would "if there is any need, put himself at disposal as player for the first team." He was taking on one of the more challenging jobs in sport: player-coach.

Drake had made a start at teaching, and then equipped himself for another more serious attempt at the profession, but the coaching possibilities in his life seemed too obvious to ignore. In 1954 he stood at a crossroads, looking back on the end of his student and amateur days, looking forward uncertainly to where and how in the world he could feed his family as a professional coach. He couldn't possibly know it, but this same junction in his life was also to prove an almost mystical node in the space/time continuum of hockey history. Clare Drake the player had learned from, and been heavily influenced by, one of the game's earliest prodigies – Frank Frederickson, NHL Hall of Famer and Canada's on-ice leader of the first-ever Olympic gold medal hockey team. And Clare Drake the coach would go on to teach, and heavily influence, leaders of Canada's most recent gold medal winning team. From 1920 to 2002, a span of eighty-two years and most of the life of the sport itself, runs a single golden thread connecting the minds of Canada's hockey Olympians – that thread, Olympian in its own right, is the career of Clare Drake, the Canadian hockey revolutionary.

CHAPTER THREE

Firsts: The Russians, A Scouting Report, A National Title

The Soviet players looked suspiciously at their Canadian rivals. The characters of the two teams are absolutely different. The Canadians coming from the little town of Penticton . . . represent a unity that achieved everything by common efforts. They are a family team, the core of which are [sic] *the Warwick brothers. Grant is the oldest one and the team's captain and coach. He is the quietest one among the rough fellows.*
Translated from the German newspaper Welt Am Sonntag,
February 20, 1955

One of Canada's greatest hockey brother acts, the Warwcks, Penticton Vees, 1952 - 53. (From left, Grant, Dick and Bill; note the autographs from these 1950s luminaries.)

In 1954, a trip to Europe wasn't just a routine matter of hopping a daily flight to London or Frankfurt. Intercontinental air travel was still in its infancy, and the few who made the trans-Atlantic journey used the old, slow and tried-and-true means of ocean liner. The *Arosa Star* took nine days to lumber from Quebec to the North Sea port of Bremerhaven, where the Drake family made landfall in the Federal Republic of Germany, the western, democratic part of what had been a whole country before 1945. The eastern lobe, the euphemistically named German Democratic Republic, was locked down under rigid Communist control; the Russians had occupied it in 1945 and never went home. In 1952, the Communist regime had closed the border between Germany's sundered halves and tensions continued to spiral upward. And just a year before the Drakes' arrival, Red Army tanks had rolled down the streets of East Berlin to suppress a workers' uprising. Construction on the infamous Berlin Wall wouldn't start until 1961, but the mentality that erected it was already entrenched. The Cold War had begun in earnest and the Drakes were now on the site of its opening salvos.

The two Germanys of the 1950s were the birthing ground for many of the forces and events that shaped geopolitics over the ensuing forty years. These same forces and events were also to have a profound effect on international sport, and they set the stage for Canada's great battle against the Soviet Union in 1972. One of the earliest preliminary skirmishes to that battle was just a few months over the horizon as the Drakes disembarked, and it would take place just across the river from their final destination on their long journey.

That destination was Düsseldorf, a thousand-year-old city on the Rhine about 300 kilometers southwest of Bremerhaven. Not much bigger than the Alberta city the Drakes had just left, Düsseldorf shared little else in common with their departure point. Pounded heavily by Allied bombers during World War II, it was in the midst of a massive rebuilding effort. Together with a fine tradition of art and music (the city boasts Robert Schumann and Felix Mendelssohn among its native sons), Düsseldorf was also proud of its two professional sports teams – Fortuna Düsseldorf, the soccer club of long standing, and *Düsseldorfer EislaufGemeinschaft*, the hockey team known to its fans as DEG. This same club still operates today in the German first division as the DEG Metrostars. At that time, the team owner was a man named Fritz Schmitter, and it was to his rescue that Dr. Gunther Sabetzki had sent the rookie coach from the plains of western Canada.

Herr Schmitter was a tightly wound German businessman, in many ways a typical European sports club owner. He made an immediate impression as a man suffering from high anxiety. Drake smiles in retrospect: "He had the shortest panic point in the history of panic." Schmitter's favorite expression was "Mein Gott! Mein Gott!" and his use of this double-barreled supplication only proliferated as his stress levels mounted. These were dramatically affected by the fortunes of his hockey club, which had taken a turn for the worse the preceding season. European hockey leagues were, and still are, organized along the same lines as that continent's soccer leagues. Teams are grouped according to their performance into divisions, with the best ten or fifteen in the top division, the next bracket into a second division and so forth on down the line. DEG had done poorly during the 1953-54 season and had been relegated from the *Bundesliga* (the German first division as it was then called) down to the *Landesliga*, the second division.

In October of '54, as his team readied for the new campaign, Herr Schmitter was smitten with angst, smarting from the sting of recent relegation and very concerned about the prospects of a rookie-laden roster under the direction of a new coach from halfway around the world. Clare and Dolly Drake had spent nine days aboard ship and most of another day hauling their toddler and their luggage on West German railways. They were tired, having barely opened their suitcases; they were wide-eyed at the foreignness of everything around them; and they were isolated by a large language gap. Although Drake doesn't remember feeling an enormous amount of pressure, Fritz Schmitter must have been the proverbial icing on this very alien cake.

The DEG team had already been through training camp when Drake arrived in mid-October, and its lineup had been set by an interim German coach. Herr Schmitter took Clare to meet the players the morning of his first full day in Düsseldorf, just as they were boarding the bus to leave town for their opening game of the season. Drake's inaugural words to his new team were, "Does anybody speak English?" After a considerable pause, two lonely hands reached tentatively upward in response. Travel-weary, culture-shocked and worried about how he would talk to his players, and with his new boss hovering anxiously, Clare Drake had stepped straight from the bucolic peace of western Canada into the frenetic world of West German *eishockey*.

But this was a man who'd been taught to "Play up! play up! and play the game!" Summoning the quiet enthusiasm his father had bequeathed him and drawing on the tactical and teaching smarts of his old UBC coach, Drake jumped on the bus and set about getting the wheels turning. Before boarding he sent someone in search of a blackboard, and once the bus was rolling he placed the blackboard across a couple of seats at the rear of the coach and had the team gather round. He motioned the two English speakers to stand nearby, bracketing him on either side, and then he began speaking in twenty- to thirty-second bursts, stopping for his translators to do their bit. Drake self-deprecatingly admits fifty years later that it may have been one of the few times in his career where his instructions to his players were so succinct.

He drew Xs and Os, circles and lines, on the blackboard as he spoke, just as he'd seen Frank Frederickson do in his UBC off-ice meetings six years earlier. It was elementary stuff — befitting a first encounter between a rookie coach and a new team, especially given the language barrier — that dealt mainly with positional play in the defensive end of the rink. These simple beginnings were the precursor to the defensive zone coverages that Drake devised in later years, concepts and terminologies that would elevate him to revolutionary status in the eyes of hockey gurus like Ken Hitchcock and Dave King. But in October 1954 it was basic survival on the playing-coach's part and intriguingly new to his curious German audience.

The meeting lasted all of thirty minutes, and even those thirty were padded by the call-and-response rhythm between the English elocutor and his translators. It turned out that these two were not your average hockey players: one was a recent graduate in medicine from Oxford University; the other was a bank manager. However, they were typical European players of the time in that, much like Canadian Football Leaguers, they had their own careers outside their sport. Drake discovered not only an interesting mix of professions on the DEG squad, but also a wide range of ages. His youngest player was eighteen and his oldest forty-one; the latter was Rainier Hillman, former West German National Teamer and Drake's senior by fifteen years. Another elder statesman was the captain, Rolf

Blankenstein, who, now in his eighties and still active in German business, remains in contact with his younger, one-time coach.

Despite the language problems, the back-of-the-bus huddle must have had some positive effect, because that night the underdog DEGs pulled off an upset against Bad Nauheim of the *Bundesliga*. The team didn't perform exactly as Drake had instructed on the bus, but they got enough of it right to produce an organized and winning effort. And they continued on from this auspicious beginning to put together a successful season. Clare, however, would have to finish that season without the company of his wife.

Dolly was already pregnant with the Drakes' second child when they left Canada in October. She'd fought sickness during the crossing, perhaps a combination of the sea and morning varieties, and brought with her some apprehension about the quality of post-war West German medical care and maternity facilities. Her additional concern about the living quarters the club would provide for her small family had been alleviated immediately upon arrival. The Drakes were given a comfortable, spacious apartment in the home of an archetypal German *hausfrau* named Paula Strau. Frau Strau, she of the rhyming nomenclature, proved a warm and welcoming landlady whose daughter Lydia occasionally babysat for Dolly. The Drakes remember the good frau and her daughter fondly for the kindness they showed to strangers in a strange land. But other than the Straus and her own two-year-old, the young coach's wife had no one with whom to while away the long hours that Clare spent at the rink or on the road with the team. True to her own upbeat way of looking at life, Dolly refuses to characterize her stay in West Germany any more negatively than "it wasn't a particularly great time for me."

Wanting her second baby born under the care of Canadian doctors in a Canadian hospital, Dolly returned to Canada with Debbie in December of 1954. Seven months pregnant and with her toddler in hand, she took a ship to New York and then the train across the continent home to Saskatchewan. She and Debbie bunked in at her parents' Yorkton home where they all anticipated the February arrival of Jami, the second daughter. Once again, Dolly waited in Saskatchewan. Clare wouldn't see his baby girl until eight weeks after her birth when he returned home in April – "the complexities of a coach's life"; indeed, the complexities of a coach's wife's life.

With Dolly ensconced in Yorkton, Clare worked on in Düsseldorf. He'd been contracted to coach both the juniors and the first team in the *Landesliga*. After league play ended in February, the first team had an extended road trip abroad slated for the post-season, so in March, Clare and the boys packed their hockey bags for a tour of Great Britain. The West Germans swept a six-game junket against teams of the weaker British league in places like Southampton in the south of England, Blackpool and Durham in the north and against the improbably-named Glasgow Mohawks in Scotland. The Düsseldorfers were welcomed and fêted in several of these British cities as the first international ice hockey team to be seen there. In Glasgow, at the Crossmyloof rink, they discovered a new meaning to the term "home ice advantage." The Mohawks' facility included an outstanding peculiarity; it featured two pillars right in the middle of the ice surface. The inherent bodychecking possibilities make the mind's eye wince, but Drake recalls no injuries from the game. As a matter of fact, *der spielertrainer* – the player-coach – led his team to a 6-4 victory with two goals.

Drake's open-air hockey home in 1954 - 55, Düsseldorf's Brehmstrasse rink, circa 1964.

It should be said that singular arena designs were par for the course in the 1950s and they were nothing new to Drake as a man of those times. He'd played in an assortment of the dimly lit, wooden-raftered barns that served as ice rinks on the prairies during those mid-century years. He'd skated in the frigid old University Arena in Edmonton that resembled nothing so much as an airplane hangar. And when he got to Düsseldorf, he encountered what was then common in big league European hockey, the DEG arena with covered seating for 12,000 and its ice surface open to the weather. Baby boomers who watched the grainy, black-and-white 1960s telecasts of Canadian Olympic Team games may recollect a strange international rule that required play to stop at the midpoint of the third period so the teams could change ends. It seemed like nonsense to most North Americans, who didn't understand that this anachronistic rule was in deference to Europe's history of outdoor hockey stadiums. Outdoor games were subject to the vagaries of changing wind and light conditions, so it was important that each team play an equal amount of time at either end of the rink. Hence, the change at the ten-minute mark of the third. Outdoor ice and split third periods aside, Glasgow's Crossmyloof arena won the prize for most eccentric.

The DEGs posted a 30-11 mark in 1954-55, their losses coming almost exclusively to first division teams as they rolled over the second division *Landesliga*. Their .732 winning percentage and nigh-perfect *Landesliga* record led to a calmer, more contented Herr Schmitter and promotion back up to the *Bundesliga* for the following season. Drake attributes the turnaround mostly to the increased ice time he gave his younger, less-experienced players. It probably didn't hurt that he could play the game some himself, and could thus model the level of intensity he wanted from his team. He's reluctant to say that coaching made the difference, although when pressed he allows with a wry smile that, "When you have a little success, the players begin to listen."

Drake's halting admission speaks to one of the great conundrums of coaching, a "chicken-or-the-egg" question for which the best don't claim to have a definitive answer. Does the success come because the players listen to the coach, or do the players listen to the coach because the team has had some success? In other words, how much of a coach's reputation is based on a fortunate combination of all the right factors coming into play at once, and how much of it is based on his ability to teach the game, build a team and motivate his players? Drake's humility, and ultimately his integrity, lie in his equivocal response to this question, a response that he's maintained throughout his career. His ambivalence shows his healthy understanding of the role of the hockey coach and of the great truism that, in the words of Robert Burns, "the best-laid schemes o' mice an' men, gang aft agley" – things often don't work out the way you plan them.

Planned or not, things do sometimes work out. Such was the case not only for the DEG season, but also for another momentous occurrence in the coach's budding career. By chance, the world hockey championships came to West Germany the same winter Clare Drake was there.

Just after the DEG season ended and shortly before their March trip to Britain, another, more celebrated team arrived in the land of *lederhosen* and Lowenbrau. To this day, the Penticton Vees enjoy a reputation as one of the great teams in the history of Canadian hockey, amateur or pro, domestic or international. When they descended on West Germany in 1955, they brought with them the flamboyant personalities of their leaders, the brothers Warwick, and the high-pressure anticipation of a hockey nation that had been badly stung at the previous year's world championships. Mix in the socio-political context of Cold War West Germany and you had all the ingredients for a heady brew of international hype and controversy.

The Penticton Senior Hockey Club had been formed just in time for the 1951-52 season of the Okanagan Senior Amateur Hockey League. The team was named the Vees, in honor of three local varieties of peaches grown in the valley surrounding the southern Okanagan town – Vedette, Valiant and Veteran. The Vees struggled to win only fifteen games out of fifty in their inaugural season. One of the core players on that first squad was Dick Warwick, former Medicine Hat teammate of Clare Drake. As part of a concerted effort to improve the team for the next campaign, Dick worked on his brothers Bill and Grant during the summer, inviting them to the pretty lakeside community in the hope they'd sign on to bolster the Vees' lineup. This was just a year after Clare Drake had driven through town in pursuit of a career in recreation.

Known affectionately as Dickie, the youngest of the Warwicks was also the smallest. Dick Beddoes, then of the *Vancouver Sun* and later to attain national prominence as sports columnist for the *Globe and Mail*, described Dickie Warwick as "a shred of muscle and a sliver of bone, no more than 130 pounds with his hands in his pockets." Beddoes's claim that Dickie was "living proof that hockey is a game for small boys" painted a stark contrast to the physical dimensions of today's players. No boy when it came to composure and skill, Warwick finished fifth in league scoring during the team's first year, tallying twenty-six goals and forty-one assists in forty-three games. He then performed an equally valuable service by entreating middle brother Billy to sign with the Vees for their second season, 1952-53.

Like his younger sibling, Bill was also vertically challenged, registering barely 5'7", but twenty-five pounds heftier than Dick. The New York Rangers had brought Billy up to the big time for a cup of coffee in 1943-44, and he spent most of the ensuing six years bumping around the high quality American Hockey League, playing for such famed teams as the Hershey Bears, Springfield Indians and Providence Reds. He was both a goal scorer and a scrapper, notching fifty goals in fifty-eight games by the time he hit his stride in the Vees' 1953-54 season, and twice leading the OSAHL in penalty minutes. Though in his eighties now, you can still see the evidence of Bill Warwick's life in hockey writ large upon his face. The flattened nose and numerous scars only enhance the sparkling character that emanates from the man. It was his combination of skill, aggression and pure dynamism that helped turn the Vees around in 1952. The Vees had other talent to build on as well – outstanding goalie Ivan McLelland, strapping defenceman George McAvoy and multi-purpose forwards like Jack McIntyre and Don Berry. The final piece of the puzzle came with the arrival of Grant Warwick.

The oldest and most accomplished of the Warwick trio, Grant had won the Calder Trophy in 1942 as the NHL's outstanding rookie, scoring thirty-three points in forty-four games for the New York Rangers. He posted three twenty-goal seasons in ten NHL campaigns with the Rangers, Boston Bruins and Montreal Canadiens, and when his little brother called he was on the tail end of a fine pro career with the Buffalo Bisons of the American Hockey League. Grant leapt at the chance to play senior hockey with his siblings in Penticton, but the politics and business rules of the game then were much tougher than they are now, lockouts and collective bargaining agreements notwithstanding.

Until the rise of the NHL Players Association and free agency, pro hockey players were owned like chattels by the teams that held their contract rights. And the pro teams were loath to cede those rights back to the player without exacting their pound of flesh. The Buffalo Bisons weren't about to allow Grant Warwick to gain reinstatement as an amateur unless they were paid handsomely for him. They demanded $7,500 for his release, a princely sum in 1952 and one far beyond the means of the Penticton Vees. But the local booster club raised $2,500 from the community and Buffalo grudgingly accepted the offer, paving the way for Grant to join the team in December. This put the Vees on a roll that culminated in their world championship a little over two years later.

In the spring of '53, in only their second season, Penticton won the OSAHL, British Columbia and Western Canadian senior championships. This propelled them into the prestigious Allan Cup, then hockey's second most venerable and venerated piece of silverware. In the 1950s, the Allan Cup was a big deal, having been awarded since 1909 to the best amateur team in the country, the Canadian Senior Champions. Senior hockey in those days was formidable, known for great teams and great players, many of whom simply chose not to play pro because they had other, more lucrative or more fulfilling career options. Senior hockey enjoyed a high profile, with great fan support and intense coverage on radio and in the papers, the popular media of the time.

For a team to play in the Allan Cup was like a journey to the promised land. But for a team from small-town B.C. to glimpse that promised land in only its second year of existence, this was the stuff of fantasy. The Warwicks and their teammates captured the imaginations and hearts of western Canadians as they took on the vaunted Kitchener-Waterloo Dutchmen. The president, general manager and coach of the K-W squad was Bobby Bauer, former member of the Boston Bruins' Kraut Line, future NHL Hall of Famer, and older brother to Father David Bauer, founder of Canada's National Team. The Dutchmen, or "Dutchies" as they were known to their fans, would post their own proud record in international hockey, winning bronze and silver for Canada at the 1956 and 1960 Winter Olympics respectively. In 1953, they did the expected and defeated Penticton to win their first Allan Cup in thirty-five years; their second was to come in 1955. The Vees returned home to a loyal and passionate fan base and readied themselves for another assault on the grand old mug in 1953-54. And assault it was. In an era when the words "mayhem" and "hockey" were synonymous, the Vees fashioned their own distinctive reputation as a hard-skating, hard-hitting, in-your-face gang. Led by their fiery troika of brothers, they garnered a new nickname for Penticton – "Warwicksville" – and an additional team moniker – "the Warwickmen." This didn't always sit well with Pentictonians but, regardless, the Vees' wild and woolly approach and their heart-stopping, come-from-behind victories made them irresistible to their fans.

With Grant Warwick as playing coach, the Vees fought their way through the West and then downed the Sudbury Wolves in a bruising seven-game series to claim the Allan Cup in only their third year of existence. In his post-series *Vancouver Sun* column of May 17, 1954, Dick Beddoes listed the great sporting spectacles of the era: Triple Crown-winner Whirlaway, the epochal heavyweight Joe Louis, the Maple Leafs' fine star Charlie Conacher. Then he said, "But believe me… until you've seen the Penticton Vees playing for the Canadian hockey title before the home town fans, you ain't been nowhere and you ain't seen nothing… nothing at all." He continued: "Extravagant that boast?… Ah, not when you've observed [them] in action. Hackneyed words are appropriate… terrific… fantastic… pulsating." Beddoes's prose may have been hyperbolic but, without a doubt, the Vees were one of those extraordinary teams that won the hearts of an entire nation. Their grip on those hearts was only to tighten in the following year.

As Allan Cup winners in 1954, the Vees were chosen to wear the maple leaf at the 1955 world championships. The '53 winners, the Dutchmen, had not been given the same honor in 1954, which fell instead to a team from East York in Toronto called the Lyndhursts. The Lyndhursts had gone off to Stockholm, site of the '54 Worlds, with standard Canadian expectations – a gold medal. And true to Canadian form they rolled over all opposition in the first six games of the tournament. They beat the usual suspects – Sweden, Finland and West Germany – by the usual scores: 8-0, 20-1, 8-1, respectively. They handled the always competitive Czechoslovaks 5-2 and were poised to take the gold by rubbing out a new team from a new hockey country, the Soviet Union, in the mere formality of their final round robin match. Much to their shock, and that of confidently waiting Canadians at home, the Russians crushed them 7-2 in the worst international defeat ever suffered by a Canadian team to that date.

So the Penticton boys were bearing a heavy burden when their plane set down in West Germany in February 1955. Canada's 1954 humiliation required revenge and it was up to the Vees to deliver. To ensure the desired outcome, the Canadian Amateur Hockey Association had insisted the Vees strengthen their lineup by adding several star players from other B.C. teams. The NHL even got into the act, with Maple Leafs' coach Dick Irvin suggesting that the Vees take two players from each of the Big Six clubs. This would have effectively wiped out most of the Penticton squad. The controversy over the roster began to build in the summer of '54 and continued through the season but the Penticton executive held firm, adamant that the Vees would go as a team or not at all.

The fuss and accompanying pressure only escalated when the Canadians got to Europe. Their first on-ice appearance was in West Berlin, where they played a couple of tune-up games against a thrown-together team that included a few Canadian ex-patriots, one of whom was Clare Drake. Feelings ran high in the former German capital, situated miles east of the closed border between the two Germanys. West Berlin was an isolated democratic enclave surrounded by Communist-controlled East Germany. The Vees and their makeshift opposition, Drake included, couldn't help but notice the blocks and blocks of rubble left from the Allied bombs of a decade earlier. And the Cold War had taken its toll as well. The Russian-dominated East German regime had blockaded all land routes to the western part of the city only six years earlier, necessitating the famed Berlin airlift, conceived by the American airforce as a way of getting food and supplies to the starving citizenry.

History and sport collided upon the high profile arrival of the Vees, when the Canadian press contingent commented on the small meals their German hosts were providing the team. This hit a nerve, given lingering local sensitivities about food shortages, and the Berlin press responded in high dudgeon. The Berliners also disapproved of what they saw on the ice. At practice, and in the two exhibition games, the Vees displayed their typical firebrand style, crashing, bashing and dropping their gloves when so inclined. The Canadians were quickly tagged as rude and rough. But regardless of the controversy surrounding them, they represented to West Berliners and their fellow West Germans,

"Der wilder Bill!" German newspaper caricature of Billy Warwick, 1955.

The Bockbeutel, *Düsseldorf, the Vees' home away from home during the 1955 Worlds (Drake, seated at right foreground imbibing with his Penticton pals).*

indeed to all of Europe on the free side of the Iron Curtain, the best hope for victory against the feared and hated Russians. The defending World Champions were seen as an extension of the occupying force that held a large chunk of Germany and all of eastern Europe in its iron grip, a force that also posed a threat to West Germany. Europe was rife with tension in 1955. If the Vees hadn't already known, they quickly got the message there was much more than hockey at stake here. Rude and rough they might have been, but in the minds of the free press, Canadians at home, West Germans and the rest of western Europe, they carried the flag for democracy against a menacing totalitarian presence that now loomed over sport the way it did over matters military and political. The Vees' flag-bearing duties were less symbolic, more actual than Team Canada's in 1972, and they were performed in a much more threatening context where the political strain was real and immediate.

Perhaps the one Canadian who best embodied this confusing role of criticized, yet hope-invested hero was Bill Warwick. He was the most incendiary player in the Vees' lineup, that rare combination of prodigious goal scorer and pugnacious disturber. He gave no quarter and asked for none, even though he was usually the smallest player on the ice except for his brother Dick. He played the game with a blazing intensity, always at a furious pace, often taking (and returning) incredible abuse in the crowded confines at the edge of the opposition crease. And the burning passion in him inspired his teammates to play with similar emotion.

Led by Billy Warwick, the sheer frenzy of the Vees' on-ice onslaught shocked the German and

European press who first saw them in Berlin. The newsmen quickly came up with an epithet for the middle Warwick brother – "Der Wilder Bill." He was caricatured by a German cartoonist who, ironically, drew him as a towering giant sweeping a pile of dazed, Lilliputian opponents off the ice using a hockey stick with a broom nailed where the blade would be. At least Warwick wasn't depicted using an axe! It's tough to tell whether the artist has Billy's face set in a maniacal grin or an evil grimace, but the piece surely illustrates the meaning of the nickname. The term can be loosely translated from the German in a couple of different ways. The Canadians understood it to mean "Wild Bill," as in Hickok. The German dictionary renders another connotation however – "the savage Bill." Savage, or just a wild Canadian player, Warwick was booed continually by the German fans for his rough play and numerous penalties. In covering the Worlds, even *Sports Illustrated* commented on "Der Wilder Bill," describing him as a "stick scarred veteran with a face stitched together like an eiderdown," but allowing that through the course of the tournament his comportment settled down and so did the attitude of the German fans toward him.

Before the Vees began tournament play, they flew to Prague for a warm-up against the Czechoslovakian National Team. Sid Godber, editor of the *Penticton Herald* and author of the stirring account, *Go Vees Go*, had an epiphany as he arrived with the team in the Czech capital. He said, "I got my first jolt in Prague seeing a wee lad with a hockey stick and skates trudging along. A little later, an open air rink… loaded with kids. And there was an open air rink on every block." Godber discovered that ice hockey had been Czechoslovakia's number one winter sport since just past the turn of the century. His conclusion: "These Czechs aren't going to be easy." He was right. Playing in the crisp, cold air of Prague's main outdoor stadium, in front of 16,000 rabid fans, the Vees squeaked by with a tie. The Czechoslovaks had beaten the Sudbury Wolves to win the 1949 Worlds, and they proved to be the Vees' toughest opposition in 1955. On February 26 in Düsseldorf, in Canada's second game of the world championship tournament, the Vees had to fight from behind twice to beat a very determined Czechoslovak squad 5-3 before 12,000 people in the home rink of Clare Drake's DEG team.

Unfortunately, the lesson that Godber and the Vees learned from their Prague visit seems to have been lost on succeeding generations of Canadians. Fast forward to March 2006, when we in the True North Strong and Free struggled to digest the failure of our men's team at the Turin Winter Olympics. On TSN's *Off the Record* sports talk show, host Michael Landsberg voiced the same question that almost everyone else had asked during the previous few days: "What went wrong?" This time he was talking to Olaf Kolzig, "Olie the Goalie," Canadian-raised goaltender of the Washington Capitals, who, by virtue of his dual citizenship, had played outstandingly at Turin for the German Olympic Team. After listening to Landsberg touch on the common wisdom surrounding the Canadian team – leadership questions, an aging lineup, an inability to gel – Kolzig took the conversation in a different direction. He commented on the true hockey parity in Turin, suggesting there were at least seven nations with a legitimate shot at winning that tournament. He paid due respect to the passion Canadians have for the game, but he also pointed out that there are other great hockey countries in the world where the players and their fans are equally as passionate. Kolzig's gentle reminder that Canada doesn't have a monopoly on hockey-mania came over fifty years after Godber's revelations in Prague, but it carried the same message. It's too bad the entire Canadian hockey nation couldn't have

Sour Soviet, happy Canucks. Vees' captain George McAvoy, world championship cup in arm, in post-game handshake with Russian star Vsevolod Bobrov, March 1955 (note the "string-of-sausages" helmet). Canada's IIHF nemesis, Bunny Ahearne, grins in the middle.

wandered the winter streets of Prague with the Vees in 1955; our expectations today might be a little more realistic.

It's no small irony that the Vees carried similar, probably even greater, hopes in 1955 than those loaded on the Canadian stars who suited up in Turin. The pressure was palpable. Canadian journalist Andy O'Brien wrote of his experience at the tournament: "The build-up for the Sunday final was more intensive than I've ever met in Stanley Cup, Grey Cup or world heavyweight fight supersituations." He estimated there were over 350 radio, TV and newspapermen from all over Europe and North America in Krefeld, site of the round robin final between Canada and the Soviet Union. Foster Hewitt, the legendary voice of the Toronto Maple Leafs who called Henderson's great goal in 1972, flew in to broadcast the final for CBC Radio to an avidly listening Canadian audience, the largest one in our history to that time. He said, "while I had been quite impressed with the clamor for victory in Canada, I wasn't fully prepared for the pleadings by Germans and other Europeans for a like result. All those national overtones indicated that [it] was much more than just a sports event."

Billy Warwick remembers the Krefeld stadium overflowing with 13,000 fans and the city streets swollen with thousands of people cheering the Vees' bus as they made their pre-game journey to the arena. Fifty years later, Dick Warwick simply says, "If we'd a lost that game, we'd a still been swimmin'." But the Vees didn't lose. They handled the pressure because, as Dick says "we were a team of characters" and "we were focused." He talks about how close the Vees were, how they hung together at their home base in Düsseldorf, just across the Rhine from Krefeld, and how they met daily during the tournament to debrief from their last game and prepare for their next one. Their favorite spot to unwind and relieve the pressure was a friendly little bistro fittingly called the *Bockbeutel*, German for "flagon." The owners had adopted the Vees, hanging Canadian flags (then the Red Ensign) on the walls and making them feel at home whenever they walked in the door during the nine days of the tournament. Speed and skill, high intensity, typical Canadian toughness and team camaraderie; these attributes carried the Vees to a gold medal win against the Russians. But they had another arrow in their quiver as well, *der spielertrainer* of *Düsseldorfer Eislaufgemeinschaft*.

Clare Drake, the connector, had made a strong and favorable impression on Dick Warwick, both as a teammate in Medicine Hat and as a UBC opponent against Warwick's Nanaimo Clippers in the B.C. Senior League. Dick talked Drake up to brother Grant, who during the 1954-55 season had become the Vees' playing coach, and they contacted him in advance of their arrival in Europe. Grant asked Clare to take on the task of scouting the Russians for the Vees, and Drake willingly obliged. Serendipity and the connector side of his personality landed him the role, and now the maven part of him kicked in.

While the Vees rolled undefeated through the tournament, thoroughly thrashing all in their path except the aforementioned Czechoslovaks and the Swedes (a 3-0 win), Drake was watching the Russians. It was a gruelling round robin format, the teams playing eight games in nine days. The Vees saw most of their action in Düsseldorf while Drake made short trips across the river to Krefeld, and northeast to Dortmund, to scout the defending World Champions, who also proceeded through the round robin without a loss. Drake's day trips usually brought him back to the Vees' Düsseldorf hotel, the Savoy, where he would make his report to coach Grant Warwick. Dick recalls Clare literally becoming one of the team during those nine, all-consuming days, hanging with the Vees most of the time whether they were at the rink, the hotel or the *Bockbeutel*. He contributed to their daily strategy sessions and played a big part in their success, says Dick.

What impressed the Warwick brothers and their teammates wasn't just Drake's knowledge, but the way he imparted it. In addition to the verbal accounts of Russian play that Drake shared with Grant, he had also noted all his observations on paper, in organized and diagnostic detail. So? That's what a scouting report should be. Easy to say now, or back in the 1980s or seventies, maybe even in the sixties. But in the 1950s, this was groundbreaking stuff. The Warwicks had been around elite hockey for a long time; Grant, with his extensive NHL experience, at the very highest levels of the game. None of them had seen or heard of anything like what Clare Drake showed them on the Russians. Even Drake himself, ever-hesitant to claim credit for an accomplishment or a new idea, says cautiously, "I don't think there were very many scouting reports done at the time."

Clare Drake's 1955 analysis of the Soviet team may have been one of the first scouting reports ever written in the annals of Canadian hockey. It was almost certainly the earliest ever compiled on the Russians. Canadians had only first laid eyes on these red-clad newcomers the year before in Stockholm. There, they'd caught the Toronto Lyndhursts unaware and unprepared; if the Canadian losers had had the advantage of any scouting they surely didn't make much of it. Dick Warwick thinks the Lyndhursts may have picked up some sketchy info from a sportswriter who'd seen the Russians, but that's about it. It's virtually impossible to prove, but logic dictates that Clare Drake was the first Canadian ever to scout the Russians. And what a job he did!

He wrote his report in a small, tidy script that filled six pages of old fashioned, letter-sized notepaper. Now, in the age of the word processor, we would describe Drake's informational style as "bullet form." He listed pointed after point, introducing each one with a dash, and had the report organized into sections entitled "Defence," "1st line," "2nd line," and "3rd line." At the end of the report were his analyses, with diagrams, of the two games the Soviets won against the Swedes and the Americans. In keeping with the politically-charged language of the day, Drake refers to his subjects throughout his report as "the Reds." Here are some of his salient points about their defence:
- all four are good skaters both ways – strong on their feet in the corners;
- they don't rush to start offensive plays – always feed to the wings then follow up fast to play the point;
- no slap shots;
- almost all shots close to the ice (forwards don't screen).

Of the Russian forwards, Drake's general observations included:
- all three lines use that opposite winger cutting behind the goal for a pass and then pass out in front to the trailing player (center or other wing);
- in opponents' end they play one man usually about fifteen feet off to each side of the goal and one man back in sort of a triangle.

While he identified all the players in the Soviet lineup by number, Drake only mentioned one by name – Bobrov. In 1955, Vsevolod Bobrov, who wore number 9 and was captain and star of the team, was the focal point of Russian hockey. At thirty-three, he was considered by his countrymen to be the greatest athlete of his generation, having dominated the Soviet Elite League for years. Between 1947 and 1957, he would score 240 goals in 130 league games and ninety-one goals in fifty-seven games while representing the Soviet Union in international play. He was selected Best Forward in Stockholm at the 1954 world championships and led his team to gold then and at the 1956 Winter Olympics in Cortina, Italy. He also happened to be a star soccer player. He was a Soviet Master of Sport, and would go on to become a "Merited Coach" and direct the great Soviet teams of the early 1970s, including the one that shocked Canada in 1972. He was inducted posthumously into the International Ice Hockey Federation's Hall of Fame in 1997. In terms of his stature within the game for his time, Vsevolod Bobrov was Russia's Maurice Richard and Gordie Howe rolled into one.

In spite of this stature and his illustrious résumé, the exalted Russian star did not overly impress the young Canadian scout. Drake identified Bobrov's line as the slowest of the three Russian forward groups. He acknowledged some of the great captain's tactics – "can fake to left and right," "hangs around the blue line a lot against the boards" – but the comment that really jumps off the page carried a damning epithet, at least within the Drake hockey canon: "Bobrov carries the puck a lot, doesn't pass too well (puck hog)." This report wasn't just the first documented breakdown of Russian hockey by a Canadian; in it we also see the first recorded evidence of a value that Drake would carry with him throughout his entire coaching career. Not one to revere reputation or raw talent for its own sake, Drake often saw greater worth in the player who served the team's needs before his own, whose contribution might not be so noticeable, or draw quite so much acclaim as that of the star.

Drake's blunt pejorative for big number 9 was out of keeping with the rest of his report, which was generally respectful and clinical in its tone. Fifty years later, the Warwicks still attest to the results of his work. The middle brother speaks of Drake's "smarts" and of the trust big brother/coach Grant placed in his hockey acumen. "Der Wilder Bill" scored twice in the game and shares credit for his second marker with Clare, who had mentioned that the Russian defence were weak at playing the body in the corner and cutting off the lane to the crease. Remembering this bit of intelligence, Billy beat one of their defencemen one-on-one, "walking the puck" out of the corner and jamming it into the net. Dick, who had labelled Drake "a real student of the game," simply says of his analysis, "He had those guys tabbed."

The final score in the game was 5-0. Bobrov and his comrades never got a sniff. And Drake really did have them tabbed. He was interviewed by CBC Radio before the game and predicted a 7-0 win for the Vees. He also put his prognostication in writing, in a pre-tournament article he wrote about German ice hockey for a Rhineland English-language newspaper. While encouraging the locals to get their tickets for the upcoming world championships – correctly suggesting that the Canada-Russia match would be a sellout – he also called that game's outcome. "My own impression… is that they [the Russians] are in terrific physical condition but are far too short on hockey "know-how" to handle this year's Canadian representatives, the Penticton V's [sic]."

Lack of hockey know-how, and perhaps an inability to match Canadian intensity and will to win – these things cost the Russians the 1955 world championship. Foster Hewitt wrote of their defeat: "On that icy surface at Krefeld, Canada had won a hockey game and a world title and, in the process, Communist nations received a severe propaganda setback." Hewitt described how the East German broadcasters in the booth next to him refused to announce Canada's third goal and missed the fourth and fifth altogether, because they went off-air early in the third period when it became obvious the Russians weren't going to mount a comeback. He said, "They just hadn't the courage to give the facts of hockey life to their own people."

The Vees, for their part, didn't have to swim back to Canada. Instead, they were welcomed home as conquering heroes and ranked high in the pantheon of all-time great Canadian teams. Clare Drake returned to his DEG boys and preparations for their British road trip, carrying with him the undying gratitude of the Warwick brothers and a gift for his team; a bundle of cherished, Canadian Northland Pro hockey sticks, courtesy of the Vees.

Drake's time in West Germany was short, lasting a little over five months, but highly significant for his own career and Canadian hockey. His first look at the Russians, really Canada's first serious look, set the wheels in his maven brain turning. Drake saw that in spite of their "lack of hockey know-how" they were inventive, adapting the game from their own perspective. He saw things worth trying in a Canadian context, for instance, that big Bobrov played on his off-wing. This tactic, virtually unknown on the western side of the Atlantic where right-handed shooters played the right side and lefties played the left, was the first of many that Drake would borrow from the Russians and other foreign sources, some with greater effect than others. He was intrigued by the odd Russian helmets, which reminded Dick Warwick of "a string of sausages tied together." Helmets weren't wholly new to Canadians. As a matter of fact, because of a head injury suffered several years earlier in a bad car accident, "Der Wilder Bill" himself wore a primitive rig of flattened leather straps that ostensibly guarded his noggin. But the concept of an entire team wearing protective headgear as a preventative measure was novel, at least within Drake's realm of experience. After he got back to Canada, he launched an unsuccessful attempt to have something similar to the Russian prototype designed and manufactured. The coming decades would see him introduce many innovations to Canadian university hockey, from where they would eventually find their way into the pro leagues.

In 1955, he was already beginning to separate himself from the run-of-the-mill, or maybe even the above-average, Canadian hockey coach. His continuous drive to improve, to welcome the unfamiliar in hope of finding a better way, set him apart from the huge majority of his colleagues. Never married to the tried and true, he rejected commonly held values like "we do it this way because that's the way we've always done it" or "that won't work here, we've never tried it before." These and similar phrases were a catechism for many Canadian coaches, not just in the 1950s but right through until the seventies and eighties. For Clare Drake, things different offered new possibilities. And he saw much that was different during his German sojourn. It was the birth of his awareness of the fertile breeding ground that was international hockey; a breeding ground for diversity and progress. What's more, through his concentrated, rewarding experience with the Vees, he saw the high drama of hockey on the world stage, and how sport and geopolitics could join to move entire nations of people to the heights of emotion. Thanks to 1955, Drake had already glimpsed many of the realities that remained hidden to the Canadian hockey establishment as it stumbled into 1972.

Europe, the Russians, the Warwick brothers… they all etched an impression on the budding hockey maven. And he'd made his own impression on both his German hosts and his Penticton pals. He'd won the respect and admiration of the Warwicks with his intelligence, his attention to detail and his hockey acumen. As for the Germans, the Düsseldorf daily paper, in a story entitled *"Der Mann, der aus Edmonton kam"* (The man who came from Edmonton), described that same man as "young, energetic, yet quiet" and spoke of his hockey expertise, his willingness and his enthusiasm. The article also referred to the Canadian's exemplary character and teaching ability, and lauded him for his playing prowess as well. The combined effect of Drake's connector personality, his on-ice skills and his coaching success with Herr Schmitter's club left a lasting mark. Six years after Drake returned to Canada, his German recruiter, Dr. Gunther Sabetzki, contacted him once again. This time, acting for the West German Ice Hockey Federation, Sabetzki proffered Drake a plum position as head coach of the West German National Team, with the express responsibility of taking them to the 1962 world championships in Colorado Springs, USA, and then to the 1964 Olympics in Innsbruck, Austria. Clare was eager to accept but, he says some forty years later with a wistful smile, Dolly stood firm, insisting that their young family be raised in their Home and Native Land.

In April 1955, Drake reunited with his family in Yorkton, meeting his eight-week old daughter Jami for the first time. More semi-pro baseball carried him through the summer and in August the Drakes returned to Edmonton, where his buddy Murray Smith had lined up a job for him at Strathcona Composite High School. This brand new facility, known as "Scona Comp" to southsiders, was located a couple of miles south of the university campus and served as a modern upgrade to the original building situated further north, where Smith had taught the previous two years. The principal, Duncan Innes, was looking for a phys. ed. teacher for the new school and Smith told him he had just the guy. So in autumn 1955, Clare Drake began teaching phys. ed. and English, and also coached senior football, track and field and junior boys basketball. Oh, and just for good measure, he said an enthusiastic yes when the call came from the U of A to stand in for Dr. Don Smith as interim coach of the hockey Bears for the 1955-56 season, while Smith was on sabbatical.

Drake was an exceedingly busy man during his first year back in Edmonton. A true appreciator of the fresh perspective, he asked for volunteers from the school staff to help with some of his coaching responsibilities. Here again his innovative streak showed itself. Reasoning correctly that a physics expert would understand matters such as trajectory and velocity, he accepted physics teacher Jim Kruger's offer of help and assigned him to the throwers on the track and field team. Consequently, Scona's shotputters and discus and javelin throwers had science working for them and, as Drake recalls, the results were very positive for the volunteer coach and his athletes. Clare's pal Murray taught math and science and in his spare time helped out with the Scona football squad while he headed the coaching staff of the Edmonton Huskies of Canadian junior football fame.

Over on campus, the Bears were preparing to defend their Hamber and Hardy Cup championships of the previous season. The rulers of the WCIAU started their late November training camp on the artificial ice at the Edmonton Gardens, before the natural ice at the University Arena was ready. Austin Smith was a fresh-faced seventeen-year-old from the small town of Sedgewick, in east central Alberta, who had played juvenile hockey in Camrose the year before. This talented young center hoped to crack the Bears' veteran lineup in 1955, but the new coach cut him at the end of camp. It may have been because of his youth, or it may have been because Drake figured he already had too many Smiths to keep track of! Whatever the reason, somebody told Drake he'd made a mistake on the kid, and the rookie coach phoned the rookie player and asked him back. For that time, indeed for any era, this behavior borders on the astonishing.

The hockey coach has always had powers akin to those of a dictator and, like a dictator, has always been loath to confess error. Drake's recall of young Austin Smith was the first of a number of such reversals during his tenure at Alberta. He still remembers the mistake: "Cutting Austin Smith was one of my first brain cramps." This willingness to confront his own lapses in judgement not only distinguished him from most others in his fraternity, it marked him as a man with an extraordinarily open mind, and as a coach whose *sole* objective was building the best team and the best players.

Austin Smith would go on to play five seasons with the Golden Bears spaced out over ten years. A bit of a vagabond, he wandered both the hockey and academic worlds before finishing his student career with a U of A master's degree in agriculture, specializing in plant science. His many decades of success in agri-business simply continued the excellence he showed on the ice with the

Bears and two other famed Alberta teams, the Edmonton Oil Kings and the Lacombe Rockets. In 1962-63, at Drake's urging, he followed his coach's footsteps to Germany and became *der spielertrainer* for Krefeld, the very site of the Vees' great victory in 1955. Using Clare's pioneering tactics – forechecking with rotating puck pressure and defensive zone coverage schemes – Smith shepherded Krefeld to a middle-of-the-pack finish in the *Bundesliga*, in spite of tension with club management. The bosses didn't like his insistence on using team depth, pressuring him instead to award all the ice time to six core forwards. Smith's commitment to distributing ice time equitably through the roster was another distinctive value he learned from Drake, one that would land the teacher in his own pot of hot water twenty years later with the Edmonton Oilers.

Smith came back from Krefeld to play one final campaign with the Bears, while he worked on his master's degree in 1964-65, and in that same season he also suited up for the Lacombe Rockets, who would win the Canadian intermediate championship. In 2006 at age sixty-eight, he was still lacing them up a couple of times a week with a few Golden Bear alumni and assorted others, every one younger than him. And he's still got "it" – that almost indefinable quality that distinguishes an elite hockey player from the rest. His smooth, effortless strides and his canny ability to let the puck do all the work cause his fellow scrimmagers to shake their heads in awe, even though they've played with him for years.

A rookie Bear in '55, Austin Smith was witness to Clare Drake's first year at the Alberta helm. Just turned twenty-seven, Drake seemed young to the players, given that he was filling in for the older Smith, he with the Ph.D. and the prestigious faculty position. Austin remembers the new coach facing "a lot of questions" because of his age and that "he had to prove himself." Just as he'd done in Düsseldorf, Drake rose to the occasion. While he was "very open" with his players, spending a lot of time in the dressing room "kibitzing and joking around like one of the guys," says Smith, he was also careful to earn their respect, so the team related to him much like they would a playing coach. They quickly recognized his hockey smarts and were eventually impressed by his commitment to, and understanding of, the role of fitness in the game. Smith thought Drake was "very much ahead of his time," especially when it came to conditioning. He saw the coach score some credibility with his team early on, when one of the players jokingly asked if he was at the same fitness level he was demanding from them. In a friendly yet purposeful response, Drake challenged the questioner to a sit-up contest on the spot. With a watchful dressing room audience, Clare left his opponent in a callisthenic cloud of dust and was still ticking away like a metronome, counting over 100 repetitions, while the sorry player lay on the floor, abdominal muscles quivering.

Austin Smith and his teammates were the first generation of Alberta players to see the experimental nature of their coach and, in effect, be his guinea pigs for many new ideas they considered "off the wall." One that sticks out in Smith's mind was Drake's introduction of ankle weights to their skating workouts, affixed by leather cuffs just above the top of the skate boot. Smith remembers scepticism turning to grudging approval as the guys felt themselves getting stronger using the hated cuffs while the weeks went by. This kind of resistance training has long since been superseded by other more modern techniques, but in 1955 it was groundbreaking and indeed off the wall. Drake's dedication to team fitness would never waver, and as the decades unfolded he would turn repeatedly to the advanced science available through his university colleagues, finding ever more effective ways to give his teams the competitive edge of greater strength and stamina.

In 1955-56, the rookie coach led his team to a repeat of the Hamber and Hardy Cup titles it had taken the year before. Don Smith returned from sabbatical the following season and Drake continued his work at Scona Comp, but all the while his unquenchable thirst for coaching knowledge drove him forward. He was an avid reader of *Scholastic Coach* magazine, an American periodical that is still running strong in the twenty-first century under the title *Scholastic Coach and Athletic Director*. Amidst the knowledge nuggets Drake gleaned from the publication he found an advertisement for a coaching clinic in Reno, Nevada, during the summer of 1957. A coaching clinic… that was something he hadn't heard of before so naturally, maven that he was, he just had to check it out. The added attraction in this instance was that the two featured speakers were a couple of legendary names from the American college ranks. Bud Wilkinson was the long time head coach of the Oklahoma Sooners, winner of three national titles and holder, to this day, of the record – forty-seven – for consecutive wins in NCAA football. Wilkinson was considered a master of preparation and precision by his peers, in part for his highly organized practices in which his drills were planned to the exact minute. The other presenter was the famed, some might say infamous, Adolph Rupp. Known as the "Baron of Bluegrass," this larger-than-life basketball autocrat coached the Kentucky Wildcats for forty-two years, posting a .822 winning percentage along the way to four NCAA titles. Rupp would later earn the dubious distinction of being the first coach of a segregated, all-white team to lose an NCAA championship game to an all-black starting lineup, when his Wildcats were defeated in 1966 by Texas Western University.

Drake was enticed by the chance to learn from these coaching giants, so he and Dolly, and Murray Smith and his wife Rean, all piled into the Drakes' station wagon and headed for Reno. The trip was a revelation for both Edmonton men. They experienced the new phenomenon of the coaching clinic and saw, for the first time, the power generated by the sharing of ideas and collected insights. They met and talked with many other coaches, and they heard at first hand what habits had wrought such great success for Wilkinson and Rupp. From Wilkinson, Drake heard about the importance of attention to detail, and particularly, the value of planned, well-structured practices – a value that would become one of his own trademarks. As for Rupp, Clare remembers him saying in his confident, lazy drawl, "Ah got mah boahs so they know every bowahd on owah floah, and they've taken 10,000 shots from one nail on one of those bowahds." Rupp was talking about what Drake would come to call the "agony of repetition." The Baron was making the point that a player only found his "spot," his place on the floor where he knew he could always make a shot no matter the conditions, through endless practice of the same series of physical movements, over and over again.

Most important, Drake came back from Reno a firm believer in the notion that football, basketball and many other sports and disciplines in life offered wisdom that was transferable to hockey. This provided abundant fuel for the innovative fires that burned within him, and it made him idiosyncratic in the hockey world, where ideas from the "outside" would long continue to be held in high suspicion.

Drake had another "clinical" experience the following summer, except this time he was one of the presenters. His old Yorkton schoolmate Metro Prystai, the NHLer who spoke so eloquently of his debt to Clare's father, was winding down his pro career in 1958 with the Edmonton Flyers of the Western Hockey League. As the summer of '58 approached, Prystai was involved in planning something new – a hockey school. This one was organized by George Vogan and staged at the University of North Dakota in Grand Forks. Vogan had also lined up Emile Francis, Fred Shero and Red Kelly as instructors, all of whom played in the NHL and would eventually coach in the big league as well. Vogan needed one more instructor to cover physical conditioning and the treatment of athletic injuries. Prystai mentioned his old friend Clare Drake, not only an elite level coach but also a UBC phys. ed. grad and thus qualified to discuss such exotica as fitness and injuries. That August, thanks to a hometown connection, Drake found himself rubbing shoulders with some of the bigger names in the hockey firmament.

The school was a two-week extravaganza for players. It covered every facet of the game from fundamentals like skating and shooting to technical refinements on positional and team play. The curriculum even dealt with the hard business truths of the time, featuring a session on contracts and the dreaded A, B, and C forms, the documents used by the NHL and other pro leagues to turn hockey players into little more than indentured slaves. We can be sure that Vogan's school made no waves, however, and offered due deference to those forms and the servitude they engendered. No one thought to challenge this system in those days except a few renegade pros led by Ted Lindsay, and evidence that this school was very much part of the establishment lies in the program's admonishment to players that this was "not a holiday from moral or religious duties."

The staff made it a fun time. Dolly Drake loaded their two girls in the station wagon and drove from Edmonton to Grand Forks in 100-degree Fahrenheit heat to stay with Clare for the latter part of the school. Her favorite memory of the event is dancing with Red Kelly at one of the evening parties thrown by the instructors. According to Dolly, the great Red Wing and Maple Leaf all-star was as smooth on the dance floor as he was on the ice, and both the Drakes found him to be an extremely pleasant and positive fellow. As always, Clare used the opportunity to learn from those around him and was particularly intrigued by Shero, whom he recognized as one of the "early thinkers in the game." Known as "Freddie the Fog," Shero would coach the Philadelphia Flyers to back-to-back Stanley Cups in 1974 and 1975 and become the very first winner of the Jack Adams Award, given by the NHL to its coach of the year.

After chumming with hockey illuminati that summer in Grand Forks, Drake returned to Edmonton and made the final move that would send him on his own path to greatness. Dr. Maury Van Vliet, head of the University of Alberta's School of Physical Education, invited both Drake and Smith, the Scona Comp pair, to join his staff on campus. The new physical education complex was scheduled to open in two years and Van Vliet was building his organization in preparation for its expanded role at the university. Drake's opportunity came in particular because Dr. Don Smith no longer wished to coach hockey. Van Vliet had noticed the fine work done by Drake during Smith's absence in 1955-56, and offered him the standing position of hockey coach, with additional duties of assistant football coach and instructor of the introductory phys. ed. courses that in those times were mandatory for all first-year students. Murray Smith got a similar load, heading up the U of A swim team, assisting with football and teaching the mandatory first year courses and an advanced course in aquatics. Murray chuckles over Van Vliet's nickname for the pair of them – "the Roadrunners" – in reference to their eighteen-hour-a-week lecture schedule on top of their coaching duties.

Except for a few sabbatical seasons, the University of Alberta was to be Clare Drake's professional home for the next thirty years. It was also to be the incubator for the development of a master coach who would transform his profession, and for an entire hockey movement that would ultimately revolutionize the game at its highest levels. Just as Malcolm Gladwell says, there are key ingredients necessary for any such movement to take root and then spread, virally infecting all exposed environments. Gladwell's Law of the Few identifies three types of people needed to start a social epidemic. Drake, we've seen, embodied the first two – connector and maven. He wasn't the only maven involved in this movement; others were already in the picture (Murray Smith for one) and more would soon enter the frame. But he may have been the most dynamic and well-traveled connector, working in the most fertile breeding ground.

Gladwell's third ingredient, the third member of "the Few," is the Salesman. If we can ignore the gender bias of his label, Gladwell's definition of this creature is intriguing and more complex than the standard business meaning of the term. For Gladwell, salesmen are not just those with persuasive verbal skills, although these count; they are people who can "mesmerize." Gladwell says they have "a kind of super-reflex" or "fundamental physiological ability" to communicate non-verbally with powerful results. In less specialized language, we might use the term charisma. It's the quality in Clare Drake that Dick Warwick referred to when he talked about the man's "panache." What makes Drake such a fascinating person, why legions of his players and coaching associates found him so captivating, is that this "super-reflex," or charisma, comes in a somewhat reserved, circumspective package.

He's the antithesis of the sales archetype. His humility, his abhorrence of hyperbole, his understated approach to life, would disqualify him from most modern sales positions. Yet, in spite of this natural reticence, Drake is one of the most positive and passionate people a body could meet. Remember the description of him in the Düsseldorf paper that juxtaposed the word quiet with descriptors like energy and enthusiasm. These seemingly contradictory qualities came together in one individual to make him an *über*salesman by Gladwell's definition. Mix in a well-tuned sense of humor and the Drake smile, emerging from behind the overcast of his intense *gravitas*, and the effect could be, and is still, immensely compelling.

Even though Clare Drake seems to be that rare individual who manifests all three of Gladwell's types of "the Few," it was his players who really became the most effective salesmen of the movement he started. He's quick to claim good fortune in the men who comprised his early teams at Alberta. Their exceptional talent as hockey players was matched by their quality as people and this combination, with Drake both leading and learning from them, generated the early impetus for the movement.

A number of names spring to the fore when discussing the Golden Bears of the late fifties and early sixties. The first, in terms of his arrival on the scene, was centerman Austin Smith. After his initial year with the Bears, Drake's stand-in season of 1955-56, Smith played with the Edmonton Oil Kings before coming back to the university squad in the fall of 1959. On his return to the Bears' lineup, he found Vern Pachal in the number one center spot. Drake's fellow Burke School student from Yorkton had come to Alberta after three seasons in the American Hockey League, then almost on a par with the NHL.

In the early 1950s the NHL consisted of six teams; its major feeder league, the AHL, fluctuated between six and ten. Hence, the two leagues combined offered barely half the teams and roster slots that are now available in the thirty-team NHL. Competition for these spaces was fierce and this gave enormous power to the owners, general managers and coaches who controlled them. One of these men, who performed all three roles at once, was the legendary Eddie Shore. Known variously as the "Edmonton Express" and "Old Blood and Guts," Shore was renowned for being the NHL's first rushing defenceman. He became the only rearguard ever to win the Hart Trophy four times, during a stellar career with the Boston Bruins of the 1920s and thirties. When he retired, he purchased the Springfield Indians of the AHL and operated and coached the team for decades. He was feared as a player and even more so as an owner and coach. Vern Pachal toiled for Shore between 1951 and 1954 for a paltry $3,400 a year, an especially mean sum given that he rang up two fifty-goal seasons as an Indian. Agreeing with the common take on Shore, Pachal laughingly says that "everybody hated him" and that he was "one of the toughest guys to play for in the world." Regardless, he got along with the old tyrant and is proud of the fact that Shore never cut him. But Shore owned the sniper's rights through the infamous C form and wouldn't release him to seek his fortunes with another pro organization. And, Pachal says, "I just realized there was more to life than hockey and decided it was time to get an education." So he looked to the U of A, where Clare Drake, the son of his boyhood mentor, was the new coach of an elite amateur team he could play for while he earned a university degree.

Vern Pachal's nickname was "Peachy," not just because of the alliterative similarities with his surname, but also for his puckhandling skills, which were as sweet and smooth as they come in hockey. Austin Smith, who would become his linemate, says that if today's enlarged NHL existed in that time, Pachal would have had a solid career in the league. Drake strongly concurs, as do Pachal's other Golden Bear contemporaries. He was twenty-six when he donned the green and gold, almost the same age as his coach, and an old hand from the upper echelons of the pro game. Most in his position would have thought themselves beyond the need for coaching, but Vern Pachal says that even though he knew the game well by this stage, Drake taught him more. Obviously, the coach couldn't have done that had the player not been willing to learn. Austin Smith was impressed with the respect the skilled veteran showed the young coach in the dressing room, and Drake himself says, "He never took advantage of our friendship." But it was a two-way street. Drake in turn relied on Pachal as a sage sounding board. "We talked things over a fair bit," remembers Vern, "and we'd discuss ideas that Clare would try out in practice." In effect, the consummate center became an unofficial assistant coach for Drake, during an era when no such role existed.

Vern Pachal credits Drake with his maturation, both on and off the ice, saying simply, "He taught me to be a man." "I grew up at the U of A," declares Pachal, "I learned to pass." What's the connection between refining a hockey skill and developing as a person? Pachal means Drake showed him that by sharing the puck he would become a leader, and one of those special players who made

Former Golden Bear, now "the Ultra Hockey Man." George Kingston, assistant coach, Florida Panthers, 2005.
Any resemblance? The enduring, Golden Bear logo sporting the smart-assed grin of its caricaturist, George Kingston.

all those around him better. During his stint in the pros, Pachal had been concerned mainly with his own game and his ability to put the puck in the net – a natural mindset given the system that held him captive. As a Golden Bear, he learned to care about the team, the greater good, and to contribute to the growth of the men with whom he shared his passion. He was among the first of legions of Drake's players who would thank the coach for teaching bigger lessons than those that applied on the ice.

Austin Smith attests to the powerful effect of Pachal's progress. Upon his 1959 return to the Bears, Smith found himself in a totally foreign position, playing right wing to Pachal's center. "Clare figured out the chemistry," says a still-mystified Smith, "Whatever it was, that was my most enjoyable year in hockey. Vern was very demanding, he'd give you shit if you didn't work your tail off, but boy he was great to play with!"

In addition to sharing the puck and tremendous on-ice success, the two also found themselves perplexed, intrigued and inspired by many of Drake's innovations. Seared in their memories is a startling tactic the coach threw into a pre-game warm-up against a big, bashing University of Manitoba squad. The Bisons had nearly run the Bears out of the rink during the Winnipeg leg of their season series, and Drake was anticipating more of the same pounding during Alberta's homestand against them. So he told the team to use half-ice line rushes with full body contact during the warm-up, forwards making sure to drive their own defence into the end boards at the conclusion of each rush. He explained to the guys that the pre-game hitting would prepare them for the Bison onslaught. Smith remembers Pachal shaking his head on the bench during the first period, muttering that he'd never seen anything like it in all his years of hockey, including his time with "Old Blood and Guts" Shore. Smith adds, "It worked though. Manitoba came out head hunting and we were ready for them."

There were other, more refined inventions that impressed these veterans and their teammates. Pachal admired Drake's early practice approach: "He didn't just drop the puck and stand at the bench, he taught you how to play. He had a personal hockey relationship with all eighteen players on the team." New to the ex-pro were things like a special breakout system for the power play, and a passing drill where the players skated in pairs from one end to the other, throwing the puck tape-to-tape at high speed, never letting it remain on one stick for more than a second. As Pachal correctly points out, fifty years later this is standard stuff at every level in hockey, but at the time it was novel.

Smith and Pachal were established team leaders when another young man came to training camp in the late 1950s. George Kingston had played junior B hockey in the Edmonton Oil Kings organization while he attended school at Scona Comp. There he played football for Murray Smith and Clare Drake, and the two positive, encouraging coaches influenced him to the extent that he dropped his plans to study architecture and instead followed his two mentors to the U of A, enrolling in physical education. Needless to say, he also tried out for Drake's hockey team. It took him several attempts to crack the Bears' lineup; in fact, Kingston laughs about his reaction to seeing Pachal at training camp: "It made me switch from center to defence!" Like Austin Smith, Kingston would come and go from the Bears well into the mid-sixties, leaving to teach school and returning to complete a master's degree in phys. ed. He would eventually earn a doctorate in that discipline from the U of A.

Kingston had changed his educational plans because of Smith and Drake. He abandoned any notions he had about playing pro hockey partly because of the stories told by Pachal and another Golden Bear great of the late fifties, Vic Dzurko. Dzurko had also played in the AHL, had also felt the iron grip of Eddie Shore, and like Pachal, was also an NHL caliber player. He was Pachal's hockey opposite – 6'1" and 200 pounds, a big man for his day and a bruising, intimidating force on the blue line. Kingston cites Dzurko as owning one of the earlier big slap shots in the game, one that scared the hell out of the opposition and his own teammates alike because, as Kingston says with a smile, "no one could hammer a shot harder, and nobody, including Vic, knew where it was going!"

Both Pachal and Dzurko told of, in Kingston's words, "the brutalizing experience of pro hockey." Now a master coach in his own right, George Kingston has logged decades of success behind the benches of university, international and NHL clubs. He's another member of Ryan Walter's and Mike Johnston's select twelve in *Simply the Best*. When George Kingston talks about coaching in the 1950s and at least one ensuing decade, a listener can hear the combined disapproval and disappointment in his voice. He doesn't mince his words as he explains what he means by "brutalizing." "Coaches motivated their players by fear; isolating, demeaning and abusing them," says Kingston. He calls it the "Punch Imlach model" of coaching, referring to the notorious manipulator who bullied the Toronto Maple Leafs to four Stanley Cups in the 1960s.

Kingston speaks respectfully of the players who survived or even thrived in the milieu created by the likes of Imlach and Shore, but he makes the point that Pachal and Dzurko were "renaissance men" who had other interests and talents outside of hockey. Pachal earned his education degree and had a long, rewarding career following CJ Drake's footsteps as a teacher and coach in Yorkton. Dzurko became a chartered accountant and a leader in Edmonton's business community for many years before his untimely death from a heart attack during an oldtimers hockey game. The alternative hockey environment created by Clare Drake at the U of A in the late fifties stood as a beacon of positivity and reason in the mostly benighted hockey world of that era. It was a place where intelligent, thoughtful men like Pachal, Dzurko and Kingston could play the game at a highly competitive and challenging level, yet pursue other interests that enriched the texture of their lives. It was a nurturing environment, an incubator, not just where Drake himself would become a "coach among coaches," but where many others would find sustenance and blossom into profound agents of change themselves. George Kingston was one of the earliest and most influential of these.

A short, ironic tangent to the story of George Kingston at the University of Alberta involves his artistic bent. A true renaissance man himself, Kingston liked to draw and later included art among his high school teaching responsibilities. When he was an undergraduate he ran for the position of athletics representative to the student council and wanted to create a recognizable symbol for his campaign posters. Working from a picture he found somewhere, he created the image of a bear's head, the face featuring a half-wink and a smart-ass grin. This image got plastered around the university during his election campaign (which proved successful) and thence evolved to become the official logo of the U of A's intercollegiate athletic teams. The irony here is that from 1967 until 1988, Kingston coached the University of Calgary Dinosaurs, the Bears' major rival through many of those years and beyond. To this day, if you surveyed the U of C campus you might not find a more detested image than the famed smirking Bear of the University of Alberta.

George Kingston won five Canada West conference championships at the U of C, winning 245 out of 373 games. He was named CIAU coach of the year twice, in 1974 and 1981. A guest assistant with the Calgary Flames in the early eighties, he moved to the NHL as an assistant with the Minnesota North Stars in 1988 and became the head coach of the San Jose Sharks in their inaugural 1991 season. He was also an assistant with the Atlanta Thrashers in their expansion year (1999). In 2006-07, he was in his fourth season as the Florida Panthers' assistant coach in charge of defence. His solid NHL résumé is eclipsed by his international record. He assisted Dave King with the 1984 Olympic Team and with Canada's bronze medalists at the 1983 world championships. He was head coach of Canada's 1987 gold medal entry at the Spengler Cup, after Clare Drake coached the first Canadian team to win this prestigious tournament. As head coach he broke Canada's thirty-three-year shutout by winning the 1994 world championship and was general manager of our silver medal team at the 1994 Olympics in Lillehammer. He was also head coach of the Norwegian and German national teams during the 1990s. Kingston is a highly approachable, articulate man who loves to discuss matters philosophical, which for him include hockey. He joins Murray Smith among the few to whom Drake ascribes "deep thinker" status. In acknowledging his remarkable career, Ryan Walter and Mike Johnston call George Kingston the "Ultra Hockey Man." The Ultra Hockey Man calls Clare Drake his mentor.

Another of Kingston's Bear contemporaries was a wide-eyed kid from northern Alberta's Peace River country named Dick Wintermute. Not as well traveled as the others, he'd played senior hockey before attending the Bears training camp in 1960, where he found himself "totally overwhelmed." Regardless, he made the team, eventually becoming Kingston's defence partner, and played his full five years of eligibility. He served as captain during his final two seasons and led the Bears to their first national championship in 1964. One of the new wrinkles he saw was a drill that presaged today's scheme of cycling the puck in the offensive zone. Drake's forwards practiced moving the puck back and forth along the corner boards under pressure, holding the defencemen off with their upper bodies. Wintermute also recalls being taught a shorthanded forechecking system that anticipated the modern-day trap in the way it forced the opposition's power play breakout to one side of the rink.

Kingston and Wintermute, Vern Pachal and Austin Smith, Vic Dzurko . . . they were great leaders and fine hockey minds in their own right. Any coach would have been foolish not to seek their counsel, but few coaches in those times would consider consulting their players. Drake, on the other hand, was more than smart enough to take advantage of the great resources in his dressing room.

Kingston and Wintermute share memories of Drake excitedly bursting into the dressing room with new tactics or training techniques he wanted the team to try. Kingston says the veterans would hear Drake's latest inspiration and give their feedback on whether they thought it would work or not. What these players appreciated about their coach was that he listened in turn, and respected their views on these matters. Kingston says it was a "breath of fresh air" playing for a man like this; Wintermute saw Drake's willingness to listen as the mark of a secure leader.

This open, empowering philosophy paid dividends and led to other coaching advances. It yielded pronounced benefits for team building, giving the veterans an influence in the room that ensured the team's identity would be impressed upon newcomers. As Drake told Walter and Johnston in 2004, this was the secret to the great consistency and continuing success enjoyed by the Golden Bears throughout and beyond his decades at the helm. Drake's leadership style has always been to teach others to be leaders. By entrusting veteran players with a leadership role, he turned a winning team into a winning program, with winning habits and attitudes passed from year to year and generation to generation by the players themselves.

Before long, this approach spawned another development. Having coached football, Drake already knew that the skipper could be more effective with a little help. He'd leaned on Vern Pachal during his first few seasons running the Bears, and he eventually concluded that if assistant coaches were fine for the gridiron, then why not for hockey, too? The success of the de facto relationship with Pachal, and of seeking input from key veterans, moved Drake to start delegating some of the work to an assistant coach.

The first of these was Ron Watson, who had started on the Bears blue line in 1962-63. Watson had played the previous four seasons with McMaster University in Hamilton, and journeyed west to Alberta to work on a master's degree in phys. ed. In joining the Bears for his final year of varsity eligibility, Watson saw a "stark contrast" between Drake's organized practices and detailed teaching techniques, and the style of his McMaster coach Les Prince. Prince was a father figure to his players, long on encouragement but short on hockey acumen. Watson says that in spite of his own years of experience before he got to Alberta, he had much more to learn about playing defence. Under Clare Drake, he refined his individual skills, such as the proper footwork for defensive turns, and he learned to "read and react," how to "fit into systems designed for strategic situations in the game."

One or two of the skills Drake was able to teach his players came from an unexpected source, through a serendipitous encounter. Edmonton's venerable landmark, the Macdonald Hotel (known affectionately as "the Mac"), was the scene of many U of A sports banquets over the years. One March evening during the 1960s, Clare Drake and Murray Smith were in attendance at one of these fêtes when, as they wandered through the hotel lobby, they ran into none other than the old "Edmonton Express" himself, Eddie Shore. While he may have been a renowned tyrant, Shore was also one of the great hockey technicians of his day, and Drake couldn't pass up the chance to learn from this acknowledged master of the game. He introduced himself to Shore and asked him a question about skating drills for defencemen and how best to teach backward crossovers. Shore responded enthusiastically and, in his smart leather brogues, demonstrated the correct footwork for Drake. To ensure he had it right, Drake then aped Shore's movements. There on the plush carpet in the ornate reception area of the city's finest hotel, in front of goggle-eyed guests and bellhops, the two danced a bizarre soft-shoe routine – forward-back, heel-toe, pivot-crossover. All this went into Drake's catalogue of skills and drills, which he duly taught to eager students like Ron Watson.

There was a junior varsity feeder team for the Bears in the late 1950s and sixties and Watson became their coach in the 1963-64 season. In the fall of 1964, Drake invited him to be assistant coach of the Bears. Other assistant coaches would follow in the next few years: Brian McDonald, a U of A administrator who had played for the Regina Pats and the University of Saskatchewan; Dick Wintermute, the former captain who would assist Drake into the mid-seventies; Peter Esdale in the seventies and eighties; and Bill Moores, who ultimately became Clare's co-coach and greatest collaborator before setting his own high standards when he led the green and gold. Drake admits that he could have delegated more to his early assistants, and neither Watson nor McDonald recall being given many responsibilities. The role expanded with Wintermute and flourished to its fullest capacity with Moores, but it started with Watson in 1964. It's difficult to ascertain when and where the first assistant coaches worked in hockey, but contemporaries agree that in the early 1960s the concept was still quite rare at any level. Bob Hindmarch at UBC was quite possibly the very first assistant in the university ranks, starting there in 1961-62 and working with Father Bauer the following season. As for the NHL, the Montreal Canadiens and the Philadelphia Flyers may have been the first teams to use assistants; Claude Ruel is listed in the position for the 1973 Stanley Cup Champions and Mike Nykoluk assisted Fred Shero with the Flyers in the early seventies.

While Ron Watson doesn't remember having many well-defined tasks as Drake's assistant, he does credit this opportunity as the foundation for his own long career in coaching. After leaving the U of A in 1965, he went on to coach the University of Western Ontario Mustangs and spent twenty years pushing that program into the upper ranks of CIAU hockey. He also completed his Ph.D. and so earned an academic position at UWO as well. "I've had a wonderful career as a coach and academic," says Watson, "and I owe a lot of that to Clare and the U of A. I took Clare's systems and teaching approach with me to Western."

Drake's use of veterans to share leadership and instil identity, his reliance on an assistant coach for input and to increase his own effectiveness; these are the trademarks of a leader with vision, a leader consciously building a framework and processes for success that will outlast his own presence. According to Harvard business professor and change management guru John Kotter, this is the kind of leadership that drives change. It "defines what the future should look like, aligns people with that vision, and inspires them to make it happen despite the obstacles."

Clare Drake's vision included a national championship for Canadian university hockey. In the late 1950s, Canadian universities had no central organizing authority for sport, but instead consisted of a number of independent regional athletic unions that each ran their own championships for the various sports they administered. The major universities in the west – Manitoba, Saskatchewan, Alberta and British Columbia – were part of the WCIAU (which would become the Canada West conference in 1972) and their hockey teams vied for the W.G. Hardy Cup, named after the U of A classics professor who helped Drake find his way to Germany in 1954. The Canadian Intercollegiate Athletic Union, which brought the regional unions under a national umbrella, was officially constituted in 1961; it became the CIS (Canadian Interuniversity Sport) in 2001. Drake's powerful Hardy Cup Champions of 1959-60, who included Vern Pachal, Austin Smith, Vic Dzurko and George Kingston and compiled an overall record of 18-2-1, incited him to lobby for a challenge series against the Ontario/Quebec Champions (in 1959-60, Laval University). His efforts produced nothing for several years, which caused him frustration and disappointment, but in the spring of 1963 the CIAU finally staged its first national hockey championship. This was due in large part to the efforts of far-sighted men like Drake and Tom Watt of the University of Toronto who, in their ongoing commitment to excellence, knew that national competition would only enhance the already high quality of university hockey.

In 1963, the McMaster University Marlins won the first University Cup. The trophy was donated by Queen's University and Royal Military College, both located in Kingston, Ontario, the site of the 1963 and '64 tournaments. Coached by Ron Watson's "father figure" Les Prince, the Marlins narrowly defeated Father Bauer's UBC Thunderbirds. The T-Birds were the first UBC squad since Clare Drake's 1950 team to win the Hamber Cup against Alberta, ending a twelve-year drought; they also took the Hardy Cup and the western title it represented. They wore the blue and gold of UBC, but the very next year, key members of this team would don red and white to earn Olympic bronze for Canada at Innsbruck, only to have it denied them on a technicality for forty-one years until the IIHF officially recognized their medal in 2005. Goaltender Ken Broderick and skaters Terry O'Malley and Barry McKenzie, Dave Chambers and Mickey McDowell all played at Kingston in '63 and on Canada's National Team the following season. And Coach Bauer and his assistant Bob Hindmarch, with Broderick, O'Malley and McKenzie, would win bronze at Innsbruck, showing that the best in Canadian university hockey could also compete with the best in international hockey. The T-Birds' 3-2 upset loss to McMaster in 1963 only whetted the Golden Bears' appetite to challenge for the national title their coach had helped make a reality. Next year it was the Bears' turn.

The 1963-64 season was a trying one for Drake and his Golden Bears. There was no league playoff in those days; the WCIAU-Hardy Cup Champion was simply the team with the best record at the end of the schedule. The Bears were atop the league, but had to forfeit points because one of their guys had played for money with another team during the season and another had been academically ineligible. The victories those players had dressed for were ruled losses by the league and, to win the title, the Bears were forced to sweep an away series against the always tough Manitoba Bisons on the last weekend of the season.

Murray Smith described Drake's coaching philosophy as "predominantly rational" and legions of his players, managers and assistants will attest to this. Many Golden Bears never, ever heard him swear and the few who did remember the occasion as a singular moment. But all who know him have also seen evidence of the great intensity that burns within – when Drake was younger this intensity would find its release point, often with humorous effect. No yeller or screamer, he was nonetheless an occasional kicker of inanimate objects, especially in the earlier years of his career. The strain of the 1963-64 season, with its aforementioned setbacks and a yearning for the new but already-coveted University Cup, generated a flurry of launched garbage cans and explosively closed doors. In good-natured recognition of their calm coach's one incendiary characteristic, the 1963-64 Bears presented him with the "Golden Boot." Not to be confused with international soccer's annual award to that game's greatest player, this piece of footwear was of sturdier, more industrial form and function. "The guys found a really solid, steel-toed construction boot," says Ron Watson, "spray-painted it gold and gave it to Clare in a fun little ceremony near the end of the season." Never shy about discussing his own shortcomings, Drake chuckles ruefully at the memory and allows that at thirty-five, he still had plenty to learn. One of the greatest things about Clare Drake is that, in his late seventies, he's still consciously working on this same process. Ken Hitchcock shakes his head in wonderment when he sees his old mentor at coaching seminars, taking notes and asking questions, because he will never outlive his devotion to learning.

The Bears overcame their troubles in 1963-64 and journeyed to Kingston as the western representatives in the four-team, single knockout University Cup tournament. They defeated the Atlantic Champions, the University of New Brunswick, 5-3 in the opener, almost doubling the shots on their opponent. Then they danced all over Sir George Williams University of Montreal, winning the CIAU's second national championship in a 9-1 cruise. The icing on the cake for Coach Drake came when his boyhood hero Syl Apps, by then a member of the Ontario legislature, presented the Golden Bears with their first University Cup.

Drake had stepped into a strong hockey tradition at the University of Alberta. It was an established institution with an attractive athletic and academic reputation that brought players like Vern Pachal from afar and encouraged the good local talent to stay, or return, home. Obviously there were many more fine Golden Bears than have gained mention on these pages, but names like Pachal, Austin Smith, Vic Dzurko, George Kingston, Dick Wintermute and Ron Watson stand as fair representation for the kind of men who influenced Clare Drake as an emerging coach and in turn were influenced by him. Only Wintermute actually remained to play with the 1964 National Champions, but what they all shared in common – whether elite pros like Pachal and Dzurko; Kingston from the local juniors; Smith, who'd been overseas; Wintermute from rural senior hockey; or Watson from the eastern university ranks – was their sense that they were onto something new and refreshingly different as they thrived under Clare Drake's tutelage. The positive, rational atmosphere, the teaching of individual skill refinements, the explicit commitment to team play and the studied, systematic approach to game strategy – this distinctive combination of elements struck all these men as evidence of a novel, enlightened philosophy that simply did not exist elsewhere within their broad realm of experience.

Counting his year as interim coach in 1955-56, by 1963-64 Clare Drake had logged seven seasons behind the bench of the Golden Bears. He'd won five league championships and one of the first two CIAU national titles. His record in league and exhibition play during those seven seasons was 101-49-14. For many NHL coaches, seven seasons have constituted an entire career. Certainly, for most coaches of pro teams, seven seasons with one club is a very rare privilege. For Clare Drake, seven seasons was just the beginning; now that he'd helped to create a national championship for university hockey and brought home its silverware, he was really starting to cook.

CHAPTER FOUR

A Man Ahead of His Time

If you can meet with Triumph and Disaster
And treat those two impostors just the same
If you can bear to hear the truth you've spoken
Twisted by knaves to make a trap for fools…
…you'll be a Man, my son!
Excerpt from "If," by Rudyard Kipling

The local "Sports Celebrity" atop, not under, the table. A dapper Drake "feels the love" from his city after winning The Double (national football and hockey titles in the same season), 1967 - 68.

When Pat Burns was named coach of the Montreal Canadiens in 1988, he quipped: "I don't want to be coach *of* the year, just coach *for* a year." He lasted four seasons with Montreal and won the Jack Adams Award as NHL coach of the year, exceeding his aspirations on both counts. He picked up a second Adams Award with the Leafs in four seasons with them, but still no Stanley Cup. The grand silver chalice eluded him yet again in Boston, where he was fired early in his fourth season even though he'd won another Adams Award during his stint with the Bruins. The only man to be awarded the Adams three times (notably with three different teams), he finally captured the Stanley Cup in 2003 with the New Jersey Devils. Burns's droll statement about his coaching goals upon taking over the Habs not only reveals his lunch pail persona, it also shows his understanding of the vagaries of a professional coaching career.

George Kingston, the hockey intellectual with the Ph.D., says the same thing using different language. While not an Adams Award or Stanley Cup winner, Kingston's perspective on the vocation he's shared with Burns carries just as much weight. In addition to his decades of experience in the university, international and NHL ranks, he's president of the NHL Coaches Association. He says coaching in the NHL is all about "the immediacy of success," explaining that pro hockey is strictly a "results-oriented business," which in turn means there's a "short fuse" for coaches. He goes further, allowing that while coaching is not a very secure calling in any of the major North American pro sports, the lack of respect accorded coaches within the NHL is distinctive. He points out that the league's financial hierarchy sees most coaches paid no more than an average player, unlike the much healthier salaries for pro football and basketball coaches, and the discrepancies between pensions for NHL coaches and those in the NFL and NBA are huge.

This lack of respect, and the brief tenure allowed most NHL coaches, creates a change-resistant culture within the NHL, says Kingston. It takes time for a coach to make changes, "to explain the whys and wherefores" so that players buy in, and NHL coaches frequently don't get that time. You can try he says, and "if the change leads to success, then it's tolerated, if it doesn't… " Just to drive the point home he cracks, "NHL, it stands for 'not here long'."

Kingston's views of the NHL are neither unique nor new. Fred Shero took much the same position in an interview with *Maclean's* contributor Trent Frayne. The eccentric bench boss of the Philadelphia Flyers was just a few months past his first of two Stanley Cups, and had been chosen the inaugural winner of the Jack Adams Award. Since Clare Drake's encounter with him in 1958 he'd become, in Frayne's 1974 estimation, "the highest-paid thinker in the history of hockey." What set Shero apart wasn't so much the remuneration as his cranial capacity. Frayne called him "the thinking man's coach" for having turned "pumpkins [the Flyers] into champions." Speaking two years after the Canada-Russia Summit Series on the matter of progress in the NHL, Shero said, "We've accomplished very little in our game in the last thirty years; in fact, we've gone back." Explaining the "reluctance of NHL coaches" to share ideas or adopt new concepts, he said, "A lot of them are afraid for their jobs. They don't want management to think they don't know it all." He also suggested that this was why the notion of assistant coaches was anathema in the league, because they were seen as a threat to the head man. "Everybody thought I was nuts when I brought in Mike Nykoluk as an assistant coach," said Shero. It should be remembered that Shero had two sides to his coaching personality; in addition to being a "thinking man's coach" he also presided over the infamous "Broadstreet Bullies," and so could be accused of being a "goon's coach" as well.

Obviously, NHL hockey has progressed in the thirty-plus years since Freddie the Fog stated his concerns, but as George Kingston asserted, the league's coaching culture has remained much the same. Coaches still live on borrowed time, and many are still loath to author changes in the way their players and teams approach the game. Dale Henwood, the president of the Canadian Sport Centre in Calgary, which includes the National Coaching Institute, sums up this basic reality quite matter-of-factly: "the NHL doesn't lead." This makes sense when you factor in Kingston's description of the coaches association membership. With thirty teams in the league, all carrying three-man staffs at a minimum, this association has close to 100 members. According to Kingston, in 2006 more than eighty percent of them were former NHL players, and as he says, "You coach the way you were coached." Hence, many of today's NHL coaches continue in the traditional, conformist mindset they learned by osmosis from the men who preceded them.

There are exceptions to this rule. Perhaps it's no coincidence that of the twelve coaches honored by Ryan Walter and Mike Johnston in *Simply the Best* ("those who have influenced the game of hockey with their strategies, approach, and team accomplishments") only three – Pat Quinn, Marc Crawford and Brian Sutter – were NHL players. Of the remaining nine, one is Clare Drake and four more (Ken Hitchcock, Dave King, Andy Murray and George Kingston) cite him as a mentor. Including Drake, five are products of the Canadian university system (King, Murray, Kingston and Mike Keenan).

There's another fascinating exception to the rule of the "old boys' network." In the summer of 2005, New York Rangers general manager Glen Sather assembled his coaching personnel for the first season of the post-lockout NHL; new head coach Tom Renney would be joined by assistants Perry Pearn, Benoit Allaire and Mike Pelino. Sather was trying a grand experiment, building the only NHL coaching staff fully comprised of men who had never played in the league. Preseason prognostications had the Rangers finishing at the bottom of the Eastern Conference, but Renney's group of savvy professionals, aided by (or maybe even responsible for) the rebirth of star Jaromir Jagr, guided the Broadway Blueshirts to a solid sixth-place playoff berth in the east. *Sports Illustrated*'s Michael Farber gave the Rangers' staff his end-of-season coach of the year award. Farber said that Tom Renney could also be *Psychology Today*'s top coach, for keeping Jagr happy, and praised him for using all four of his lines effectively and for bringing "structure to a slovenly team." Farber acclaimed Perry Pearn the "NHL's best assistant," credited Pelino as a "sharp mind" and noted Allaire's technical and personal skills. Again, perhaps it's no coincidence that Renney and Pearn both count Clare Drake as a major influence on their careers, and that Pelino is a former CIAU player and coach. In fact, Renney met with Drake and his fellow Alberta colleague Bill Moores before the season to glean a few refresher tips from his old mentor on penalty killing and other fine points of the game.

These exceptions prove the rule. Coaches in the NHL are, as Kingston asserts, still mostly members of an exclusive fraternity, constrained by their longstanding bonds of job insecurity and its attendant conservatism.

It's not the same for university coaches. They live and work in a different culture. Like their pro hockey counterparts they are professional coaches and most of them in Canadian institutions are hired on a contractual (as opposed to tenured) basis to run a hockey program. And like their counterparts, university coaches face intense pressures, although these are as chalk is to cheese compared to the pressures faced by pro coaches. A certified master coach through Canada's National Coaching Certification Program, Dave Adolph of the University of Saskatchewan is about as professional as they come in the world of hockey. In 2006 he said:

> You can define pressure in a thousand different ways. It can be mid-February and I'm not frozen by the possibility I might lose my job, while Marc Crawford [the Vancouver Canucks coach who was fired just a few weeks after Adolph spoke] has his team fifteen games above .500 and he doesn't know if he'll survive the season. But the last five or six years I've felt enormous pressure because our program's been successful. The expectations are there now and it's all on me to make it happen... recruiting, budgeting, planning practices, planning road trips, everything but driving the bus. My assistants help, but the responsibility's all on me.

Pressure aside, Adolph loves his job and exults at running the bench of one of Canada's top amateur teams: "It's three hours of the best ride in the world!"

Eric Thurston, who as rookie head coach took the Golden Bears to a CIS-record twelfth national title in 2006, can empathize with Adolph. With a friendly laugh he relegates his Saskatchewan rival's "ride" to "second best," and concurs on the issue of pressure: "When you have a program with the tradition ours has – thanks to Coach Drake, Billy Moores and Rob Daum – the expectation is that you have to win it all. It's not good enough to finish in first place, or win a Canada West championship; if you don't win the nationals it's like a failure."

At the upper levels of university hockey in Canada, coaches face extraordinary job demands and an intense need to win, but this pressure generates consequences unlike those in the NHL. University hockey is a product of its surrounding environment, and so has long been heavily influenced by the cultural values upheld in universities, where questioning the status quo and independent thinking are celebrated. And while university coaches aren't tenured faculty members (even in Drake's era many weren't), they profit from working in a context where job security is believed to enhance creativity and innovation.

So if you apply pressure to win on a coach operating within this distinctly different milieu, where instability and orthodoxy are supplanted by confidence and curiosity, you get distinctly different results. You get new ideas, growth and progress. You get the charge led by Clare Drake in the early 1960s as he took the coaching bit between his teeth and started to run. You get the first awakenings of a movement, a nation-wide network of collaborative professionals, fomented by a maven-connector-salesman who just happened to be a hockey coach.

This movement started percolating in the mid-1960s, its nascent stirrings rooted in gatherings of university coaches who began to share hockey knowledge the same way academics impart their research findings at conferences. Two of the earliest gatherings were held at MacDonald College in Montreal in 1965, and the following year at Queen's University in Kingston. Some of the key movers and shakers during this mid- to late-sixties flowering were Father Bauer and Bob Hindmarch from UBC and Canada's National Team, Tom Watt from the University of Toronto, Paul Arsenault of Montreal's Loyola University, George Lariviere of the University of Montreal, Bob Boucher from St. Mary's University in Halifax, Ron Watson from Western Ontario, George Kingston, coaching at the University of Calgary by 1967 and, of course, Clare Drake.

These men would assemble, usually at a university facility, to present seminars on many elements of coaching, from the philosophical to the technical. The proceedings were open to all comers, and were targeted especially at minor and elite coaches of amateur teams. Among the presenters was the occasional pro coach. As Bob Hindmarch says, "We used to bring the pros in because people felt they had all the answers. We found out pretty quickly that they didn't." Howie Meeker, former Maple Leafs star and coach, later to win national affection for his enthusiastic work as a Hockey Night in Canada analyst, spoke at the Montreal seminar in 1965. During his talk he suggested to his listeners, many of them amateur coaches of youngsters, that they instruct their defencemen to use an elbow to clear an opposing forward from in front of the net. When Hindmarch asked from the front row if Meeker was advocating that coaches teach rule-breaking to their players, a rather strained silence ensued. Forty-some years later, Hindmarch magnanimously downplays the moment, instead remembering the positive post-session discussion he and Father Bauer had with Meeker. In that exchange, Bauer demonstrated to Meeker the entirely workable, yet legal, technique for a defenceman to use on a forward at net-front and the former NHLer bought the concept.

Another memorable meeting was hosted by UBC during those same mid-decade years. The star of this event was Anatoly Tarasov, the "father of Russian hockey" and coach of the reigning Olympic Champions. Bauer and Hindmarch met him at their 1964 Olympic debut in Innsbruck and Hindmarch, who took over as coach of UBC thereafter, invited him to do an on-ice clinic in Vancouver. Tarasov was a legend in the Soviet Union, but he was no model coach by any humane standards. Described by Russian sportswriter Yevgeny Rubin as a "villain character" with "absolutely no moral principles," he was a ruthless dictator, feared and intensely disliked by his players. His totalitarian methods reflected those of the political regime he represented, and it was this aspect of Soviet sport that inflamed Father Bauer's desire to beat Tarasov and his robotic Russians.

Nonetheless, Tarasov was a proponent of team play to a degree virtually unknown in Canada at that time, and men like Bauer, Hindmarch and Drake respected him as an innovator and hockey tactician from whom they could learn. In his 1969 work *The Road to Olympus*, he said, "Our school of hockey differs from the Canadian school in that Soviet hockey players pass the puck much more frequently than do the Canadians." Evidently, things had changed since 1955, when Drake laid the "puck hog" label on Vsevolod Bobrov. Tarasov had the statistics to prove his point, citing the 1963 world championships in Stockholm as an example. There, he proudly declared, his team outpassed Canada's Trail Smoke Eaters 110 to sixty in their 4-2 victory. More noteworthy than the superior passing ratio is that Tarasov kept track of such statistics, something unheard-of in Canadian hockey until decades later.

Bob Hindmarch remembers being surprised at Tarasov's arrival in Vancouver because he came alone, without the usual Communist party watchdogs that hovered around Soviet representatives traveling abroad in those times. Drake can still picture the image of Tarasov standing on the ice in running shoes, waving a stick and shouting directions in Russian at the Canadian kids being used for demonstration purposes. The coaching icon appeared sans skates because his enormous girth made it impossible to bend over and lace them up, consummate irony given his fanatic insistence on the fitness of his players. Language barrier and faulty footwear notwithstanding, Drake learned valuable lessons from Tarasov's visit. He was impressed with the way the Russian had structured the mock practice so that all areas of the ice surface were in continual use and all the players were moving almost ceaselessly. This style of practice would become a Drake trademark; Golden Bear training sessions were renowned for being well planned, creative, intense and exhausting.

Clare Drake's revolutionary instincts around sharing provided much of the impetus behind the movement — we'll call it the "method movement" for its studied approach to the game and intent to teach what was learned to others — that burgeoned in Canada's universities and colleges during the 1960s. National seminars were becoming an annual occurrence and regional clinics run by university coaches had evolved into regular events. In Alberta, B.C., Ontario and Quebec, provincial hockey associations were starting to align themselves with the community extension work being supported by the post-secondary institutions. With the full encouragement of their respective universities, George Kingston and Clare Drake would hit the road every spring, traveling to small towns up and down their own province to teach amateur coaches how to coach, spreading the gospel of the method movement. As these clinics for coaches grew in popularity, the Alberta Amateur Hockey Association began to help organize them and sponsor them formally. Similar advancements were underway in other provinces, in most cases led by university and college coaches.

The fascinating thing about this groundswelling of method applied to hockey, this new rationality intruding into a game long ruled by emotion and tradition, was that few, if any, of the men involved were conscious that it was indeed a movement. They didn't keep records, they didn't document their proceedings or, in the beginning, even their teachings. That was to come later in the form of published proceedings of their seminars and manuals for the National Coaching Certification Program. These men weren't aware that they were leaders of profound change, that they were in fact making history. They didn't have a name for what they were doing or for themselves, the group doing it. Their motives were purely and simply to improve the game and contribute to the development of their profession. Murray Costello, who became president of the CAHA in 1979, by which time this tide was rolling at full bore, says of this "bunch of university guys," "they weren't opportunistic like a lot of others in the game. They saw a need for an educational process for coaches and they just wanted to make the game better."

While this metamorphosis began to take shape, there was hockey to be played and championships to be won. The U of A Golden Bears had brought the University Cup home from Kingston in 1964 but failed to make a return trip to the tournament the following year. Their tough, intra-league rivals from Manitoba laid another western beating, 9-2, on an eastern school, St. Dunstan's University of Charlottetown, now the University of Prince Edward Island. But the season after that — 1965-66 — an ominous presence, at least to Albertan eyes, emerged from Ontario. The classic blue and white uniforms of the University of Toronto, adorned with their historic emblem of a maple leaf superimposed on a T, appeared at the nationals for the first time. Meeting the Golden Bears in the tournament final, hosted by Laurentian University in Sudbury, the Varsity Blues announced their arrival at the pinnacle of the CIAU by thumping Alberta 8-1. It was the first meeting between Tom Watt and Clare Drake, two men who would dominate university hockey over the next fifteen years as mighty, but friendly, rivals.

The Blues' perch at the pinnacle would be protracted and secure; they wrapped their arms in a chokehold around the University Cup, clutching it for nine of the next twelve seasons. Expertly coached by Watt, the Blues also enjoyed a gushing pipeline of talent from southern Ontario, especially Father Bauer's old stomping ground, St. Michael's College, and the powerful Toronto Marlies of major junior fame. Between 1966 and 1977, only the Golden Bears and the University of Waterloo Warriors managed to penetrate the "blue fog" enveloping the Cup – the Bears winning in 1968 and 1975, the Warriors picking up their sole national title in 1974.

In spite of the ascendancy of Watt and the Varsity Blues, the mid-to-late sixties were an exciting and fulfilling time for Clare Drake, marked with several notable achievements. In the 1964-65 season, immediately following his first University Cup, Drake took on another coaching appointment extra to his duties with Alberta.

His love of the game made him reluctant to hang up his skates; in the late fifties he had occasionally suited up with his Bears on their exhibition swings through northern Alberta against local senior teams. And he'd also played with the Lacombe Rockets through several seasons in the early sixties while he coached the Bears. In those years, with the university schedule being so brief, it was possible, and still allowed by the CAHA, for athletes to be listed on another team's roster at the same time as they carried their varsity colors. Some Golden Bears did double duty in the green and gold of Alberta and the red and white of the Rockets, and stalwarts like Vic Dzurko, Al LaPlante, Dave Carlyle, Dick Dunigan, Austin Smith and Doug Messier (father of NHL legend Mark) went full time with Lacombe after they graduated from Alberta. This strong Golden Bear connection, and Drake's previous service for them, moved the Rockets to recruit him in September 1964 for a special, short-term coaching assignment.

Lacombe is a small town located in the central Alberta parkland, about 100 kilometers due south of Edmonton. The Rockets played in Alberta's tough senior-intermediate league against hard-nosed outfits like the Red Deer Rustlers, the Ponoka Stampeders and the Drumheller Miners. In the spring of 1964 they won the Canadian intermediate championship, almost on a par with senior hockey's Allan Cup. This was a big deal for the town and the league they came from. It became even bigger when, by virtue of their championship, the CAHA chose them to represent Canada on a three-week-long, thirteen-game tour of Europe. The highlight was an appearance at the Ahearne Cup, a prestigious tournament in Stockholm that in 1964-65 would feature four Swedish club teams, the Rockets and the Russian National Junior Team. The Rockets were also scheduled to play in Switzerland, East Germany and Czechoslovakia. Knowing they would be up against some very challenging European opponents, the Lacombe management asked Drake to come along as a playing assistant coach. Drake served as a "strategy guy," remembers Austin Smith, providing much appreciated input for coach Art Park. Smith and his fellow Bear grads, with the exception of Messier, also made the trip. In addition, there was another key U of A man in the lineup, defenceman Ed Zemrau, the university's director of athletics and former pro from the ranks of the American and Western Hockey Leagues.

As with most Canadian teams in the sixties, and like the Penticton Vees who'd gone before them ten years earlier, the Rockets were expected by their European hosts to be brutish and undisciplined on the ice and equally ill-mannered away from the rink. But they won over the Swedes with their comportment and skill, representing Canada admirably at the tournament with two wins and three losses against competition that many anticipated would be above their heads. This was Drake's second look at the Russians, except in this instance he was able to take the ice against them. They weren't such strangers this time, because the Rockets and the Russians, both away from their homes and families at a special time of year, celebrated Christmas together at Stockholm's Christinaberg Hotel.

Clare Drake is well known among his friends for being a rallying force when it comes to a party,

Drake's good friend and fierce adversary, all in one. Tom Watt as an NHL head coach in the 1980s, after nine University Cups in twelve years at the University of Toronto and a season as co-coach, with Drake, of the Canadian Olympic team.

with a regulated yet unmistakable affection for the odd libation or two. But bon vivant that he is, he confesses he was in tough against the Russians that Christmas. Their affinity for the fieriest of undiluted vodkas, and their imbibing technique – "they didn't waste time getting to the bottom of the glass," says Drake – forced him to the realization that he couldn't stay with them. The Soviets bested Drake and his mates on the ice as well, squeaking out a 3-2 victory even though they were outshot 31-17 by the Canadians.

In addition to the quaffing lesson, Drake also learned some new hockey tactics from the Russians. "That was the first we saw of their puck control game, their patience offensively," he recollects, describing the "regrouping and circling back with the puck" that would make the bewildered NHLers shake their heads a few years later during the Summit Series. He also noticed the Russian forwards interchanging positions, criss-crossing at the opposition blue line to break free from the table-hockey, up-and-down-the-same-wing groove that Canadians had long patrolled on the strict orders of their coaches. This tactic in particular was one that Drake brought back to use with the Bears.

The Rockets left Sweden with their heads held high and flew to Czechoslovakia, where they became the first foreign team in ten years to tour through the country undefeated, winning two and tying four in hard-fought matches against the National Juniors and two club teams. In all four countries they visited on the tour, they excelled as ambassadors of Canadian hockey, repairing the damage done to Canada's image by some of the thuggish squads that had gone overseas in the years since 1955. The goodwill engendered by the Lacombe Rockets paved the way for an improved hockey exchange between Canada and Europe, which in a broad sense helped set the stage for the great series that came seven years later.

Drake returned to the Bears in late January of 1965, taking back the coaching reins from his assistant Ron Watson, whom he'd had the foresight to install in the position in the fall when informed about the Lacombe opportunity (necessity played a major part in invention when it came to Drake's use of an assistant coach). The Bears failed to get past Manitoba, who would be that year's CIAU Champions, and the next year came their first, fateful meeting with the University of Toronto at the nationals. Then, in 1966-67, the Saskatchewan Huskies nosed the Bears out for first and went winless at the nationals, hosted in the West for the first time by the universities of Alberta and Calgary. The Bears sat idly by, watching Toronto win its second University Cup in their own backyard. It was in the season after, 1967-68, that Clare Drake would pull off one of the most remarkable feats in the annals of coaching.

When Clare Drake was first appointed to the phys. ed. staff at the U of A, his duties included helping coach the Golden Bears football team. The U of A footballers had their own proud tradition dating back to the 1920s, which had reached its zenith in the late 1940s with Maury Van Vliet, the new Dean of Physical Education, as head coach. Sadly, having won two western titles in three years, the Golden Bears were forced to fold in 1948 owing to lack of viable competition. Those late-forties teams included future Alberta premier Peter Lougheed and a young halfback named Murray Smith. Although the Bears were mothballed, their green and gold uniforms carried on (along with Lougheed and several other Bear grads) to serve the second edition of the Edmonton Eskimos during their inaugural 1949 season.

Ten years later, intercollegiate football in the West was revived, and so also, the next year, were the Bears' championship ways. Under now-head coach Murray Smith, with Drake assisting, the U of A won the Western Intercollegiate Football League title in 1960. Drake took over as interim head coach from his pal Smith in 1962 and the team surged to a 7-1 record and another WIFL title. Then Maury Van Vliet brought in Gino Fracas, a just-retired Edmonton Eskimo linebacker with eight pro years and two Grey Cup championships under his belt. He was also a teacher and coach in Edmonton's Catholic high school system and it was his pedagogical background, in addition to his football experience, that moved Van Vliet to hire him. The highly esteemed Fracas guided the Bears for four seasons, winning three WIFL championships and losing to the University of Toronto in the very first Vanier Cup, played in 1965. That initial national championship game featured two noteworthy names among the assistant coaches involved, Tom Watt on the blue and white side, Clare Drake on the green and gold. After the '66 season, Gino Fracas returned to his roots in Ontario and started the University of Windsor football program, where he remained for twenty years.

So in the summer of 1967 the coaching reins of the football Bears passed once again to Clare Drake. Ed Molstad was a veteran defensive lineman at training camp that August and, to this day, he remembers Drake's first speech to the team: "Gentlemen, I'm not going to pretend that I know a lot about football. But I've surrounded myself with some really great assistants and we're going to work hard, have fun and play some good football this year." Molstad says this discourse struck the players as unusual in its honesty and humility – "not the kind of speech you heard from a head coach" – and it earned Drake, already respected as an assistant, instant credibility as the new boss.

Molstad and linebacker Val Schneider were part of a veteran team core that had quality but lacked depth. There were concerns about the fourteen rookies in the starting lineup, and Schneider recalls the pressure this added for Drake, who was already expected to fill the large coaching cleats vacated by Fracas and to carry on the Bears' winning tradition. Both Schneider and Molstad marvel at the way Drake brought the rookies along and pulled the team together. Speaking separately but singing from the same song sheet, they talk about his way of drawing the best from individuals – "you didn't want to let him down," says Schneider – and his uncanny ability to build team chemistry. This wasn't the first time Drake had shown faith in rookies and it wouldn't be the last. And he was true to his word about the quality of his assistants. Molstad says, "He was right; they were outstanding football men."

Drake's staff, small by today's standards, consisted of Roy Stephenson, Arnie Enger, Don Barry and Jim Donlevy. The latter, by coincidence, had been Drake's student manager for the Golden Bear hockey teams of the late 1950s and early sixties. It was no coincidence that, with lessons learned from Drake, Donlevy eventually became head coach of the football Bears, winning five WIFL titles and two Vanier Cups. Retrieving Drake's opening speech from his own memory banks, Donlevy challenges the man's self-deprecation regarding his football knowledge: "Clare knew football, and he had that knack, that magic, that got great performances out of teams and individuals."

The Drake magic certainly worked its spell during that fall of '67, guiding the rookie-laden Bears through the WIFL to a 6-1 record and the league title. This landed them a berth in the Vanier Cup, and so in November they journeyed east to Toronto's Varsity Stadium to face a heavily-favored veteran squad from McMaster University. The game was a tough defensive battle, tight to the very last minute. Having traded touchdowns in the first half, the two teams held each other in check through most of the second, the Bears clinging to a one-point, fourth-quarter lead thanks to a field goal scored off a fumble recovery deep in enemy territory. McMaster drove the ball to the Alberta seventeen-yard line with less than a minute remaining and looked poised to win, but the Bears intercepted an attempted touchdown pass and sealed the 10-9 victory. Val Schneider, who had lined up at fullback, punter and linebacker, and as a result barely had time to grab a drink of water, won the Ted Morris Memorial Trophy as the game's most valuable player.

Like Donlevy, Schneider watched Drake and learned. After university he coached junior football in Red Deer and then moved to the University of Saskatchewan, where he was head coach of the Huskies for ten years and won two WIFL championships. He became athletic director at U of S and continued to assist with the football team, which captured two Vanier Cups while he was on the staff. What did he pick up while playing for Drake? "There were two major things I saw Clare do that I tried to emulate. I tried to let my assistant coaches coach, and I tried to treat people with dignity and respect." But he didn't stop at just two: "Like Clare, I always measured my success in terms of seeing kids become successful, confident individuals who made their mark on society."

That brings us back to Ed Molstad, the exemplar of a coach's success by this form of measurement. Molstad graduated from the Bears to play six solid seasons on the Eskimos defensive line and, more importantly, take his place as a member of the Alberta bar. Now one of Edmonton's most respected lawyers, a Queen's Counsel and counsel to the CFL Players Association, he speaks from the perspective of a lifetime in and around sport when he says, "Most athletes will tell you they've had one or two coaches who touch your life in a special way. For me, Clare was one of those guys." That's his observation on Drake's personal imprint. As for the way the coach ran a winning program, Molstad says, "What made us champions was that we played as a team. He created the chemistry for that." Echoing Dale Henwood's comments about Drake being a "standard bearer for coaches in all sports," Molstad concludes, "His ability to coach transcended a single sport. You could put him in a sport he'd never seen and by the end of the season he'd be an expert in it; he's a student of any game."

How fitting then, that Clare Drake performed it – that championship dance – all over again during that same university season with another team in another game. When the pigskin Bears came home from Toronto, Drake had no time for celebration. That September, he had left the hockey Bears in the capable hands of Brian McDonald, the junior varsity coach who succeeded Ron Watson as Drake's assistant. McDonald took the team through training camp and into the first weeks of the schedule and then turned it over to Drake.

As with the football team, the 1967-68 version of the skating squad was a green one, dressing fourteen rookies at the nationals. They got there by fighting their way through the tight WCIAU, having to sweep an end-of-schedule series at UBC to nip both Saskatchewan and Manitoba by two points for the league title. Then it was off to Montreal, where the University Cup was being hosted by Loyola University, Sir George Williams University and MacDonald College. The first two schools have long since joined to form Concordia University and the third was incorporated into McGill University.

The Bears were almost completely discounted as a factor in the tournament; the two-time defending champion Blues were the overwhelming favorites. Alberta opened against St. Francis Xavier University of Antigonish, Nova Scotia. It was a sweet start for the westerners, given that some St. FX players had been heard to say that if they could get by Toronto, they'd be okay. The Bears rolled over the Atlantic Champions 12-3, scoring three short-handed goals along the way. Next they dispatched Laurentian University 7-2 and caught a big break when the hometown Warriors of Loyola toppled Toronto in a 1-0 overtime thriller. This set the table for one of the greatest finals in CIAU history, played in front

"His ability to coach transcended a single sport." Head football coach Drake teaching championship technique to Golden Bears' running backs on the way to the Vanier Cup, 1967.

of what is still the largest crowd ever to witness a University Cup.

Loyola's unexpected victory had primed Montrealers for what they thought would be a coronation, and they poured into the fabled Montreal Forum, site of the championship match, to the tune of 12,000. The hallowed hockey shrine was in an uproar from the opening face-off and the Warriors really took it to the Bears, outshooting them 47-27 during the game. But the Bears hung on bravely, and were only down 4-3 at the end of the second period. The final stanza was especially lopsided, with the shots 18-6 in favor of Loyola, but Alberta hero Ron Cebryk tied the game at the mid-mark of the period. The clock was ticking down with the score still even when the Bears' Jack Gibson stole the puck and put it once again on Cebryk's stick, sending him in all alone. A contemporary newspaper account reported that while the "avid Loyola fans screamed in disbelief, Cebryk calmly shifted one way and then, when goalie Andy Molino went for the fake, flicked the puck over the netminder and into the gaping net." There were only seventeen seconds remaining when the puck crossed the line. Clare Drake had won his second University Cup in an upset, only five months after winning the Vanier Cup, also in an upset – two national titles in two sports during the same university season. The realities of sport today make the feat impossible; in that time, it was only highly improbable.

The Bears were under no illusions about their victory. Dale Halterman, the stalwart goalie, who turned away twenty-one more shots than his opponent, said, "We won it on coaching, that's all. Everybody knows that." Tom Devaney was one of the freshmen, a forward on an all-rookie line with Dave Couves and Don Falkenberg. Drake credited this trio with sparking the team through the second half of the season and especially during the third period of the final. Devaney turns all the credit back on Drake: "Most of us had never played in front of big crowds before, but it didn't seem intimidating because of the way Clare had taught us to play our system. He was so calm and cool on the bench and in the room, always thinking about the next step. We were down with a few minutes to go, but he didn't get rattled and neither did we."

Devaney sees the Montreal victory as "an example of taking a system and using less-talented players to beat teams with more talent." Talk to many of Drake's players, colleagues and competitors and you'll hear the same thing. UBC's Bob Hindmarch, who himself had no great wellspring of talent to draw from on the Pacific coast, says that while the Bears plucked the prime fruit in the West, Drake was usually at a disadvantage compared to Watt and other coaches at the big eastern schools, with their deeper player pools. Dale Henwood concurs: "Most of Clare's teams were less talented than the competition but better prepared."

Ever the deflector of praise, Drake lauded his players, and told a journalist that he was "lucky" to have young men in the Bears program, year in and year out, who brought enthusiasm and dedication to practice every day – luck obviously had nothing to do with it. In summing up this great championship double, another reporter wrote that "Canadian championships in both hockey and football must climax the most satisfying year of Clare Drake's life." The man hadn't yet seen his fortieth birthday, early days for most professionals to reach the apex of their careers. Looking back across the broad vista of his life from his septuagenarian observation deck, Drake allows that the 1967-68 season "ranks as pretty special." He talks about the unique set of circumstances that made The Double possible, and says the achievement registered more with him a few years later when he realized he was never going to do it again. No one's done it… before or since. But Drake also refuses to pick a single year as the culmination of all his dreams. That's partly because he's always been more of a goal setter than a dreamer, and partly because his self-imposed standard of success includes markers other than championships, and experiences beyond winning. Again borrowing from John Wooden, Drake finds common cause with the American icon's bit of verse on the subject, from *They Call Me Coach*:

> Success is peace of mind
> which is a direct result of
> Self-satisfaction in knowing you
> did your best to become the
> Best you are capable of becoming.

Regardless of how Clare Drake rates 1967-68 in his lifetime ledger, there's no denying that it made him a master coach in the eyes of his athletes, his University of Alberta colleagues, his coaching peers, the Edmonton sports community and the media. The City of Edmonton, which couldn't possibly have anticipated The Double, was impressed enough by his fall championship to name him Sportsman of the Year for 1967. *Edmonton Journal* sports columnist Wayne Overland lionized him, proclaiming, "It is a shame college sports in Canada don't have the vast spectator appeal they do in the U.S. Otherwise Drake and his University of Alberta teams would be well on the way to becoming a national legend such as Knute Rockne, Bear Bryant and other U.S. college coaches established over the years." The fickle nature of media fawning would become painfully evident a few years later as Overland turned from Drake booster into Drake basher, but in 1968, "the Duck" (as he'd been affectionately dubbed by his community) was riding the wave. Overland was right in this instance; if only on a Canadian scale, Drake was nonetheless a coaching legend in the making. He had become "The Coach."

Stephen Scriver, the Canadian hockey poet, has captured the gritty truth of hockey, its violence and profanity, its courage and heart-swelling emotion. His down-home, free verse renderings evoke the joys and sorrows of this tough yet graceful game. "Coach," Scriver's ode to the hockey coach, doesn't portray Clare Drake – it wasn't intended to. But it does sketch certain traits of many successful coaches: the ability to inspire performance, knowledge of the game, an attention to detail and the urge to win and to celebrate, not just the victory but that part of the game that brings out the boyish jubilation in the men who play it.

> *By the Jesus, boys, if I go to hell for swearin', it's your fault!*
> The coach is a nice guy
> except where the team is concerned
> he's like a mother badger
>
> in practice – snarling at us
> in games – ready to destroy anything
> between him and us
>
> And we'll bust our butts to win for him
> because of his savvy
> *You pass into your man's skates again*

The second half of The Double. A less-than-happy looking Drake on the left (nobody knows why!), amidst the Bears' University Cup celebration, Montreal Forum, 1968.

    and he'll be three rows into the stands
    his rebukes
    Don't go into the corners
    like you got a dozen eggs in your pocket
    his despair
    Well you guys sang O Canada shitty
    and things got worse from there

    and because when we win
    he's one of us for awhile –
    a crazy, tender man
    exulting over a kid's game

    More! All Star Poet, Stephen Scriver

There are some common qualities connecting Scriver's "Coach" with The Coach, Clare Drake, but it's the dissimilarities between the lyrical portrait and the real man that are telling. Drake doesn't swear, and he doesn't despair… ever. His commitment to positivity, to encouragement, to building up his team, is unrelenting. You can see another dissimilarity in the last stanza. Once past the early stages of his career, Drake was rarely one of the boys, and few of his players would have called him "tender." When asked about things he might have done differently if he could do it all over again, Drake chews his lip for a moment and muses, "I'd have tried to be closer to my players. I don't think it helped, me being as distant as I was."

In addition to his capacity for fearless self-examination, this statement reveals the enigmatic side of the man that is Clare Drake. His career flourished thanks partly to the connector side of his personality and his salesman (charismatic) attributes. His peers knew him to be approachable, gregarious, sociable, one of the guys who was usually up for a party, enjoyed a good joke and told a good story. Yet his wife, who knows him best, will also describe him as a "bit of a loner." And a significant number of his players, after they've finished extolling his virtues as a coach and role model, will recall that he could be impersonal, at times cool and hard to read. Some of this can be put down to his intense focus, which was always first and foremost on the team and its success. But some of it was just the man himself and his own particular style of dealing with athletes. Howie Draper saw both factors at work.

In 2006, Draper remained the first and only head coach of the U of A women's hockey team, the Pandas. He'd spent nine seasons at the Pandas' helm, guiding them to eight Canada West titles and a remarkable five CIS national championships. A winner of two CIS coach of the year awards, Draper has become a master coach in his own right and credits much of his progress to lessons he learned from Clare Drake.

Draper was a smallish but gifted rookie defenceman on the Bears 1986 national championship squad and played five full seasons under Drake and his successor, Bill Moores. He came to the team from the Sherwood Park Crusaders of the Alberta Junior Hockey League, where his coach was Al Hamilton, a former New York Ranger and local star as captain of the WHA Edmonton Oilers. Draper had thrived under Hamilton's affable, "players' coach" style, but when he stepped up to the comparatively big league Bears, he found the environment imposing and impersonal. It was imposing because of the big learning curve he was climbing, struggling to absorb a highbrow hockey lexicon and complex systems beyond anything he'd seen before. It was impersonal because of Clare Drake. This coach didn't have the warm and friendly manner of his junior coach; he was reserved and, at the rink, he was all business. Draper found out early that easy familiarity wouldn't wash when speaking to, or about, his coach. In a training camp chat with his defence partner and team captain, Ron Vertz, he referred to Drake as "Clare." Vertz promptly corrected him, explaining that nobody, not even the most senior of veterans, addressed their leader using any term except "Coach." This convention wasn't Drake's idea, it was a mark of the respect his players held for him and by then, it had become longstanding tradition.

Draper saw the ultimate manifestation of Drake's team-first fixation during a hard-hitting tilt in his freshman year, when an opposing forward caught him admiring a pass he'd made and just about "de-skated" him. As he sat on the bench trying to shake out the cobwebs, the coach bent over and said to him, in not unfriendly tones, "Try to keep your head up, Howie; it's not good for team morale when you take a hit like that." Draper's not whingeing about this; in fact he tells the story with a grin on his

Mentor coach with master coach. Drake and Howie Draper, surrounded by Draper's winning, grinning U of A Pandas at Clare Drake Arena, circa 2002.

face, laughing at himself for his propensity to get clobbered and at Drake for being so absorbed with the greater good of the team. Draper's deep respect and affection for his old coach are readily apparent. He tempers this anecdote by qualifying it as an anomaly, stressing that over time he understood the depth of Drake's commitment to the young men who played for him. "It wasn't until I matured and became a coach myself that I saw how effective his style was. He was there to do a job and that was to help you become a better person and a better player."

Dale Henwood, who backstopped the 1975 Bears to a national title, also noticed the distance Drake maintained with his players. It didn't have the same impact on the goaltender because he was older and more experienced, and enjoyed the same, closer relationship with Drake that many of the veterans did. But Henwood admits that some of his teammates would see Drake coming down an arena hallway and "duck into the washroom to avoid him" because they felt awkward in his presence.

Steve Carlyle elaborates on the same theme. Like Draper, he was a small defenceman, with enough talent to win All Canadian honors in both his seasons with the Bears (1970-71 and 1971-72) and to carry him, despite his lack of size (5'9", 175 pounds), through four seasons with the WHA Edmonton Oilers. He says of Drake, "My interactions with him were fairly personal… I was his captain, but some players, especially the younger guys, viewed him [as aloof]." The coach cared though, says Carlyle: "He took an interest in you as a person. He cared about how you did at school, how you fit in socially on the team, and he taught you how to treat people." Carlyle explains that Drake worked through his captains and senior veterans to reach players who were younger or not part of the team core, asking his leaders for a reading on how an individual was fitting in, on how he was handling academic pressures, or disappointment with a lack of ice time. He used his assistant coaches in a similar capacity.

Here we have the paradox of Clare Drake as coach. He could be single-minded to the point of occasional insensitivity and he was distant enough from his younger players to create tension, which can sometimes be the enemy of performance. Yet almost to a man, they instinctively grasped the notion that he had their best interests at heart; they knew they could count on his integrity and honesty; they saw, like Ed Molstad and the football Bears, his humility. Above all, they had enormous faith in his ability to teach the game and build great teams. "Drake's knowledge base was the hook, that's what guys respected," says Carlyle.

And when it came to player relations, the coach had another weapon in his arsenal. In addition to communicating through his assistants, captains and veterans, Drake also relied on another key influence within the team community – his wife. Dolly Drake holds a special place in the hearts of many Golden Bears. She never blew a whistle at practices or set foot inside the Bears dressing room, but she was an integral part of the team nonetheless. She hosted many team gatherings over the years and attended many others. When her two daughters became independent, she often rode the bus with the coach on road trips, and she led the participation of the wives or girlfriends of assistant coaches, players and managers in most team social activities. She was around the team a lot, and she made her presence known quietly but effectively, with a warm smile and a positive, upbeat manner. Tom Devaney says, "I don't know if it was by design, but Dolly did a lot to help the players feel like they belonged, like they mattered. She was always talking to us at team parties, especially the rookies, and she could sense who needed a pat on the back or a little encouragement. She was like a second mother to a lot of us."

No, it wasn't by design; it was just Dolly's way. She says of her role, "It just kind of happened" and expresses nothing but gratitude for the opportunity her husband's profession afforded her. "There were so many quality kids on those teams. We got so much out of having those boys in our lives." When Clare speaks of his wife's "sharing and understanding of the complexities of a coach's life," one of the main things he's talking about is the way she supported his relationship with the young men in his charge. With Dolly's help, the sometimes distant coach was able to inspire great loyalty in his players, and partly through her efforts, they understood that while he could be impersonal, he was nevertheless committed to them as persons.

The completion of The Double in 1968 marked the beginning of an Alberta drought at the nationals. Toronto's blue wave would roll almost unabated over CIAU hockey for the next seven seasons. And the same year Drake pulled off The Double, his eastern adversary was adding to his own remarkable résumé. Tom Watt's Blues may have missed the mark in Montreal that spring of '68, but they'd done themselves and Canada proud a few weeks earlier in Innsbruck, Austria, at the Winter Universiade. Records are sketchy for Canada's early involvement in world student games, but Watt believes his team was the second to represent Canada, the first having been a University of Manitoba team in the early sixties. The Blues took on both the Russians and the Czechoslovaks in the tournament, losing to the latter and managing a 5-5 tie against a Soviet squad comprised, as Watt wryly recalls, of a "bunch of

WHA meets NCCP. The new league's shining star, Gordie Howe, with Drake at a national coaching seminar in the early 1970s.

older guys from the Institute of Roads or something." In other words, the Russians, as was their wont, sent pros to an event intended for amateur, student athletes. The U of T boys came home with a bronze medal and a justifiably proud coach. Their upset loss at the nationals that year couldn't have fazed them too much; they simply ran off five University Cup titles in a row starting with the 1969 season. The Blues' trip to Innsbruck, organized by Watt and Olympic Team coach Father Bauer, was the harbinger of the important part university hockey would play in maintaining Canada's tenuous connection to the international game. Already associated with the Olympic movement through Father Bauer and his use of student athletes on the National Team, the universities would also forge a strong link with Hockey Canada, established in 1969 as the organization to coordinate Canada's international hockey presence thenceforward and through the increasingly dark years following the '72 Summit Series.

There's no small irony in the role that Hockey Canada played. It was founded, and originally funded, by the federal government as an arm's length agency and adjunct to the CAHA. Its mandate was to promote "best-on-best" international competition, continuing and improving on Father Bauer's National Team efforts the CAHA had helped to birth in 1963. The irony was that within a year of assuming responsibility for the National Team program, Hockey Canada shut it down and officially withdrew from Olympic and world championship competition. This was because Canada's longstanding beef with the International Ice Hockey Federation had finally erupted into open warfare. The British president of the IIHF, John "Bunny" Ahearne, was reviled by Canadians as the man who rigged a last-minute rule change on tiebreakers at the 1964 Olympics, robbing Father Bauer's team of the bronze medal they had rightfully earned. In 1969, Ahearne at long last gave in to Canadian protests about the faux amateurs being used by the Russians at world championships, and agreed that Canada could send a team with up to nine non-NHL professionals to the 1970 Worlds, which had been planned for Winnipeg. But the IIHF, under pressure from the Soviets and their European cohorts, reneged on the agreement. In response, Hockey Canada withdrew from the tournament, which was moved to Stockholm. Canada wouldn't compete again in the world championships until 1977, nor in the Olympics until 1980; but we would, under the auspices of Hockey Canada, send our best pros up against the Russians in the fall of 1972.

The same year that Hockey Canada came to life, a few guys got together over beer and pizza. It was during the spring in Denver, the occasion being the NCAA hockey finals. The participants were Clare Drake; Ron Watson, then coaching at the University of Western Ontario; Paul Arsenault, the Sir George Williams coach who had lost the second University Cup to Drake in 1964; and Bill Mahoney of McMaster University. As the four washed down a disc (a favorite moniker for the Italian pie among a certain group of Edmonton hockey fans) with anaemic American suds, they discussed a meeting they'd attended as observers while at the NCAA tournament. It was an official proceeding of the NCAA hockey coaches association, and the quartet agreed it was high time they started their own such association in Canada. Their informal resolution led to the first official meeting of the Canadian University and College Hockey Coaches Association in Charlottetown, at the 1970 University Cup hosted by UPEI. This association created an administrative, organizational face for the method movement that Drake and his like-minded colleagues had been pursuing for at least ten years. As former CAHA president Murray Costello mentioned, these men weren't really looking to make a statement, nor were they aware of the long-term implications of their actions. They were educators, just trying to improve the game they loved by doing what they did best, which was study and teach.

Drake and his university colleagues were a peculiar and pretty much anonymous bunch by the standards of Canada's hockey mainstream. Bob Hindmarch places their unofficial, below-the-radar movement in context, explaining that they had little status within the CAHA's amateur hockey culture because they weren't community volunteers like those who coached youth hockey – they were professionals, working within the semi-cloistered halls of academia. And they certainly didn't rate within the pro environment; none of them held the cachet of having played in the NHL or its feeder leagues. The men of the method movement were in no way part of the old boys' network. But remarkably, because of their expertise and dedication, they became a pervasive, if unsung, influence on the development of the Canadian game in the ensuing three decades.

They were able to exert this influence because, serendipitously, Hockey Canada needed something to do. Having folded the National Team and withdrawn from the international scene, the organization still had employees and an administrative infrastructure. So it turned its attention to improving the game within Canada, to making Canadian hockey more competitive for whenever we might return to international play. The warning from Jack Ludwig, the *Maclean's* writer who in the post-Summit glow of '72 would call for better skill development and coaching, had actually been anticipated by the Hockey Canada bosses. Though they'd shut down the National Team, they had a healthy vision for the longer term, and they turned to Canada's university and college coaches to make it happen. In September of 1971, exactly a year before the clash of the titans, they brought a group of head instructors together for a train-the-trainers session that kicked off Hockey Canada's first attempt at a coaching certification program. Every one of these men, except for a couple of Hockey Canada officials, was a Canadian university or college coach. The most senior of them, as both a coach and coach of coaches, was Clare Drake. Accompanying him from the west was his self-proclaimed disciple, George Kingston. Also part of the group were Bob Boucher, the St. Mary's University coach who'd become a method movement leader in the Maritimes; Dennis McDonald, the coach at Centennial College in Scarborough, Ontario; and Cec Eaves, of the University of Windsor. This first Hockey Canada braintrust planted the seeds for the National Coaching Certification Program.

The NCCP started to grow a year later when Hockey Canada collaborated with the CAHA to form the Canadian Hockey Development Council. The council consisted of representatives from the provincial amateur hockey associations, the CIAU and the Canadian Colleges Athletic Association, the CCAA being the junior college version of the CIAU. The council chairman was Bob Hindmarch of UBC and its membership included Cec Eaves and Dennis McDonald. Its mandate was to develop the content for the NCCP, which would be funded by Hockey Canada and administered by the CAHA. The Hockey Development Council held its first meeting in Toronto in November 1972, just two months after the Summit Series sounded the alarm bells for those Canadians who were listening. As the Council began its work on content for the NCCP, it turned once again to the men of the method movement, the same basic resource group that Hockey Canada had enlisted the year before.

And why not? The university coaches were academics, teachers and students of the game. As with Drake and Kingston in Alberta, many were already teaching coaches how to coach in their own backyards and now, along with the support of men like Gary Aldcorn, a former National Teamer and one of Hockey Canada's first full-time employees, they were driving the Hockey Development Council and

Men with bad haircuts but good hockey minds. The "method movement" morphs into a program as Hockey Canada starts training instructors, 1971. (Drake, standing far left; Cec Eaves, standing third from left, George Kingston, standing fifth from right; Gary Aldcorn, standing far right; Bob Boucher and Dennis McDonald, seated far right).

the creation of the NCCP.

In 1973, Cec Eaves would become the CAHA's first technical director on a one-year, start-up basis; Dennis McDonald would take over the permanent job in 1974 to continue developing and operating the NCCP and later, the CAHA's National Resource Centre. In the spring of '73, barely eight months after the Summit Series, these two, along with Gary Aldcorn and the rest of the Hockey Development Council, went on a fact-finding mission to that year's world championships in Moscow. The council members met with officials from the Russian Ice Hockey Federation and the Central Red Army and Moscow Dynamo sports clubs; they also traveled to Prague to learn from Czech sports administrators. The ideas they brought back helped construct the framework for the NCCP. In the summer of that year, the Hockey Development Council held its first seminar for NCCP "master course conductors" at the Guildwood Inn, on the Lake Ontario shoreline in Toronto. The keynote speakers and presenters at that seminar were the usual suspects – university coaches. Again, Clare Drake was the most senior among them.

There was a young westerner in the audience that summer, a recent graduate of the University of Saskatchewan who was just getting his coaching feet wet as an assistant with the Huskies hockey team. According to many, including *Simply the Best* authors Johnston and Walter, Dave King is now one of hockey's greatest teachers and tacticians. In 1973 he was just twenty-six years old and eager to learn. The diminutive Drake already stood tall in his eyes, because of the way Drake's Golden Bears were always so well prepared and so tough to play against when King skated for the Huskies in the late sixties. In '73, King saw Drake as the unofficial leader of a group of presenters consisting, as he remembers, entirely of Canadian university coaches, "not a pro coach in the bunch." In fact, there was one pro coach at the first seminar – Fred Shero. The brutish tendencies of his teams notwithstanding, Shero may have been more at home with this gang of academic eggheads than with his NHL colleagues, who branded him "the Fog" for his off-beat, cerebral approach to the game. Perhaps Shero's criticisms about the reluctance of NHL coaches to share or embrace new ideas sprang out of the different mentality he encountered at the NCCP seminars.

Another star from the NHL ranks graced some of the NCCP's early proceedings in the 1970s. By then, Montreal's Scotty Bowman was well on his way to becoming the most successful coach in pro hockey and dean of the NHL branch of the profession. Like Shero, he presented at more than one NCCP seminar in the program's first decade and his reputation was already such that the assembled hung on his every word. Dave Dryden, older brother of Bowman's goaltender Ken, tended goal himself for seven NHL seasons with Chicago, Buffalo and Edmonton and also suited up for the WHA Oilers. He was an eager member of one of Bowman's first NCCP audiences, pen poised, ready to glean wisdom from the master. Dryden remembers Bowman's answer to a question about why he'd had so much success: "He said it was 'Having the right people on the ice at the right time'."

Juxtaposed against the highly analytical offerings Dryden had heard from the other presenters, Bowman's comment left him "amazed at the gulf between the pro game and the university game." The gentlemanly ex-goalie intends no disrespect for Bowman's elementary, pragmatic position; he's simply remarking on the differences between the disparate worlds of NHL and CIAU hockey. Bowman's world, in which he was king, was all about results, and he knew intuitively how to deliver them. The world of Clare Drake, the method movement and the NCCP – the world that Dave King was entering in 1973 – was more about studying the hows and whys of the game, finding the ways and means to make it better, and communicating those ways and means to other coaches so they could implement them.

From the outset, Dave King saw the same thing in Drake that Ken Hitchcock referred to when he called Drake the "grandfather of the sharing of information." As King reminisces about his 1973 epiphany, he tells of his sense of wonder as he watched Drake just "give it all away. He was so generous with his time and his knowledge." That was the whole point of this and the other seminars in the years to come. Dave King and Ken Hitchcock eventually made their own huge contributions to the NCCP over the years, as did Drake's fellow pioneers like Kingston, Watt, Boucher, Watson, Lariviere, Arsenault, Hindmarch and others in the seminal circle. And while these men provided the content, they assign credit to Dennis McDonald, as CAHA technical director, for supplying the organizational drive behind the program.

There's no doubt that the method movement, which morphed into the NCCP, drew its life and ideas from a whole group of talented, committed coaches working in universities all across the country. However, Kingston, King and Hitchcock don't mince words when they lay the credit for the movement's earliest stirrings at Clare Drake's feet. Like Hitchcock, King uses the term "grandfather" as he puts Drake's name at the head of this sharing ethos. Dale Henwood is another disciple. He coached at Edmonton's Northern Alberta Institute of Technology after playing for Drake and, like the others, has contributed to the NCCP as a presenter and author himself. Henwood confesses his bias toward his mentor, but he's unrepentant in his agreement with the other three that Drake was the fountainhead for the movement. Granted, these men are westerners all, and so had much more direct contact with Drake than their eastern counterparts, but their position on this matter holds up under scrutiny.

Drake started his university coaching career in 1955, years ahead of any of his method movement fellows. By 1964, he had already launched his first protégé in Ron Watson. At the time of the NCCP's inception, he'd been busting the hallowed coaches' code of secrecy for almost twenty years. He set the example, not just with his generosity, but with the innovations he'd been inflicting on his own players since the mid-fifties, (witness Austin Smith's stories about body-checking line rushes in warm-up and ankle weights for skating drills). Dan Smith (no relation to Austin), a former Western Ontario Mustang under Ron Watson and graduate assistant with Clare Drake in 1977-78, later became Dennis McDonald's assistant technical director at the CAHA, and in this position managed part of the NCCP in the early 1980s. As Watson's player he was a protégé of a protégé, if you will, and like Watson, Smith was an easterner who gained western exposure, becoming yet another admirer of the Drake way. He describes the CIAU of the early seventies as "a community of coaches with sound academic backgrounds and good coaching practices," but he also picks out Clare Drake as the original counter-cultural pioneer.

Does it really matter who started it all? Drake himself would insist that it doesn't. As he'll remind anyone who asks, "It's amazing what can be accomplished when no one cares who gets the credit." So perhaps the more important question here is what was accomplished? What's the big deal about the National Coaching Certification Program? NCCP – it's a bunch of initials, an acronym by-product of the Canadian sports bureaucracy. What does any of this have to do with hockey, with the blood and sweat, tears and joy of what happens on the ice; or with the Stanley Cup, to Canadians the holiest of grails; or with our national identity and the pride we feel when we win on the international stage, the burning shame when we lose?

Ken Hitchcock's story of his lockout-bound search for a hockey fix offers one answer to these questions. His comment that Philadelphia minor hockey coaches were "barking all the same stuff" that he used in major junior in the 1980s points to the influence the NCCP has had on hockey both within and outside of Canada. It's not only significant that American amateur hockey uses the Canadian NCCP content and materials; what's even more important is that regardless of country or culture, the game of hockey now has a common language and structure understood by all who play and coach it. As a Stanley Cup winner, Hitchcock uses that language and structure and so, says he, do most of the successful coaches in today's NHL.

Dale Henwood points to another impact, saying the coaching education program has helped the game get past the traditional Canadian hockey mentality that claimed, "I played, therefore I can coach." Most coaches outside the NHL are now taught, and practice their calling, in a "more professional and cerebral way" thanks to the NCCP, says Henwood. In The Show itself, this influence created the environment wherein Tom Renney and his New York Rangers' staff got their opportunity for the 2005-06 season. Indeed, Renney and his colleagues would credit the program for a good deal of their success. As for Canadian performance relative to the rest of the hockey world, Henwood cites the NCCP for the "sophistication of how hockey has developed in Canada, allowing us to stay at or near the top internationally."

In the early seventies, however, sophistication was not an accurate descriptor for the mainstream face of Canadian hockey, especially in the international arena. The NHL pros were outmaneuvered, outprepared and outsmarted by the Soviet hockey machine in the '72 Summit Series. The win-loss record for those eight monumental games, decidedly the most critical measure, was the only way Canada

"A tough little son-of-a-gun." Former Golden Bear star and coach Bill Moores, assistant coach, Edmonton Oilers, circa 2004.

"A pair of shorts." Protégé and mentor, best of buddies; Bill and Clare, late 1990s.

managed to outdo the Russians in '72; oh, and, as Anatoly Tarasov postulated, we beat them on the heart-and-desire meter. For Pete's sake, we won eh? Victory aside, no image conveys the "sophistication gap" more graphically or accurately than that of Canada's gap-toothed hockey urchin Bobby Clarke, cutting down the elegant Russian star Valery Kharlamov in Game Six with a well-aimed two-hander to the ankle. The gap widened in 1974, with the abysmal effort of the WHA's Team Canada against the Russians, and we couldn't narrow it through the rest of the decade and into the ensuing one. North American pros flailed away against the Soviet machine, notching occasional victories when the stars aligned, but running up an overall record of failure and futility.

With no presence at the Olympics or the world championships, and largely unsophisticated and unsuccessful professional representation, it would seem that Canada was dead in the water during those lost years of the seventies. But Dennis McDonald and his posse of university coaches were toiling away, working in obscurity to change the game from the grassroots up. And unbeknownst to the rest of the Canadian hockey nation, the CIAU carried the maple leaf abroad with distinction and refinement. Clare Drake continued to buzz away at the center of this activity.

While working diligently in the off-season on various method movement projects (mainly NCCP seminars and provincial coaching clinics), Drake continued to mount challenge upon challenge against

Tom Watt's unstoppable blue wave. He also worked on his own professional development, in keeping with the academic standards of the university environment and with his personal commitment to lifelong learning. In the late 1960s, through summer and long distance course work, he had completed his Master of Science from the University of Washington. So in the 1969-70 season he was ready for a sabbatical and he, Dolly and the girls moved to Eugene, Oregon, where he enrolled in the University of Oregon's Doctor of Education program in educational and coaching theory. He took the required courses and wrote the comprehensive exams but didn't complete his doctorate because his thesis adviser left Oregon that year. True to form, Drake blames himself for not finding another adviser and finishing his thesis, but it all worked out twenty-five years later when the University of Alberta conferred an honorary Doctor of Laws degree on him. By 1995, the coach was already a venerated professor emeritus when he finally became Dr. Drake. Ron Watson, a Ph.D. himself and long-time professor at Western Ontario, stresses the enormity of this honor, explaining how rare it is for a Canadian university to accord such a mark of distinction to a faculty member whose primary role was that of an athletics coach.

When he returned to Edmonton in the fall of 1970 with valued knowledge he'd gained at Oregon, he was still just Coach Drake, sans doctorate. And in spite of two Canada West championships in the ensuing four seasons (1972, 1973), he was also sans University Cups since The Double; he and his Bears couldn't crack Toronto's dominance at the nationals. An intense, but rather one-sided rivalry had developed between the two schools since their first meeting in 1966. In the ten seasons between then and 1975, the Blues and the Bears faced off at the nationals in eight games over five tournaments, with Alberta only managing two wins and a tie against five losses. The record was even more lopsided when it came to national titles – two for Alberta, seven for Toronto. Remarkably though, and this is a tribute to the character of both coaches and the fraternal culture in which they operated, Tom Watt and Clare Drake became collaborators. The relationship grew partly through post-game chats and shared analyses of wins and losses, but it really blossomed as the two contributed to the method movement through their presentations at NCCP seminars. As Watt says with a laugh, "We tried to beat each other's brains out, but we were friends."

The friends finally got to work together toward a mutual victory when the CIAU, with Hockey Canada support, commissioned the two pre-eminent coaches in Canadian university hockey to take a team to the 1972 Winter Universiade, staged during February in Lake Placid, New York. This Student National Team featured a half-dozen All Canadians and other elite CIAU players. It included four Golden Bears – captain and future Edmonton Oiler Steve Carlyle, forwards Jack Gibson and Dave Couves and goaltender Barry Richardson – and six Varsity Blues. A number of players on this roster made it to the major pro ranks, such as Loyola University's Larry Carriere, who played five NHL seasons with the Buffalo Sabres, the Atlanta Flames and the Vancouver Canucks; Toronto's John Wright, who saw three seasons with the Canucks and the St. Louis Blues; Ken Lockett of Guelph University, who tended goal for the Canucks for two years; and Carlyle, Gibson, Gavin Kirk (Loyola) and Bob McAneeley (UBC), each of whom logged time in the WHA. Drake and Watt were co-coaches of this team, and the head of the CIAU delegation to the games was Drake's boss and old Lacombe Rockets teammate, U of A athletics director Ed Zemrau. Zemrau was no stranger to university hockey, having been an All American at Denver University in the 1950s, and he would go on to become president of the CIAU and chairman of the 1983 Summer Universiade held in Edmonton. He was a key supporter of Drake at the U of A for many years, and played a significant administrative and funding role in helping build the Golden Bear hockey dynasty.

There were only three teams in the 1972 Lake Placid tournament; Canada, the USA and the Soviet Union. Coached by Boris "Chuckles" Kulagin, the Soviets' feature line consisted of Vyacheslav Anisin, Yuri Lebedev and Alexander Bodunov, who would all become international stars just seven months later as emerging young heroes on the Soviet Summit Series team. "They gave us a headache," says Drake of the trio. In keeping with Russian custom, some of the Soviet players seemed a little old to be students. The tournament was a round robin, consisting of three games against each opponent. The CIAU boys defeated their American NCAA counterparts handily in all three of their head-to-head contests, but it was a different story against the supremely talented Russians. After getting badly spanked ("maybe 9-2," remembers Carlyle) in the first game against the Soviets, Drake and Watt did some serious strategizing to help the overmatched Canadians close the competitive gap. In their second game the score was a lot tighter and they managed to tie the Big Red Machine in their third and final go. This was a signal achievement for a bunch of Canadian student athletes and they were just as proud of the tie as of the silver medal they brought home.

What Drake brought home was more food for thought, more new ideas to be tried out in his U of A hockey laboratory. He saw yet again the Russian regrouping system that he and the Rockets encountered at the Ahearne Cup in 1965, the circling back with the puck that would give the NHLers fits just a few months hence in the Summit Series. He also got his first look at what he came to call the "controlled change," a method of changing on the fly used by the Russians to maintain puck possession while they moved a fresh batch of players onto the ice. Changing on the fly wasn't so common in that time when long shifts were the professional standard and, when it did happen, it usually involved dumping the puck deep into the offensive zone while the tired group went to the bench. The result may have been a fresh line or defensive pair, but it almost always meant losing the puck. The Russians, on the other hand, would advance the puck up the ice and then pass it back to their defence while the forwards rotated off. They would keep circling back with the puck like this until an entirely new five-man unit was out on the ice, maintaining all the while.

Drake used the controlled change with the Golden Bears from this time on at Alberta and then introduced it with the Winnipeg Jets when he moved to their staff in 1989. "It's not the kind of thing that'll win you a championship," says Drake. It is one of those little extras however – the fine details that go into getting an edge on your opponent – for which Drake became known.

Another new wrinkle the Russians brought to the Lake Placid tournament was the tactic they used to generate intense forechecking pressure. Steve Carlyle remembers them "overloading," bringing all three forwards to one side of the offensive zone to bottle the Canadians up in their own end for long periods of time. Both the tactic and the pressure it generated were new to Canadian hockey then, but before long they became a Golden Bear trademark, having mutated into Drake's distinctive 2-1-2 forechecking system. This was one of several such systems Drake developed in the seventies, but it was the Bears' signature when it came to creating offensive pressure.

Pressure forechecking can't happen without other key elements in place. It's based on an up-tempo, high-speed style of play, which in turn requires well-conditioned athletes taking short shifts at very high intensity levels. And short, high intensity shifts work best when a team has depth. Drake has

Gimme a drink outta that thing! Drake's third University Cup, Varsity Arena, Edmonton, 1975. (John Horcoff, reaching, immediate left of Cup; Kevin Primeau, future Olympian and Oilers' assistant coach, to Horcoff's left; Bears' assistant coach Dick Wintermute, in checked shirt, leaning in above and to Horcoff's right; captain and Student Nat Steve McKnight, to right of Cup; Student Nat and future Hitchcock assistant Brian Middleton, immediately behind McKnight; All Canadian and Student Nat Ross Barros, bottom front, far left; Student Nat Bruce Crawford, standing, outside right front.

Above: Rinkside roster analysis at a Student National Team camp, 1974. (From left, Drake; Bob Boucher of St. Mary's University; Tom Watt of University of Toronto).

Left: Another European tour, more banners and baubles to show for it. Drake with memorabilia from his trip to Czechoslovakia as head coach of the Student National Team, 1975.

always been a proponent of giving each player as much ice time as possible; he's no believer in the "star system" where key players get a lion's share of the ice time, reasoning that such treatment detracts from team depth and can retard the development of other players on the roster. In the fifties and sixties, roster sizes were smaller and didn't allow for four full lines, but by the seventies this had changed. Steve McKnight, the captain of the 1975 National Champions, recalls the coach rolling three lines steadily and "spotting" a fourth, getting everyone on the bench into the game. By the late seventies, the fourth line had become part of the rotation. This use of team depth, combined with Drake's long-established commitment to fitness and the new forechecking tactics, allowed the Bears to generate pressure in the offensive zone to a level virtually unseen in North American hockey at that time.

The success of this emerging strategy was born out most vividly in a December 1972 game against the Golden Bears' old and sometimes bitter crosstown rivals, the Edmonton Oil Kings of junior fame. The Oil Kings and Bears had battled on and off in a series of "town and gown" exhibitions since the 1950s; perhaps because of its final score, the 1972 match would be their last head-to-head contest. The favored Oil Kings brought a loaded roster into the '72 affair. Their lineup featured junior stars such as John Rogers, Darcy Rota, Harold Snepsts, Dave Inkpen and Doug Soetaert, all of whom would soon play in the NHL or WHA. But this talented bunch of local heroes hadn't met with, and couldn't handle, the waves of pressure the anonymous Bears threw at them in their own zone. One of Steve McKnight's favorite Drakeisms was, "When the other team's defence have their faces pushed up against the glass all night, they don't play very well." He was talking about both the pressure of strategic forechecking and physically finishing the check. Thanks to the efforts of McKnight and his fellow forwards, the Oil Kings outstanding D-men, including the hulking Snepsts (a future star for the Vancouver Canucks), spent most of that game pasted to said glass. The effects were noticeable in the shots for-and-against (54-18 for the Bears), on the scoreboard (10-1 Bears), and in the continuous parade of overwhelmed and frustrated Oil Kings to the penalty box.

Now, in the twenty-first century, it has become fashionable among NHL coaches, players and TV analysts to talk about "taking away the other team's time and space." Rick Wyrozub, the smooth Bears forward who won the Canada West scoring title that 1972-73 season, says that while Drake's forechecking systems might have seemed complex (and they were by the standards of the day), his way of teaching them in practice made it all easy to understand. "He'd say, 'Take away their time; take away their space.' You wouldn't forget that," says Wyrozub. McKnight concurs, as does Brian Middleton, a standout defenceman with the early seventies Bears. In separate conversations they use identical words to describe the way their coach imparted these innovative schemes to his players: "He made the game simple." Almost thirty-five years ago, Wyrozub, McKnight, Middleton and the rest of Clare Drake's Golden Bears walloped the Oil Kings with this new brand of high tempo hockey and strategic, pressure forechecking; they were simply taking away their opponents' time and space.

The 1972 Universiade was Drake's third exposure to the Soviets and Tom Watt's second. They'd had an up-close and personal look at the style of play the Russians favored, the systems they were using and even some of the personnel that would take the ice against Team Canada in September 1972. Their CIAU colleagues, George Kingston of the University of Calgary and Bob Hindmarch of UBC, had also seen plenty of the Russians. Hindmarch had managed Canada's 1964 Olympic team, and Kingston, it could be argued, had penetrated the mysteries of Soviet hockey further and deeper than anyone before him.

In the summer of 1971, the ever-curious George and his wife Wendy had taken their two youngsters to Germany, where they'd purchased a Volkswagen bus and crossed into the "forbidden territory" behind the Iron Curtain. They motored all the way through Poland and the Soviet Union to far-off Moscow, where Kingston spent three weeks meeting with Russian coaches and observing the Central Red Army team at something almost unheard of North America, off-season training. It's hard to comprehend in our CNN-shrunken, twenty-first century world what a bold and courageous journey this young family made into the darkest recesses of Communist Eastern Europe. There were no shopping malls and water parks for Wendy and the kids to visit while George picked the Russians' brains. They all survived however, and Kingston came back with few illusions about how our mighty pros would fare against the despised Communists in 1972.

A less circumspect man than Drake, Kingston didn't wait in vain to be asked about the Russians. In the summer of '72 as pre-Summit hype burgeoned, he volunteered his well-formed opinions to Calgary media acquaintances, and was branded a "traitor" because of his assertions that the Soviets would thrive in the series. He'd seen first-hand evidence of Russian fitness, skill and strategy. As for the sketchy Canadian scouting reports that promised a lack of Soviet goaltending and firepower, he knew them for what they were – quick, superficial glimpses that in no way told the whole story.

The accumulated wisdom and experience of men like Drake, Watt, Kingston and Hindmarch went untapped and unheeded in 1972, and the NHL, under the auspices of Hockey Canada's international mandate, stumbled unwittingly into the ambush laid for them by the Soviets. The guys at Hockey Canada got the message though, and two months after the end of the Summit Series, they launched the Hockey Development Council. In addition to sponsoring the fact-finding trip the council members took to Moscow for the 1973 Worlds, Hockey Canada funded a Moscow junket for fifty Canadian amateur coaches to study the Russians at the 1974 Team Canada-Soviet series involving the WHA. One of the fifty was a diminutive, bespectacled Edmontonian named Billy Moores.

Moores was a former Edmonton Oil Kings captain who played junior hockey while getting an education degree at U of A. In his final year of university, with his junior eligibility gone, he donned his school colors and logged one momentous season for the Golden Bears in 1971-72. It was momentous because of the impression he and his coach made on each other; the two quickly developed enormous mutual respect. Many in the Golden Bears community have noted tongue-in-cheek that the affinity between the men must have been rooted in their shared close proximity to the ground. Drake had finally found someone his own size, not to pick on, but with whom he could identify! Actually, the relationship that grew between player and coach, and that eventually blossomed into an incredibly successful coaching partnership, was founded upon much stronger stuff than the bond between a "pair of shorts."

Drake admired Moores the player for his smarts and determination. "He was a tough little son-of-a-gun," says the old coach of his greatest protégé, "a fine team-first player who never backed down and always went wherever the heaviest contact was." Moores, who had enjoyed his Oil Kings experience, grew further with the Bears thanks to the teacher-coach who brought to the game a level of detail he'd never seen before. For his part, Moores brought speed, skill and intensity to the rink every day, whether for a game or practice, and he became the Bears' most valuable player and leading scorer for the 1971-72 season. Already an intelligent, focused athlete, he rose to the challenge of how much more he had to learn, how closely he had to pay attention to follow Drake's systems, and how the coach used "the agony of repetition" through creative drills to ensure his players "got it." Moores appreciated that with the Bears, "we always knew what we were doing in every part of the rink" and more, how Drake achieved all this with honor and respect, for the game and his players: "We never heard him raise his voice," says Moores.

After graduation, Moores went to work as a teacher and started coaching in Edmonton's minor hockey system. He also pursued his coaching certification through the Alberta Amateur Hockey Association clinics that would soon tie in with the NCCP. This was how he qualified for the Hockey Canada trip to Russia in 1974. Like his mentor, Moores has a passion for learning. His quick development as a coach, and the pronounced statement he made in his one year in green and gold, inspired Drake to call him when seeking an assistant in 1976.

It was the beginning of a coaching marriage made in heaven; Moores and Drake clicked together behind the Bears bench like rum and coke (their choice for many a post-game tipple). The younger man assisted his mentor for three seasons until taking over as interim head coach in 1979-80, when Drake went to the Olympic Team, and won a University Cup in Drake's absence. He made his second tricky transition from assistant to interim head coach in 1983-84 when Drake was on sabbatical, merely winning the Father George Kehoe Award as CIAU coach of the year. And after a season as head coach of the junior Regina Pats, he returned for a third stint with the Bears as Drake's co-coach, finally taking over as sole head coach from 1989-90 until 1993-94. In seven seasons running the Golden Bears, Moores rang up a astonishing .717 winning percentage, tallying four conference championships and two University Cups (1980, 1992), and earning CIAU coach of the year honors twice (1984, 1991). As Drake's assistant or co-coach, he won five conference titles and another national championship. After leaving the CIAU for good in 1994, he guided the Kokudo Bunnies to the All Japan championship and later joined the New York Rangers staff. In 2000, his Rangers colleague Craig MacTavish asked him to assist with the Edmonton Oilers, where 2006 found him as a key architect of the Oilers' outstanding penalty-killing unit on their inspiring playoff run.

It would be a mistake to think of Bill Moores as a Drake *doppelgänger*, their physical similarities notwithstanding. The mentor points out one of the key differences between himself and his protégé. "Bill added a different touch to the team," says Clare. "The players found him more approachable than me and he encouraged them to play tougher, because of the kind of player he'd been. He was feistier than me, although he still insisted on discipline. We were a good complement to each other."

Moores's assessment rings consistent: "I'm probably a little more emotional in my approach, Clare probably a little more contained, but his teams always played with passion." Former Golden Bear goalie Ted Poplawski, an All Canadian in 1979 and 1980 who became a long-time assistant with the team, offers the best insight into the main difference between the two coaches: "If a Clare Drake team skated up to a wall, they could go through it, but they'd probably think their way around it. If a Bill Moores team skated up to the wall, they could think their way around it, but they'd probably go through it."

Differences aside, it's what Drake and Moores had in common that made this pair so dynamic, that made their influence on the game so telling. Even though Moores started out as Drake's student, and will heap praise on the man he calls his mentor at any opportunity, Drake in turn sees Moores as someone from whom he has learned as well. Once again, we see the Gladwellian maven in operation here. The two put their keen hockey minds together to take Drake's work of the fifties and sixties to another level. Their new ideas or refinements in the areas of defensive zone coverages, breakouts, forechecking, faceoff strategies, power play and penalty killing formed a significant part of the content for the NCCP. And they did all this from the noblest of motivations. They fed off their mutual drive to better the game and the professional standing of the coaches in it. Their synergy inspired them not just as collaborators, but also as continuing catalysts in the method movement while it rolled from the seventies on into the eighties and fueled the NCCP. Bill Liskowich, who coached the highly competitive University of Regina teams of the 1990s, says it all about these two and their great contribution: "These hockey concepts might seem to be obvious, but they're only obvious because Clare Drake used them, and emphasized them and shared them. To me, he's the pope of hockey, Billy's the archbishop and the rest of us are just their disciples. They would beat you, and all you had to do was ask them how they'd done it. It didn't matter that you were playing again the next night. They'd share everything."

Another fine coach in the making, another disciple, came along just about the same time as Bill Moores. Perry Pearn enrolled at the U of A in 1972, a graduate of the Red Deer Rustlers junior A Centennial Cup Champions. He attended Golden Bears training camp but couldn't stick with the main squad and so played for Dick Wintermute on the junior varsity team. When he finished his degree he moved across the river to Edmonton's north side, where he became ex-Bear Dale Henwood's assistant coach at the Northern Alberta Institute of Technology. The NAIT Ookpiks play in the Alberta Colleges Athletic Conference, part of the CCAA, and in 1976 they were Henwood's first coaching charge, before he went to the NCAA to join the staff at St. Lawrence University. Pearn spent two years learning the Drake way from Henwood – again, a protégé of a protégé – and took over the Ooks in 1979 to build one of the great dynasties in Canadian small college hockey.

Between 1979 and 1992 his teams won six CCAA national titles and dominated their conference year in and year out. Pearn continued to soak up everything he could, by attaining the top level of NCCP certification and through occasional sit-downs to pick the master's brain, where he'd grill Drake for hours at a time. Pearn's gratitude extends not just to Drake's tremendous generosity; it also includes key lessons he learned and coaching values he adopted. One of the most important of these was that "you can't compromise your principles for one player; the team has to come first." "I lived by that the rest of the days I was a head coach and sticking to it made a big difference," says Pearn.

He offers an example from his turn as head coach of Canada's team for the 1993 world junior championships in Gavle, Sweden. That squad boasted a number of future NHL greats, such as Chris Pronger and Paul Kariya, and it also included Alexandre Daigle, Canada's most exalted junior of the time whose star would fade quickly once he reached pro. Although he was one of the team leaders, Daigle showed poor discipline with a cross-checking penalty in a tight game against the Swedes. To hold him accountable for his behavior and send a message to the rest of the players, Pearn took a big risk and sat him out for two periods. Daigle responded with a multiple-point game in a 9-1 win over the Russians and the team gelled to bring home a gold medal, the first of Canada's five-in-a-row run through the mid-1990s. In a revealing statement about the intestinal fortitude it takes to be an elite level coach, Pearn says of benching a star, "The courage to do it came from knowing that a guy like

Another Drake student; according to Sports Illustrated, *the "NHL's best assistant" in 2006. Perry Pearn, assistant coach for the New York Rangers, 2006.*

Clare had said this was his philosophy."

Perry Pearn also won two world junior championships as an assistant (1990 and 1991), assisted Dave King with the Canadian National Team and, after he left NAIT, was head coach of Ambri-Piotta in the Swiss Elite League and the Medicine Hat Tigers of the WHL. He started his NHL career as an assistant with the Winnipeg Jets and then spent eight seasons on Jacques Martin's staff with the Ottawa Senators. In 2005-06, his work with the Rangers won him kudos from *Sports Illustrated* as "the NHL's best assistant." Three of the seasons Pearn spent in Ottawa were in the company of Roger Neilson, one of the most inventive and highly regarded coaches in the history of the game.

Pearn talks about the new ideas Neilson introduced, the enormous influence he had on so many Ontario-based coaches – men like Jacques Martin and Mike Keenan – and draws a parallel: "Clare Drake is the Roger Neilson of western Canada. Clare was the guy who was ahead of his time in terms of his innovations and teaching the game. Every part of what he did as a coach is now part and parcel of what every NHL coaching staff does." As Pearn casts his mind back to the early eighties, when he was at the lower end of the learning curve and attending every NCCP seminar he could, he cites a small but telling indicator of the power of Drake's influence. The NCCP had picked up steam by this time and, while its key contributors were university coaches, some of the pro guys were starting to show up both as presenters and to watch and learn themselves. Pearn says that at most of the sessions the audiences consisted of young coaches like himself, but when it was Drake's turn to present, the room was always packed and the pro coaches were all in attendance, listening intently and taking notes. This jibes with Ken Hitchcock's appraisal of the impact Drake had on the NCCP: "I've been in many clinics that he's taught at, and you can't get a seat when he presents. That shows how highly he's thought of by the people in our community."

In addition to mentoring and influencing several generations of coaches, Clare Drake and Roger Neilson share another, less fortunate, similarity. They were both renowned and lampooned during their careers for their propensity to be so intensely focused on hockey brainwork that they could appear incompetent when it came to simple, daily matters. In Drake's case this character trait, when combined with his university position, often earned him the epithet of "absent-minded professor." Cam Cole, Canada's twenty-first-century version of Jim Coleman, wrote a touching tribute to Neilson a few months before Neilson's 2003 death from cancer. In his *National Post* column, Cole mentioned the legion of stories about Neilson's forgetfulness and his tendency to get muddled by technology; on an appliance-shopping run for example, when he confused a microwave oven with a TV monitor, asking the sales clerk if they didn't have something "with a bigger screen." Drake-watchers boast the same number and type of stories. You can't talk to a former player or coaching colleague without hearing them – everything from misplaced car keys (an almost daily occurrence if all accounts are to be believed) to comical battles lost with overhead projectors at coaching seminars. Ask Bill Moores about this aspect of the Drake mythology and you see the feistiness his old mentor talks about. Moores's penetrating eyes flash darkly as he vents his frustration about how some folks derive a little too much enjoyment out of Drake's absent-mindedness. Moores himself will smile affectionately at Drake's idiosyncrasies, but his point is that the joking can get taken too far and detract from the old coach's tremendous body of work and the respect he deserves. Moores is right.

Before Clare Drake and Bill Moores established their mutual admiration society, and before Perry

Pearn launched his distinguished career, there were a couple of other signal events in Drake's career. There was another high point, and then the first, and possibly lowest, of the lows.

The high point was a third national hockey championship. This came in the 1974-75 season and was special for several reasons. Since being crushed 8-1 by Toronto in the 1966 national final, Alberta had lost four straight games to the Varsity Blues at various University Cup tournaments between 1969 and 1973. Adding to the frustration was that, in 1973-74, George Kingston and his Calgary Dinosaurs were finally able to crack the Bears' stranglehold on the conference title; sadly for Kingston, they lost to the eventual champions, the University of Waterloo, at the nationals that year. The next season, the Bears were a pre-season choice for also-ran status, but defying predictions, they ran away with the Canada West conference and began the CIAU's new (and short-lived) playoff format comprised of a number of best-of-three elimination series between conference champions.

After knocking off Brandon and Loyola universities, the Bears hosted the Ontario Champion University of Toronto for the national final, staged in what was then called Varsity Arena in Edmonton. This building had replaced the old, Quonset-style University Arena where Clare Drake had skated as a Golden Bear. Opened in the fall of 1960, it still stands today at the western edge of the U of A campus, now bearing the name of the man who patrolled behind its south bench for nigh on three decades. Even after nearly fifty years, it's an oddly attractive edifice by hockey arena standards, built into a shallow hillside with an all-window, upper level entry hall that looks down onto the ice surface. There's room for 2,800 bums on its bench seats, but in March of 1975 the rink was crammed with close to 3,500 for the showdown against Tom Watt's mighty Blues, winners of seven of the previous nine University Cups. In those days, the Bears' fan base held a much higher percentage of students than it does in the twenty-first century, and the noisy, well-lubricated undergrads filled every nook and cranny of the arena, sitting in the stairways, piled deep into the corners above the stands and taking up every available inch of standing room. It was a fire marshall's nightmare, but a home team's dream. Alberta's organist Rick Leblanc, who parlayed his Varsity Arena performances into a big league turn with the Edmonton Oilers, had these fans singing in one voice, like the thundering choral crowds of English soccer stadiums.

Spurred on by this uproar, the Bears took down their eastern rivals in three hard-fought games. They relied upon the superb goaltending of Dale Henwood, an undersized but tough and intelligent defence corps, led by All Canadian Ross Barros and his partner Brian Middleton, and a strong platoon of forwards with no great stars, but every one of whom skated tirelessly and read the game like a book. This seamless, finely tuned team passed the puck on a string and forechecked the more talented Blues incessantly, taking away their "time and space" shift after shift, no matter which of their four lines was on the ice. It was another coaching triumph for Drake.

The respect these players had for their coach was deep and abiding, and in at least one case, it was handed down to a succeeding generation. One of the stalwarts on the '75 National Champions was John Horcoff, a dogged, determined centerman from Castlegar, B.C., who had a nifty touch around the net. To the surprise of many, he won the Canada West scoring title that season, his last in the CIAU. A few years later he also produced a son, Shawn, another dogged, determined center with finishing ability who, in 2006, carried the mail on the Edmonton Oilers' top line. For his father's mentor, the son shows due reverence: "Clare Drake is one of Canada's greatest coaches, one of hockey's greatest coaches, and my dad had a chance to play for him and win a championship at U of A," says Shawn Horcoff.

The 1974-75 season also marked a further taste of international hockey for Drake. The CIAU and Hockey Canada decided to send another Student National Team to the '75 Winter Universiade in Livigno, Italy, but the hockey tournament at these games was canceled for lack of participants. Drake, Watt and Bob Boucher of the St. Mary's University Huskies had worked to assemble this team since the previous summer, running selection camps in Halifax, Toronto and Edmonton to cull a final roster from a nationwide pool of top CIAU players. The end product included bunches of Blues, with Huskies and others sprinkled in to leaven the mix. Among them were four Alberta boys: Barros, Middleton, Steve McKnight and Bruce Crawford. To get some competition in lieu of the Universiade tournament, officials hastily organized a tour of Czechoslovakia, where they played eight games over the Christmas-New Year's break against the Czech Junior National Team and some military and senior club squads. They handled the juniors well but struggled a bit against some of the club teams. From an Alberta perspective, the Student Nats' record wasn't as important as something the four Golden Bears noted. It was seeing their teammates, the cream of the CIAU crop, up close that convinced Middleton and his fellow Bears they could compete with the best that season. Another benefit that derived from the tour was the model that Drake, Watt and Boucher had designed to form the team. Drake, Watt and Father Bauer would also employ cross-country selection camps to pare down a pre-identified player pool into a working roster for the 1980 Olympic Team.

All careers have their peaks and valleys. In March of 1975, Clare Drake was at one of his higher peaks; less than twelve months later he would hit the bottom of his deepest valley. In March 1975 he was the ascendant coach of one of Canada's two finest amateur hockey teams, having just beaten the other one for his fourth national championship. He'd won the incomparable Double in 1967-68. In seventeen seasons behind the Bears bench he'd won twelve conference championships and been named Edmonton's Sportsman of the Year twice. He knew international hockey as well as anyone in the country, and he'd stared into the implacable eyes of the Russians probably more than any other Canadian except for David Bauer. He was the father of an entire coaching movement that by 1975 had grown into Hockey Canada's National Coaching Certification Program. His university peers and many other coaches in amateur hockey looked to him as a sage of the game. Finally, someone in the professional ranks decided to break the "brain barrier" and take a risk on this university professor. It had only been tried once before, when the Detroit Red Wings hired Ned Harkness, the coach at Cornell University of the NCAA. Harkness lasted for a few months in the fall and winter of 1970, winning only twelve out of thirty-eight games before the Wings unaccountably bumped him upstairs to general manager. The Drake experiment didn't work out much better.

He was hired by Edmonton Oilers owners Dr. Charles Allard, Mitch Klimove and Zane Feldman in the early summer of 1975 to take over a team that had posted a mediocre 36-38-4 record in the previous WHA season, having missed the playoffs for the second time in its three years of existence. His immediate boss was the larger-than-life Bill Hunter, former Edmonton Oil Kings owner, general manager and coach, and now the Oilers' general manager. He was also a part owner of the team and one of the original architects of the upstart league that emancipated pro players and their salaries by offering an alternative to the NHL. Hunter was a dynamic individual and one of hockey's true characters. Much loved in Edmonton for his color, his drive and his optimism, many who knew him had no illusions about certain other aspects of his personality. Ed Willes, in his affectionate, anecdotal account of the WHA, *The Rebel League*, called Hunter "a windbag, full of himself and certain of his path."

He was also a coach-killer, having earned a reputation for firing coaches almost as quickly as he hired them. Hunter's own unique twist on this trait was that he usually replaced the fired coach with himself. In the three seasons prior to Drake's hiring, Hunter fired coaches Ray Kinasewich and Brian Shaw and each time went behind the bench to inspire the team with his enthusiasm, if not his tactical acumen. Steve Carlyle, the former Golden Bear All Canadian who played four seasons with the Oilers and witnessed each of Hunter's takeovers, makes a quiet but incisive comment about the man's hockey knowledge: "He would get us all pumped up and say, 'C'mon guys, you just need to go out there and play the system.' Except there was no system." Carlyle contrasts this with Drake's technical depth, which exposed the Oilers to different powerplay strategies and forechecking rotations, all new to the world of professional hockey in 1975. Goaltender Dave Dryden, who backstopped Drake's Oilers squad, says of the coach, "He was very obviously a good coach, so well prepared. He put a strong stress on fundamentals and systems and the players we had weren't used to that. It was one of those cases of a guy being ahead of his time."

Al Hamilton, the Oilers' captain and a local hero, having been one of Hunter's junior stars with the Oil Kings, lists off some of the innovations Drake tried to introduce with the Oilers: defensive zone coverages, forechecking systems, shorter shifts and changing on the fly, and pre-season conditioning. The battle-scarred old pro says, "So many things we see now in the NHL he wanted to bring into the game then." As an example of the entrenched attitude the coach encountered, Hamilton tosses out an earthy remark referencing Drake's gospel on short shifts: "Nobody looked at that shit back then. When your ass was tired, you came off!" And by Hamilton's own account, there were at least a few tired and inept asses filling out the blue and orange pants of the 1975-76 Oilers. In what many would view as an understatement, Hamilton says of the team Hunter assembled, "[Drake] didn't inherit a great hockey club." The owners agreed at the time, saying after Drake's departure that the blame for the Oilers' poor performance lay with Hunter, who had selected the players. And the Edmonton fans saw things the same way; in an *Edmonton Journal* poll, sixty-one percent of them named the GM as the source of the Oilers' woes, while only 4.2 percent identified Drake as solely responsible.

General manager, players and coach… together they all stumbled to a 22-29-2 record by January 22, 1976, when Dr. Allard apologetically informed Drake that he was fired. Bill Hunter took over the team for the last time, and they managed only five more wins against another twenty losses and three ties for a final, dismal tally of 27-49-5.

In twenty years of coaching, it was the first time Clare Drake had been fired; it was the first time he'd experienced a major failure in his career. As Murray Smith points out though, it wasn't really a failure so much as a "judgement passed by others" that Drake had to live with. In the moment, he was typically taciturn, saying simply that he was "very disappointed" and that he felt "the team was coming around a little." He even invoked some of his characteristic positivity, telling the *Edmonton Journal*'s Terry Jones, "I really enjoyed [the Oilers]. It was a continuous learning experience and I think I was getting better and better at the job I was asked to do." Looking back, Carlyle sees it the same way. Being as diplomatic as possible, he says, "I thought it was… uh… 'opportune' that Hunter took over when he did, because I really thought the guys were starting to come around. We had a lot of old pros who didn't like new ideas, but the guys were starting to believe that what he was telling them was going to work."

The grace and dignity Drake demonstrated under pressure and throughout his five months at the helm of the Oilers had earned him the respect of the team's owners, at least some of the players and most media commentators. Dave Dryden told the *Edmonton Journal*, "[Drake's] a good coach and I'm sorry we didn't win more games for him." An Edmonton weekly newsmagazine said of the firing, "The move seemed pathetic, even desperate, the selection of a scapegoat to suffer consequences that properly belong elsewhere." But regardless of all the people Drake had in his corner, the key missing ingredient was an influential group of players. And another factor was the vitriolic criticism of Wayne Overland, the *Journal* sportswriter who, in the greatest of ironies, had seven years earlier compared Drake to Knute Rockne and Bear Bryant.

Overland and the players, some who went on record and some who remained anonymous, leveled three charges most consistently at Drake, all of which were proven over time to be absurd. One had to do simply with who he was – a university coach. Overland said, "Flying a Piper Cub doesn't qualify you to pilot a Concorde. And that's the difference between college hockey and pro hockey, the reason college coaches have never lasted amid the mercenaries." The profusion of university coaches, or coaches trained by university coaches, who followed Drake into pro hockey negated this prejudicial, nonsensical argument. The other two criticisms were about his most contentious attempts at innovation; the interrelated issues of conditioning and short shifts.

Drake's fervid commitment to team fitness had been on record since the mid-1950s and incorporated the notion that players should come to training camp already in shape. This seemed hare-brained to most pros, including the majority of the NHLers who formed the Summit Series team and the Oilers who attended Drake's '75 training camp. As Al Hamilton says, "You worked yourself into shape at training camp." Drake got off on the wrong foot with the players at the outset when he sent them an enthusiastic summer letter, exhorting them to work at an off-season conditioning program he'd prescribed that included running, stretching and weight training. Things got worse when he opened training camp with a compulsory twelve-minute run in Edmonton's Hawrelak Park that was meant to serve as a fitness test. The media were in full attendance for this unheard-of spectacle, and some reacted with glee when veterans bitched about having to run, or simply jogged with cheeky indifference through the allotted time. Most notable of these was the Montreal Canadiens' legendary goaltender Jacques Plante who, at the very tail end of his long, distinguished career came to Edmonton to serve as a part-time goalie and "trophy" acquisition for the Oilers. Forty-six at the time, only a year younger than Drake, Plante showed up at the starting line in loafers, grumbling loudly, "I don't run." Drake made him trot around the park all the same, and there was much laughter over the professor's newfangled idea that running could in anyway relate to hockey. Now, of course, there's scarcely a pro or amateur anywhere in the game who doesn't invest countless hours in rigorous off-season training, including running, stretching and weightlifting.

While there were other complaints that arose over the season, none got as much attention as Drake's belief in rolling four lines during games and distributing ice time among his players, not necessarily equally, but equitably. He believed then, as he still does (along with the many NHL coaches he's influenced), that using four lines serves two important ends. One, it affords valuable playing time to fringe or developing players, increasing their confidence and worth to the team; and two, it allows all players to take shorter shifts, more in the range of thirty to forty-five seconds, which in turn provides for an up-tempo, high-pressure forechecking style of hockey, the style that visitors to Varsity Arena had come to fear. As Steve McKnight observes, "It makes more sense to go hard for forty seconds than to cruise for a minute and ten." But the old pros were having none of it and some of the team's so-called stars complained to Overland, who lambasted Drake for not giving them enough ice time. As usual, Drake takes responsibility for the breakdown, mildly castigating himself for not doing a better job of "selling" his ideas to his players. He also says he failed to understand the "different agendas" at work in pro hockey, where ice time affects contract negotiations, which take precedence over team performance in the minds of many players.

Different agendas aside, Clare Drake opened the four-line debate within the pro context and thirty years later, it's pretty well closed. As Hamilton said, it's one of Drake's innovations that is now commonplace in the NHL. Andy Murray, who logged seven good seasons with the L.A. Kings and in early 2007 was hired by the St. Louis Blues, swears by Drake's philosophy: "If you're out there more than forty seconds, you're cheatin'. We can outwork the other team by being fresh." Perry Pearn made the same point at the 2005 CIS coaches' forum. Sharing the podium with other NHL experts like Ken Hitchcock and Craig MacTavish, Pearn stated, with heads nodding in agreement, that "success in today's NHL comes from consistently outchanging the other team, from getting fresh players on the ice against tired ones." It's no coincidence that Pearn ended up on Tom Renney's staff. The New York head coach is another believer in "rolling four" and he credits Drake as the source of his conviction. Renney faced a particular challenge in maintaining this team strategy when he took over the Rangers in 2005, given that he had the NHL's highest paid, highest profile star of the time in his lineup. A prolific goal scorer who came to Broadway with a me-first reputation, Jaromir Jagr responded to Renney's adept touch and bought into the four-line concept with the Rangers. If anyone was likely to chew up ice time it would be Jagr, but in a late-season team meeting he stood up and spoke about the great contribution made by the third- and fourth-liners. The coach sees this statement as a testament to the strategy itself, to Jagr's own character and to the work of his less-celebrated teammates. Renney admits freely there are situations within a game when a coach has to shorten his bench – power plays being one example – but he and his staff went into every game with the intention of rolling four lines and succeeded, with Jagr's cooperation, the great majority of the time.

Common practice in the twenty-first century NHL has vindicated Clare Drake. Like many prophets, he was sacrificed on the altar of narrow-mindedness and mediocrity. Unlike many prophets, he's lived to see the changes he was advocating actually come into effect. Although his maven-connector-salesman abilities weren't enough to overcome his "outsider" status within the entrenched world of pro hockey when he first entered it, his ideas and values would be carried forward by others – colleagues, disciples and protégés of protégés. As the 1990s and the new millennium unfolded, the NHL would become more accessible to those from outside the old boys' network, and the Canadian game would once again become a respected force in international hockey.

Of Drake's 1975 fling with the pros, Al Hamilton says, "If it had been ten years later, it would have been a helluva lot easier for him." Hitchcock, the man who sees Drake as a revolutionary, stood on the threshold of his minor hockey coaching run in '75 and was there as all the drama played out in Edmonton. He says, "The problem was that Clare was too far ahead of his time, probably by ten years." These two aren't alone; it's remarkable how many Drake watchers use the same expression — "ahead of his time" — and the same time period — a decade. They've got one part of it right; he was indeed a visionary who had outstripped his own era. But they could be wrong about the timing — the gap may have been closer to a quarter of a century.

CHAPTER FIVE

The Russians... Again!

*They ask me why I teach,
And I reply,
Where could I find more splendid company?*

John Wooden quoting Glennice Harmon,
They Call Me Coach

Surrealism in Japan, 1978. Solemn Bears stand at attention for "O Canada" after winning the Pacific Rim Tournament in front of 20,000 at Tokyo's Yoyogi Stadium, host venue for swimming and diving (note the platforms) at the 1964 Summer Olympics. (Randy Gregg, future Olympian and five-time Stanley Cup-winner, flanked by Bears' teammates Darrell Zapernick, to Gregg's right, and Stan Swales.)

Not that he's been there a whole lot, but Clare Drake is uncomfortable in the glare of the media spotlight, even when it shines favorably. And it certainly didn't during most of his five-month role in the Edmonton Oilers' soap opera, which drained him of the positive energy he'd always radiated. Dolly Drake says of his reaction to the January '76 firing, "he was in a funk." Being in a funk is the rarest of conditions for Drake, and at that time, it basically meant silence. As Dolly elaborates, "he wasn't miserable, but there wasn't too much communication." On the spur of the moment, with only two days' notice, Clare did manage to communicate a need to get away, so off he and Dolly went to Hawaii for two weeks. That was all he needed to recharge his batteries and he was soon back to being his old positive self, focusing on the lessons he'd learned with the Oilers and how he would put them to good use. One mitigating factor in the process was the fortuitous presence in Hawaii of the Drakes' good friends, Wes and Val Montgomery. Wes Montgomery was an Edmonton radio personality whose nimble wit earned him great popularity and affection during his life. His death in April 2005 was a sad event for many Edmontonians, the Drakes among them. In 1976 Montgomery was in fine form, helping to tease his old buddy out of the doldrums, not just in the privacy of their tropical resort, but on air after their return home. He wisecracked to the city's largest morning radio audience that he'd last seen Drake "swimming out to sea." Drake's own irrepressible sense of humor and ability to laugh at himself, a trait he shares with Dolly, stood him in good stead as he took stock of his career and tried to decide "What next?"

While Dolly reflects that her husband's decision to accept the Oiler challenge might have been "a bit hasty" (given the instability of the organization), he'd had the foresight to negotiate a one-year leave of absence from the university. This ensured that he had his faculty position and coaching job to fall back on should the pro experiment not work out, and so he returned to Varsity Arena in the fall of 1976. Years later, he told Ryan Walter and Mike Johnston that he'd been happy to go back to the U of A because "there's more opportunity to sell concepts to university players and more opportunity to influence them." He contrasted university players with some he found in the pro ranks, whom he described euphemistically as "somewhat noncommittal." Drake has always enthused about the passion and commitment that elite amateurs have for the game, and the privilege he considers it to coach them. In the fall of '76, he may have appreciated that privilege more than ever before or since.

With his new assistant Bill Moores at his side, Drake set to work building a Bears squad that had great things in store. His reconstructed team would once and for all end the University of Toronto's ascendancy at the University Cup. There were just a handful of holdovers from the Bears' 1975 national championship club; the majority of players in September 1976 were strangers to their coaches and vice versa. But before long, Drake and Moores could tell they had a pretty talented bunch on their hands, and the players figured out that their renowned coach was every bit as smart and demanding as his reputation suggested. The core of this group would propel Alberta to four consecutive appearances in the national final, winning three, and five of these players – John Devaney, Randy Gregg, Kevin Primeau, Dave Hindmarch and Don Spring – would represent Canada at the 1980 Olympics. Four of these five would go on to play in the NHL.

In their first season together, this fresh young crew waltzed through the Canada West conference preparatory to hosting the University Cup tournament in March of 1977. With Varsity Arena rocking on its foundations much as it had two years earlier, the Bears once again met the Varsity Blues in the final game. This time, however, the rookie-laden Bears couldn't dent the composure of the veteran Blues, and although they were outshot, Toronto opened up an early lead and hung on for a 4-1 victory, its very last against Alberta at the nationals. The Blues won their ninth, and penultimate, University Cup in 1977; their final one, as of 2006, came in 1984 with Mike Keenan as head coach after Tom Watt had left for the NHL.

The 1976-77 Golden Bears had gotten a whiff of glory, the following season nothing could stop them. The nationals were situated in Moncton in 1978 and the Blues, as defending champions, were the focus of all attention. But the Bears, with eighteen returning players and depth from the center line to the goal line, steamrolled their way through the tournament. They had at least three different forechecking systems at their command, but relied on their stifling 2-1-2 formation, four good lines and dominant play from their big, mobile defence to leave no doubts about which team was Canada's best. The 6-5 score against the Blues in the final was closer than the actual play and tribute to Toronto's gifted forwards, who made the best of their opportunities.

The 1977-78 season was noteworthy not only because it yielded Drake's fourth national hockey title. It also featured the Golden Bears' first opportunity to represent Canada internationally as a complete unit. While individual Bears had played on various Student National Teams, the whole team had never gone overseas before. In this case, the University of Alberta had been selected by Hockey Canada and the CIAU to be Canada's entry at the Pacific Rim International Tournament in Japan. This was a three-team, double-round-robin affair that pitted the Golden Bears against the American Senior Amateur Champions – the St. Paul (Minnesota) Parkers – and the Japanese National Team. The games were played in Tokyo and Sapporo, site of the 1972 Winter Olympics (to which Canada sent no hockey team). The Makomanai Ice Arena in Sapporo was built for the Olympics and in 1978 was a beautiful modern structure with seating for 12,000 and all the accoutrements of an NHL facility. The Bears played to full houses there and in Tokyo, where the final game was staged in Yoyogi Stadium. It had been the swimming and diving venue for the 1964 Tokyo Summer Olympics and also had the capacity to host ice-based sports. Here the Albertans performed in front of 20,000 curious and excited Japanese fans, the largest crowd ever to witness a Golden Bears hockey game. The Bears went through the tournament undefeated, which allowed them to savor the surreal post-game experience of hearing "O Canada" as the maple leaf flag rose slowly above the Olympic ten-meter diving platform that towered over the ice surface in the huge, packed stadium.

In another interesting historical twist, the Bears also won a non-tournament game against a team of all-stars from the northern Japanese island of Hokkaido, where Sapporo is situated. Their playing coach was Vyacheslav Starshinov, a center on the Soviet '72 Summit Series team and by 1978, thirty-eight years old. Winner of two Olympic gold medals and a Soviet Master of Sport, this former Russian great couldn't keep up with the younger, faster Bears. At one point, frustrated and struggling behind the play, Starshinov delivered a violent two-hander to the helmet of Alberta forward Kevin Primeau. In an outburst of anger, the Bears' student trainer shouted from the bench, "You've got nothing left old man. You oughta hang 'em up." Drake, who always monitored the comportment of his team, understood Starshinov's action against the wider context of his distinguished career and quietly tapped the young man on the shoulder and shushed him, saying, "Show some respect."

The Golden Bears traveled halfway across the world on their Japan junket, playing and winning seven games in fourteen days including intercontinental flying time. This was some achievement, especially given that their opponents were no patsies. At that time the Japanese were ranked at the top of the IIHF B pool and the American team was comprised mostly of graduates from the 1976 NCAA Champions, the University of Minnesota Golden Gophers. The Japanese coach, Nigashi Makino, told Cam Cole, then a young *Edmonton Journal* beat reporter covering the trip, that he thought this Canadian team could compete in the IIHF A pool. Two years later, their coach and five of their players did exactly that, at the Lake Placid Olympics.

The Golden Bears learned some valuable lessons on this exhausting but exhilarating journey to the Orient. For most of them, it was their first exposure to something Drake already knew well – the beauty of international sport. The players felt the thrill of representing Canada abroad game after game when, as per international tradition, the winner's anthem was played at the end of the contest. The Japanese gave these young Canadians a warm and respectful reception; they found themselves, and particularly their coach, admired and celebrated by the Japanese media and fans alike for their intelligent, fast-paced brand of hockey. They discovered after their arrival that they looked exceptionally good to the Japanese when compared to the WHA's Winnipeg Jets, who had come to Japan in December 1977 for an exhibition series against a Soviet team. The Japanese had been very disappointed with the Jets' behavior both on and off the ice, and their estimation of Canadian hockey rose dramatically with the Golden Bears' performance just two months later. This was a distinct point of pride for Canadian ambassador Bruce Rankin, a U of A alumnus who fêted the Bears at an embassy reception in Tokyo.

The power of international sport to educate, break down cultural barriers and build new friendships is well known. Dave Bidini, guitarist for the Canadian rock band the Rheostatics, is also a hockey addict and vagabond. His book, *Tropic of Hockey*, is the colorful tale of his global rambling in search of hockey wherever and however. Through his wanderings he found the frozen game in Hong Kong, Harbin, Dubai and the city of Ciuc, Romania. In Ciuc, Bidini met a bunch of local kids and gave them Team Canada hockey pins, watching their joy and amazement as they treasured these maple leaf insignia in the palms of their hands. Many of the '78 Golden Bears could share their own similar stories with Bidini, besieged as they were by legions of rosy-cheeked Japanese children. These guileless youngsters, wide-eyed and grinning from ear to ear, sought autographs, hockey pins or just a smile and a wave from their newly adopted Canadian heroes.

The attention lavished by the Japanese on the Golden Bears and their esteemed coach was quite different from what they knew at home, where their place in the hockey pecking order ranked well down the scale. Some players were even a little startled at how the throngs of media and Japanese hockey people hung on Drake's every word at the news conferences and receptions that filled their days off. In a culture that venerated the old, the wise and the experienced, the man the Bears respected within their own little world as "Coach" was seen by the Japanese as an international hockey *sensei* and treated accordingly. Honored more by strangers than on his home turf, Drake took all the hoopla in stride, encouraging his players to get the most of out their traveling experience but at the same time keeping them focused enough to go undefeated on the trip.

Coming home posed another challenge, one that led to a new wrinkle that would find its way into pro hockey many years later. The Bears had one game remaining in their 1977-78 schedule before playoffs started. It was against the UBC Thunderbirds in Vancouver, where their ten-hour, trans-Pacific flight landed on the way back from Tokyo. The team cleared customs during the morning of their first day back on Canadian soil and grabbed just a few hours of sleep before they took the ice on the UBC campus that night. As Alberta's major Canada West rivals in those years, the T-Birds were "loaded for Bear," licking their chops as they anticipated crushing this fatigued, jet-lagged team that had played seven games in fourteen days while traversing half the globe.

But the Bears' *sensei* had them prepared for this eventuality. As 1971 All Canadian Steve Carlyle says, "Drake wasn't just winning today's game, he was always thinking ahead, coaching for the next game, or the next season." No finer example of this exists than the new checking system Drake and Moores had introduced in practice earlier that winter. Although the Bears made their living on the aggressive 2-1-2 forecheck and had two others in reserve if needed, the coaches cooked up a new scheme for situations when the team didn't have the energy necessary to execute these high intensity systems. They called this scheme the "stay-up" and it consisted of one forward, the center primarily, crossing over the opposition blue line to harass the other team's breakout. The other two forwards stayed in the neutral zone, occupying the outside lanes along the boards so the defence could stand up in front of or at their own blue line, forcing the play in the neutral zone – hence the name "stay-up." The rubber-legged Bears played this system to perfection that late-February evening in 1978, scoring early in the first period and then hanging on gamely for a 1-0 shutout win against the frustrated and confounded Thunderbirds.

Most Canadian hockey fans will recognize this formation as the dreaded neutral-zone trap seen in the NHL since the mid-1990s. As with many of Clare Drake's innovations, it's difficult to verify if he was indeed the first author of this strategy, given that hockey records are about wins and losses, not technical development. But anecdotal evidence suggests that Drake's 1978 stay-up was the original version of the trap; if not, it was certainly one of the very earliest. Like so many good ideas, this one came to be used for different purposes than its inventor intended. Drake saw this strategy as an emergency measure for extreme situations such as the one the Bears faced on their return from Japan. Some NHL coaches would employ it years later as a season-long platform from which they could eke out victories against faster, more talented opponents. Bill Moores suggests that the trap is a weapon every team can have in its arsenal, to use only when conditions call for it. But it's not the kind of system that's suited for exclusive use, as a team's bread and butter – it doesn't do the game justice.

One other outcome of the Golden Bears' 1978 sojourn across the Pacific was the pipeline it opened between the U of A and Japan. Father Bauer had forged the initial link between Canadian and Japanese hockey years earlier, when he helped the Japanese build their national program. Because Father Bauer's 1960s home base was at UBC, that institution had maintained a connection with Japan, providing development opportunities for a few Japanese players and training staff, and in turn seeing some T-Bird and Canadian National Team grads (such as Terry O'Malley, Barry McKenzie and Doug Buchanan) travel west to play and coach.

After '78 however, this Tokyo-Vancouver axis sprouted a Tokyo-Edmonton tangent. Before he became part of the Edmonton Oilers' Stanley Cup dynasty, Golden Bear and Olympic Team grad Randy Gregg crossed the big pond to suit up as playing coach for the Kokudo Bunnies, the oddly named but very successful club whose logo bears a striking resemblance to a cartoon rabbit named Bugs. About a decade later, Bill Moores coached the same team to the All Japan championship. While there, he was given a fascinating object lesson in power, authority and pressure to win. As Kokudo's coach, Moores was in the employ of Yoshiaki Tsutsumi, head of the Seibu Corporation and considered during the 1980s to be the wealthiest man in the world. (In 2005, he began serving a thirty-month prison sentence for violations of Japanese securities law.) Working for Tsutsumi-*san* carried an imperative to produce results, and the effects of this pressure, and Japan's traditional culture of power and hierarchy, were vividly brought home to Moores one day when the big boss showed up at a Kokudo practice. "I was talking to the players in a group on the ice," says Moores. "When they saw him they skated away from me while I was in mid-sentence. It was like I didn't exist. They lined up in a row where he stood at the boards, took their gloves off and arranged them neatly on the ice at their feet, palms up, sticks all lined up on the ice as well. Then they all bowed to him at the same time." Moores adds with a laugh, "And I thought *I* was important!"

"Power plays" and cultural differences didn't get in the way of an enduring Alberta-Japan connection. After Drake's first trip there in 1978, he went back with the Olympic Team for exhibition play in preparation for the 1980 Games, and later paid two visits to Moores, assisting him with team development work for Kokudo. The traffic wasn't all one-way. The Japanese National Team joined the University of Denver Pioneers in Edmonton for the 1979 edition of the Pacific Rim Tournament, again won handily by the Bears. The Bears rolled over both the Japanese and a talented young Denver squad that included two 1980 Canadian Olympians and future Edmonton Oilers, Glenn Anderson and Ken Berry (whose father Don had played for the '55 Penticton Vees). Afterward, during the 1980s and nineties, both the Japanese Nationals and Kokudo held training camps at the U of A.

As for the Bears crew who won in '78, they moved on to their second and third national titles in a row. The 1978-79 team lost only a handful of players from the previous year and stormed through the CIAU season, the playoffs and the University Cup tournament, hosted by Concordia University. The Bears served up a businesslike 5-1 win in the final over the Dalhousie University Tigers, who were coached by future NHL headman Pierre Pagé. One of the Tigers' stars was Paul MacLean, who would join the 1980 Olympic Team, play eleven solid NHL seasons and eventually become an assistant coach with Anaheim and Detroit.

The '79 Bears were one of Canadian university hockey's greatest powerhouses, loaded with talent experience and coached by Drake and Moores to finely honed precision. Alberta's third straight University Cup the following year was quite remarkable, gutted as they were by the loss of their head coach and the stellar Olympic quintet; it was also proof of Bill Moores's own outstanding coaching chops. Only half a dozen players stayed for all three seasons of the Bears' national championship hat trick. Along with the five who departed for the Olympics, these young men joined the program through two training camps, in 1976 and '77, and were bolstered by other arrivals to fill out the roster, which was ravaged in the fall of '79 by the Olympic exodus.

Golden Bear training camps were, and remain to this day, open to all comers. Unlike now though, in the seventies very few of the players who came to camp were recruited. It may have been just serendipity, but those training camps Drake and Moores ran in September of '76 and '77 produced a rare assemblage of talent that created, in Drake's assessment, "a golden era" in Golden Bear history. Their great run of four University Cup finals and three national titles in a row was eclipsed only by their predecessor dynasty, the U of T Varsity Blues of the late-1960s to mid-seventies. In addition to the five Olympians, these championship teams featured many other fine players, most of whom made their way to Europe's

"Smart-tough personified. "Terrible Teddy" Olson creates space at netfront against the Japanese National Team, Tokyo, March 1978. (Bears' center Dave Breakwell, #17, lines up a shot while future Olympian Kevin Primeau looks on.)

professional leagues after graduation or found employment in the North American minor pro ranks. And most, if not all, were true student athletes, leaving the U of A with degrees in disciplines such as physical education, education, agriculture, engineering, commerce, law, pharmacy and medicine. In this matter, they were no different than the legions of Golden Bear hockey players who came before and after them. Drake points out that talented though this bunch was, the team chemistry and personal bonds they formed were every bit as important to their string of championships.

Among these exceptional individuals was one young man whose transformation under Drake is a testament to how the coach touches lives; it also says a lot about the character and intelligence of this player. Ted Olson (sporting the moniker "Terrible Teddy") came to the Bears at mid-season in 1976-77 after a tumultuous major junior career in the Western Hockey League. A powerfully built two-sport athlete, Olson played linebacker for the football Bears and brought a fearsome reputation with him to the hockey team. At the time, he held the career record for penalty minutes in the WHL and still ranks third on their all-time list. He had a short fuse, quick fists and a quicker mind. Olson was even smarter than he was tough and temperamental (bordering on genius, figures Drake), and possessed a wry and excoriating wit. In an era where fighting was still tolerated in university hockey (no game misconducts) and bench-emptying brawls still occurred, Olson ran roughshod over Golden Bear opponents with his stick, elbows and pugilistic skills, marking himself as one of the most penalized and controversial players ever to wear the green and gold. The fans loved him, but his relationship with his coach, and even some of his teammates, was initially tenuous.

Not one to suffer lack of discipline and regard for team goals, Drake considered cutting Olson during his first months with the Bears. But he hung in there with this rampaging bull of a player, quietly but firmly engaging him through one-on-one dialogue and dangling the ice-time carrot. Olson came around. His intelligence and respect for his coach and teammates won through, and he eventually became an overwhelming physical force on the ice, within the rules. His tenacious puck pursuit and crushing but legal bodychecks made him one of the CIAU's most effective forecheckers in his time. With Drake's help, Ted Olson became a highly valued team contributor, and an exemplar of the Drake philosophy on toughness.

Ken Dryden, in his fine hockey memoir *The Game,* speaks eloquently on the issue of fighting in the NHL. He says the "venting" theory in justification of fighting is "nothing more than violence tolerated and accepted, in time turned into custom, into spectacle, into tactic, and finally into theory." Dryden offers an alternative, suggesting that "anger and frustration can be released within the rules, by skating faster, by shooting harder, by doing relentless dogged violence on an opponent's mind." This is the same message Clare Drake preached to Ted Olson and generations of Golden Bears, although Drake's list of ways to release anger and frustration contained one more item: "Driving your shoulder into your opponent's chest." Drake is not an anti-fighting crusader, but he consistently held his players accountable to play a game of disciplined toughness within the rules – what he calls "smart-tough" as opposed to "dumb-tough." Terrible Teddy Olson was one of his greatest successes in this aspect of the game.

When Olson left the Bears he signed a contract with the Minnesota North Stars and played two seasons for their Central Hockey League team in Oklahoma City before returning to the U of A to complete his law degree. He was called to the Alberta bar in 1986 and went on to a first-rate career with ex-Bear footballer Ed Molstad's firm in Edmonton. Molstad describes Olson as "an excellent lawyer who was very much a team player" within the firm; Olson credited his team-first ethic to lessons learned from Clare Drake. Sadly, Ted died of a heart attack at forty-six, in 2002; his fellow Golden Bear alumni miss his unique character, marked by his keen intellect and dry, trenchant sense of humor. Together, Clare Drake and Ted Olson overcame a wide gulf between player and coach, and in so doing, they set a standard for toughness balanced with intelligence in amateur hockey.

The late seventies were a time of tremendous growth in Drake's technical repertoire, thanks to the synergy he and Moores generated and the profusion of talent channeling through the U of A program. The systems Drake had tried to sell to the Oilers at mid-decade, which had seemed so far-fetched and complicated to some pros, were enhanced and expanded in the ensuing years. What the pros couldn't or wouldn't buy, the elite amateurs hungrily ate up, eager guinea pigs in the professor's hockey laboratory.

Drake's historic ability to break the game down into a constituent series of elements – one-on-one fundamentals, defensive zone coverage, neutral zone attack, forecheck, penalty kill, power play – was on its way to becoming the stuff of legend. His players, among them fine future coaches like George Kingston and Ron Watson, had long been impressed at his ability to "see" the game as a composite of interconnected movements and configurations. Many have said over the years that Drake has a "video camera" for a brain, capable of rerunning the play in slow motion or freeze-frame to analyze the most intricate patterns on the ice. His other great strength, working in concert with his analytical powers, is his ability to teach these elements of the game to players in a developmental, progressive flow that moves from the simple to the complex. It was during the late seventies that two individuals, both of whom would become highly influential, first witnessed this compelling tandem of analytical and pedagogical skills at work. One of them was Ken Hitchcock; the other was Dave King.

In the late 1970s, Ken Hitchcock worked at one of Edmonton's oldest and best known sporting goods stores, United Cycle. Owned by longtime Golden Bears supplier and supporter Wilf Brooks, United Cycle is located in Old Strathcona, a couple of kilometers east of the U of A campus. Its proximity to the campus was important for Hitchcock, the guy in charge of team equipment sales at the store. Then a young volunteer coach in the Sherwood Park minor hockey system, a satellite community on the eastern outskirts of Edmonton, Hitchcock had a thirst for knowledge and a will to improve. So on his shift break, he would jump in his car, drive the five minutes to campus, park at the back of Varsity Arena, and slip in to watch Drake's late afternoon practices, stealing as many minutes away from the store as he could manage. As he sat in the stands observing the continuous flow and scripted movement of a Bears practice, Hitchcock knew this was something beyond his ken. "There were things happening on the ice I couldn't understand," he recalls, "but I could see groups of players working constantly in all three zones, and there seemed to be a purpose and design to everything going on out there." He gives the example of how Drake worked on fitness with his players: "There were hardly any of those mindless skating drills we all knew – up and down the ice, back and forth across. Instead, the fitness stuff was all with the puck, so the players were also developing other skills at the same time. And he had them doing anaerobic stuff to get the intensity levels higher. He always had them working hard and smart."

As Hitchcock continued to visit Varsity Arena, laboring to understand the arcane goings-on there, he pursued his coaching certification and rose through Sherwood Park's minor system to become head coach of the midget AAA team. He didn't consider approaching Drake to ask him about his well-conceived practices, wrongly assuming the master would have no time for a young minor hockey coach. So he invited Brian Middleton, one of Drake's former players and a fellow minor coach, to assist him with the midget team. Middleton was a Bears rookie in 1971-72, Bill Moores's sole season with the team. He'd had the great advantage of seeing Moores's intensity and commitment, and he'd also learned from All Canadian Steve Carlyle, his first defence partner. Middleton blossomed under Drake's demanding coaching and in 1973 became one of the first CIAU players to be drafted by the NHL while at university. He accordingly went off to the Detroit Red Wings training camp in the fall of that year and what he saw left him sadly disillusioned. "I found out right away that it was nothing but a *meat* business," Middleton emphasizes. And while he respected individual players for their talent, the training camp practices seemed quite basic to him. "At U of A," he explains, "everything we did on the ice led to something else. It made sense. At the pro camp, we never did anything that came close to even our simplest drills with the Bears. It was just scrimmaging and senseless skating drills." Turned off by his experience, Middleton walked out of training camp and returned to Alberta to finish his degree in commerce. Almost twenty years after Vern Pachal and Vic Dzurko came back from the pros, things hadn't changed much.

Middleton continued for two more seasons with the Bears (winning the nationals in 1975 with another All Canadian defence partner, Ross Barros); two more seasons of working hard and working smart under Clare Drake, whom Middleton says taught him the value of "the agony of repetition." "Coach had a detailed plan drawn up for every practice, and he followed his notes to the minute." Drake's astute drills wove individual fundamentals into the patterns of a sophisticated team game, and his words ring in Middleton's head to this day: "One more time, Brian, one more time." Middleton chuckles as he recalls his response to this exhortation. "Coach, I'm working hard here!" And Drake's constant rejoinder, "That's good… one more time now."

In 1981, after coaching several seasons in Edmonton's Capital Junior League, Middleton joined Hitchcock in Sherwood Park and became the latter's intermediary to the "Drake way." It was only after he hooked up with Middleton, says Hitchcock, that he began to understand the carefully orchestrated practices he'd been watching, and more importantly, how those led to the intense, high-pressure hockey with which the Bears dominated their opponents year in and year out. Middleton and Hitchcock worked with their young athletes to instil Drake's team principles, starting with defensive zone coverage ("we take care of our own end first") and moving up the ice to address all facets of the game. They built the Alberta Chain midget hockey program in Sherwood Park, which quickly became competitive provincially and nationally. From there, Hitchcock went to the Kamloops Blazers of the Western Hockey League and it was only after he'd left town that he himself approached Drake, finally tapping directly into the man's vast knowledge of the game. Why did he wait so long? "I was in awe of him," says Hitchcock. Had he ever just walked up to Drake any of those afternoons at Varsity Arena, he would have known years earlier of the master coach's supreme generosity and willingness to impart everything he knows. With Drake's encouragement and shared wisdom, and Hitchcock's own determination and intelligence, his career eventually reached the heights of NHL success.

After Hitchcock moved on, Middleton left coaching to concentrate on his burgeoning property development business, and to continue using the lessons he learned under the coach. Hitchcock's statement that Drake's "fingerprints are all over the game" resonates with Middleton, who adds, "That man's fingerprints are all over the people too." He's making no accusations of impropriety here; instead, he's commenting on the way his old coach touches lives. "Coach Drake was the best thing and the worst thing that ever happened to me. He was the best, because he taught me to never stop pushing to get better, at whatever I was doing. And the worst, because he taught me to accept nothing less than excellence, and now I'm never satisfied with anything but."

And the practices that so intrigued Ken Hitchcock? By the time the midget coach started lurking around Varsity Arena, Drake had been designing and refining drills for nigh on a quarter of a century. His earliest tinkerings had impressed men like Austin Smith, Vern Pachal and Dick Wintermute. George Severin, from Wintermute's era, chips in with his own testimonial on Drake's practices: "They were fantastic for ice utilization; you never saw players standing around. You were moving from start to finish." And this was before Drake saw Anatoly Tarasov's Vancouver demonstration of efficient, high-speed practices in the mid-sixties. Then we hear from Dan Bouwmeester, another of Brian Middleton's defence partners in the early seventies, who in the twenty-first century has watched over his son Jay's career with the Florida Panthers. Himself an accomplished minor hockey coach and member of the Golden Bears staff, Bouwmeester has witnessed many pro practices involving his son and says, in disappointment and wonder, "Thirty years later [after Drake showed the way], and there are still guys standing around waiting for the next drill to start." To be fair, the NHL is not a practice-friendly environment, given its overloaded schedule and the limited practice time available, but that should motivate coaches all the more to make the best use of the practice time they have. While the league has its Renneys and Hitchcocks, there are those who have not yet heard about or bought into the Drake method.

Technical wizard and big believer in Drake's 2-1-2 forecheck; "you'd swear to God there were eight [Bears] on the ice." Dave King as assistant coach with the Montreal Canadiens, mid-1990s.

Ken Hitchcock began watching Clare Drake from the stands at Varsity Arena. Dave King first saw him from the ice in the late 1960s, as a player in the green and white of the Saskatchewan Huskies. Then, during the 1970s, he listened to many Drake presentations at NCCP seminars, but his first direct contact with him came in 1978. During that summer, Drake and Tom Watt, under the auspices of Hockey Canada and the management of Father Bauer, began identifying the pool of players that would feed Canada's reborn national program and comprise the Olympic Team for Lake Placid in 1980. Following the model they'd created in 1974 with the Student National Team, they set up selection camps in Toronto and Edmonton, with Watt in charge in the east and Drake in the west. They invited the best of the CIAU to these camps, leavened this time with some Canadians playing in the NCAA and a few juniors who had indicated an interest in international hockey. To help him with his western camp, Drake recruited his own assistant Bill Moores, his disciple and friendly adversary from Calgary, George Kingston, and Dave King, who just that year had won the Western Hockey League's coach of the year award while heading the Billings Bighorns. Father Bauer dropped in for several days to meet with the coaches and deliver an inspiring address to the players on what it means to wear the maple leaf.

King's memories of that camp in the summer of '78 border on blissful. He talks about being among "the idols" – Drake, Moores, Kingston and Bauer – and how he soaked it all up, taking meticulous notes on every drill and asking Clare question upon question about every aspect of the game. One of the things that stood out most for him was Drake's famous drive-skating progression, a series of drills that taught forwards the skill of driving hard to the net with the puck by beating the defenceman to the outside. This was a four-step process that began with simple crossover drills on the face-off circles. The next step had the players performing this same exercise in pairs, with a defender on the inside applying light body pressure on the puck carrier. This moved to half-ice drills (running concurrently), with a defender chasing the puck carrier from behind, to give the latter a speed advantage and confidence going at the net while being harassed. The final stage was a full-ice, full-speed drill that involved an all out race to the goalmouth, the attacker taking the puck off a pass and fighting for body position with the defender all the way to the post. King marveled at the simplicity of this progressive form of skill development, at the way Drake had broken it down and taught it so effectively to produce the end result, a powerful attack on the net.

Former Bears Dave Hindmarch and Randy Gregg, who both attended the selection camps and eventually earned their places on the Olympic roster, consider the drive-skate drills and the results they produced to be a staple of Golden Bears hockey. Hindmarch, son of former UBC coach Bob and the first CIAU player to be drafted as an eighteen-year-old, played three seasons with the Calgary Flames until a devastating knee injury ended his career in 1984. He says, "If you played for the Bears, you drove the net – that's the way it was." Gregg, the physician who won five Stanley Cups on defence with the Edmonton Oilers, remembers one of the constants in Drake's U of A practices: "Every day at 5:30, the same place in every practice, it was time for the drive-skate drill." He remembers not initially understanding the need for this reiterative "agony," but in due course he saw how the repetition made his team's forwards almost unstoppable, and how the tactic became an indispensable part of the Bears' offence. Glenn Anderson, whom Drake coached on the 1980 Olympic Team, was perhaps the ultimate practitioner of drive-skating, making it his bread and butter throughout his stellar NHL career with the Oilers, Leafs, Rangers and Blues.

Drake had a number of Golden Bears at the '78 selection camp, in addition to the five who made the Olympic roster. He used them all to demonstrate the systems he was teaching the rest of the participants, and King remembers being amazed at what he saw then, and a season later when he took over as coach of the Huskies and had to compete head-to-head against the Bears. The Bears' command of fundamentals was exceptional, and their team strategies were even better. To Dave King, Drake's array of forechecking systems was sublime, in particular his patented 2-1-2 formation with its seamless five-man rotation and aggressive pinching: "The pressure they created was so intense – with all five guys on the same page – you'd swear to God there were eight players on the ice!" exclaims King, who still lives by Drake's 2-1-2 to this day, especially if his team is down and needs to get back into a game.

King was also astonished by Drake's attention to detail. Moores, Hitchcock, Perry Pearn and many others comment on Drake's thorough insistence that all "I"s were dotted and "T"s crossed when it came to the players, practices, game plans and team organization. King saw this at work in '78 as Drake stopped drills in mid-action, to correct players and make them do it over, the right way. In one instance, recalls King, Drake was so intent on this that he wheeled out into the flow of a high-speed, full-ice drill with his eyes fixed firmly on an out-of-position player, disastrously ignoring the backpedaling defencemen bearing down on him. There was a tremendous collision that sent Drake flying, as King says, "ass over teakettle," his clipboard and whistle swinging wildly from his neck. But he bounced up off the ice and went directly to the guy he was looking for to make sure he understood where he should have been situated in the play, to make sure he got it right.

This intense focus on the littlest things, while still maintaining the larger perspective, was what made Drake's teams so well prepared. Both King and Wayne Fleming, the 2002 and 2006 Olympic Team associate coach who headed the Manitoba Bisons in the early 1980s, remark on how league games against the U of A were always like the playoffs. It wasn't just the intensity level the Bears brought every night, but their refined excellence at the minute aspects of the game. Tom Watt told Fleming that when he and Drake co-coached the 1980 Olympic Team, Drake "drove him nuts" by never letting up on the little things, but by the end of the season he could see that his old colleague was right, and that the team was better for it. Bob Murdoch, head coach of the Winnipeg Jets from 1989 to 1991, and the 1990 Jack Adams Award winner, also learned the value of Drake's thoroughness during those two seasons when Clare served as his assistant. "He was a stickler," says Murdoch, "He'd get on something you might think was trivial but then you saw how it fit into the big picture."

This facet of Drake's character, sometimes exasperating yet ultimately the mark of excellence, has endured throughout the years. In 2005, the University of Alberta hosted the University Cup. Drake was long retired from the university and had for years made a point of not imposing his presence on the hockey program, to give his successor coaches room to operate. But he'd been invited to serve on the tournament organizing committee and was at a pre-tournament meeting with Bob Kinasewich, the university's acting athletic director. When he attended the Bears' Canada West playoff game a couple of nights earlier, he'd had to wait in the line of vehicles slowly entering the Stadium Parkade, across the avenue from the arena. Eternally the detail man, Drake made a special point of telling Kinasewich that he should make sure to have extra parking staff on duty when the tournament started, to cut down on the parkade lineups and get fans into the games more quickly. The Golden Bear legend had noticed a wrinkle that needed smoothing out.

When considering the cumulative effect of Drake's contribution to the game, Dave King mentions another realization about Drake's teams: "I couldn't believe how much the Golden Bear defencemen talked on the ice, and the great calls they used with their goaltender." Drake coached his players to communicate clearly and consistently, especially when under pressure, with precisely worded terminology that carried specific meanings about where the pressure was coming from and where the puck should go.

This was one manifestation of what Ken Hitchcock means by his signal statement that Clare Drake "brought terminology to shinny." The vocabulary the Bears used in their on-ice chatter was part of a greater lexicon that Drake created to define and explain the game. It gave him and his fellow coaches a way of organizing the game and then teaching that organization to the players. It helped him describe positioning responsibilities and how they fit into the various zones he'd identified on the ice, the guts of his defensive zone coverage system. He had names for every zone, from one end to the other, and the various positions players should take within those zones depending on the whereabouts of the puck.

Hitchcock casts his mind back to his first involvement with Hockey Canada's Program of Excellence, in the early 1980s, when Drake, Kingston and King were mentoring coaches in the national under-seventeen and under-eighteen programs. Drake's hockey language permeated the classroom work, manuals and instructional videos for this program and was passed on through Hitchcock and the many elite coaches who participated (Tom Renney, for example). Both the Program of Excellence and the NCCP were mechanisms for "spreading the virus" of Drake's philosophies, his technical innovations and the terminology that described them. And through these channels, this terminology found its way to American minor hockey, so that Hitchcock would hear it being "barked" at Philadelphia youngsters during his lockout-induced wanderings.

Dave King talks about the ingenious "cue words" that Drake cooked up, which made every coach's job of communicating with his players a bit easier. A King favorite is "head-on-a-swivel," one he shares with Dan Smith, the '78 graduate assistant who became the CAHA's assistant technical director. Before he got to Alberta, Smith had never heard this descriptive epithet (perhaps derived from Frank Frederickson's 1950s instructions to his UBC squads) applied to hockey. For Smith, "it says everything" about how the backside defenceman should keep an eye on the slot while watching the puck in the corner. Another gem for King is "back-post, skates up-ice." This describes the foot positioning for that same netfront defenceman, which then indeed allows him to keep his head on a swivel.

After meeting Drake in 1978, King went back to the Western Hockey League for one more season before re-establishing the University of Saskatchewan as a CIAU power. In 1983, he won Saskatchewan's only University Cup to date, with future Huskies coach and Drake admirer Dave Adolph on defence. While at Saskatchewan, King began his long and distinguished career in international hockey, coaching Hockey Canada's first entry at the world junior championships to a gold medal in 1982 and assisting with Canada's bronze medal effort at the world championships later on that March. The following year he became head coach and general manager of Canada's National Team, where he stayed until the NHL beckoned in 1992. During his stint with the national program, he coached Team Canada to world championship silver in 1989 and 1991, and two Olympic fourths (1984 and '88) and one silver (1992).

In the NHL, King was head coach of the Calgary Flames for three seasons, winning consecutive division titles in 1994 and '95. He followed that with two seasons as an assistant with the Montreal Canadiens and then served as head coach for the Columbus Blue Jackets during their first two and a half seasons in the league. He made the long journey to Siberia in 2005 to take over the coaching reins of Metallurg Magnitogorsk in the Russian Super League, where his team (which included *wunderkind* Evgeny Malkin) finished first in the regular season and won the famed Spengler Cup in Davos, Switzerland. Thought by many to be the most technically brilliant coach in the game today, King's final statement leaves no doubt about his regard for the man he first met in the summer of 1978: "I've coached against Scotty Bowman, Mike Keenan, Roger Neilson, all of the greats. Tom Watt is also a terrific coach and innovator. I happened to spend more time with Clare though. I'd have to say he's the best I've ever seen."

In 1979, after Clare Drake had won his fifth (and second consecutive) University Cup, he made his second departure from the U of A, this time to work for Hockey Canada. Father Bauer, a member of the organization's board of directors, had managed to convince the board to reinstate the National Team program, with a view to returning Canada to the Winter Olympics set for Lake Placid, New York, in 1980. Bauer was to be the managing director of the program, with Clare Drake, Tom Watt and Lorne Davis as co-coaches. Drake and Watt were long-time rivals and collaborators; Lorne Davis was a former Regina Pat who saw pro duty with the Canadiens, Red Wings and Bruins during the 1950s and spent time with the National Team in the 1960s. As an ex-National Teamer, he brought a thorough understanding of Father Bauer's vision and values for this second edition of the national program.

Drake was excited about the opportunity because he "wanted the experience of coaching an elite team and to be involved in the renaissance of the Olympic program." It was a chance to work with the very best amateur athletes in hockey and, perhaps, to take another swing at the pitch he'd passed on twenty years earlier, when he'd had to turn down the West German invitation to take their team to the Olympics. In a sense, it was a culmination of the forays into international hockey he'd made over the years. His ringside seat for the Penticton Vees' world championship in 1955 had whetted his appetite for the rush of international sport, and the 1980 Olympics was the ultimate banquet that could feed that appetite.

Even though the work had started unofficially the summer before, the program formally kicked off on July 31, 1979, when sixty players, most of whom had been identified in '78, showed up at Calgary's old Stampede Corral for training camp. The Corral – a 7,000-seat arena opened in 1950 and, as forerunner to the Saddledome, Calgary's major hockey facility – was home ice for the team. The Olympic hopefuls were lodged four to a room in what the players came to call "Rig 80," a collection of bunkhouse trailers from a drilling rig camp, parked on the asphalt of the Stampede Grounds just a stone's throw from the Corral. Once the roster for the seven-month pre-Olympic season was set at about twenty-five, the players had the "luxury" of living in pairs in these humble digs.

The rooms were furnished with bunk beds, and some of the guys lobbied for permission to cut off the upper bunks so they could at least sit on their beds upright, without having to hunch under the overhead sleeping tier. Even in the relatively less affluent days of the late seventies, asking elite hockey players to live two to a room in a camp trailer was asking a lot; it would be unthinkable with today's pampered athletes. This was only one part of the commitment these dedicated young men made on behalf of their country. They ate their daily meals in the Calgary Exhibition cafeteria located on the Stampede Grounds, where the monotony of the food ground down even the heartiest believers in the Olympic ideal. John Devaney, one of Drake's ex-Golden Bears, recalls with particular revulsion the chicken *à la* king, which he says "started off okay but when you had it every third day or so it got pretty bad."

Insipid food and cramped quarters were compounded by the penurious sum the players were given as a living allowance to supplement their free room and board. The $4,000 they received for the entire season could in no way be construed as a salary; it paled by comparison with the money they could have earned playing pro hockey or working professionally, given that almost every one of them either held or was close to completing a university degree. Yet they signed on for this purest of Olympic experiences because, to a man, they bought into Father Bauer's gospel of amateur Olympic hockey.

Bauer, known simply as Father to his congregation of hockey faithful, was a visionary with a driving conviction that education and sport could work together to build character in, and make fine citizens of, Canada's young men. This was partly why he'd founded his 1960s National Team program at UBC, and later on in the decade, when it relocated to Winnipeg, why he preferred that National Teamers be graduates of, or enrolled in, university. Canadian sportswriting giant Scott Young put Father Bauer's countercultural attitudes in perspective in his 1976 work, *War On Ice:*

> While most junior coaches never let education get in the way of hockey if they could avoid it, Father Bauer carried five or six extra players so that any in need of extra study could skip a game or two. He also had the quaint (for hockey) notion that a player could be rugged without being dirty, and that mental discipline and development of the mind were as important as physical development and hockey skills.

Drake and Bauer saw pretty much eye-to-eye on these values, but Bauer was exceptional in his belief that sacrifice (playing for your country, playing for a greater cause than your own wealth or advancement) was part of being a true amateur and Olympian. This idealism, and the limited budget Hockey Canada provided for the program, combined to set the conditions under which the 1980 Olympians lived and trained. Drake and his co-coaches were concerned at the outset that the Spartan lifestyle might prove debilitating to player morale, but he says, "It seems that it kind of grew on them, and over the long run I think they were reasonably happy." Randy Gregg concurs. Even though he chafed at the lack of privacy, the big doctor (who became part of the Oilers' Stanley Cup dynasty and retired from hockey to open his own sports medicine clinic in Edmonton) says of his Rig 80 days, "it was the time of my life." Dave Hindmarch, a couple of years younger and a fair bit zanier than Gregg, says that Rig 80 was "the perfect place for someone like me – simple and straightforward." And John Devaney, in spite of his aversion to the chicken *à la* king, remembers the experience as "great fun."

All this dedication aside, there were those from the original player pool who, presented with the lure of a pro contract, simply couldn't resist. Two juniors who would go in the first round of the 1979 entry draft, Brad McCrimmon and Ray Allison, had attended Drake's 1978 selection camp but signed contracts with the clubs that chose them, the Boston Bruins and Hartford Whalers respectively. Laurie Boschman and Paul Reinhart, who both turned up at the Stampede Corral in July '79, were also first-rounders in the '79 draft; Boschman taken ninth by Toronto and Reinhart twelfth by the Atlanta Flames.

Two out of three Olympic Team coaches and the GM; Drake, Lorne Davis on his right and the boss, Father Bauer, on his left, Calgary, December, 1979. (Tom Watt was in Moscow, coaching a mixed squad of Olympians and pros at the Izvestia Tournament.)

Father Bauer's vision appealed especially to Reinhart, who resisted the siren song of the NHL long enough to suit up with the National Team for the month of September. But Boschman and Reinhart each succumbed, understandably, to the blandishments offered by the Leafs and the Flames and went on to long and successful careers in The Show. Another training camp attendee who followed Boschman and Reinhart was Vincent Tremblay, Toronto's fourth-round pick in '79. Had he stuck around, things might have gone better both for him and the Olympic Team. A major junior all-star in the Quebec league, Tremblay was a goaltender, the position that proved to be Canada's Achilles' heel at Lake Placid. With the benefit of all the practice time and coaching excellence built into the Olympic program, he might well have blossomed into the performer Drake, Watt and Davis kept searching for but never really found. Instead, Tremblay signed with Toronto, spent parts of two seasons with their AHL farm team, and got shelled each time he was called up to backstop the Leafs' woeful defence. Whether it was about ability, or just being in the wrong place at the wrong time, Tremblay never caught on in the NHL

– one can only speculate about the possibilities for all concerned if he'd held off for one season instead of reaching for the mediocre bucks that came with a two-way pro contract.

The siphoning-off of talented youngsters by NHL clubs certainly didn't help Canada's chances. In his post-Olympic comparison of the Canadian and American programs, the *Edmonton Journal*'s Terry Jones said the USA was able to "convince more first-rate kids than [Canada] to wait a year on pro" and it "convinced more NHL clubs not to pressure the kids into signing." George Kingston, a guest coach with Canada's team, said before the tournament, "I'm sorry that in some areas the talent wasn't made available. I'd like to have seen a lot of kids sign their NHL contracts to take effect [after the Olympics]." Of course, Alan Eagleson, Hockey Canada board member, boss of the NHL players' union and the NHL's international front man, put a different spin on this issue. He glibly declared to Jim Coleman during the Corral training camp, "the NHL club owners really have been extremely helpful in assisting our Olympic program." It would be another fifteen years before most Canadians would awake to the disturbing similarities between Eaglesonian prevarication and the propaganda of *Pravda*.

Although there's little denying that the likes of Boschman, Reinhart and Tremblay would have bolstered the Canadian lineup at Lake Placid, the team wasn't nearly as short on talent as many assumed. Ten of Canada's Olympians played in the NHL after 1980, with Randy Gregg and Glenn Anderson collecting eleven Stanley Cup rings between the two of them. And Gregg, Anderson, Paul MacLean, Tim Watters and Jim Nill would have all qualified for corporate long-service awards had they been white-collar workers, combining to log over sixty NHL seasons. Compare this to the much more celebrated USA team, many of whose players became household names in North America after their Miracle On Ice, and there's not much difference. Only two more Americans made it to The Show, and of these twelve, Ken Morrow of the Islanders and Neal Broten (with New Jersey in 1995) managed to win a total of five Stanley Cups.

The quality of Canada's roster was unknown to the country though, and the Canadian amateurs carried the same stigma that dogged Father Bauer's 1960s teams, that of "boys sent to do a man's job" against the veteran, de facto professionals of the Soviet Union and Czechoslovakia. It's true they were very young, even fresher-faced than their fabled American counterparts. Except for Terry O'Malley, the thirty-nine-year-old veteran from the 1960s National Team, the 1980 Canadian Olympians averaged a scant twenty-one years of age. Standouts like John Devaney, who led the team in scoring at Lake Placid, and Glenn Anderson, were twenty-one and nineteen respectively. But as the season unfolded the kid Canucks began to look quite capable of doing a man's job.

The youngsters got their first blooding in early September of '79, winning an overseas brace of matches against Finnish club teams and then on to Prague's prestigious Rude Pravo tournament, where they met the cream of international hockey, the Russian, Czech, Swedish and Finnish national teams. They won only one out of four games, but gave a good account of themselves for a newly assembled squad. Their tenacious forechecking and refusal to be intimidated in a hard-fought 5-3 loss to the Soviets caused Anatoly Tarasov to make a remarkable admission to Father Bauer. As the two old adversaries sat watching the game together, Tarasov turned to Bauer and told him it was time for the fleet-footed Valery Kharlamov (two-time Olympic gold medalist and great Russian star of the Summit Series) to retire because he could no longer keep up with Canada's blazing young forwards – Kharlamov was only thirty-one. John Devaney said of the Canadian effort against Kharlamov and comrades, "We [were] playing against the best teams in the world. I'll never forget that first shift we played against the Soviets. All of a sudden I had the puck and I passed it to Kevin Primeau and he shot and scored [against Tretiak]. It was only twenty-one seconds into the game."

Next in the Canadians' patchwork schedule was a six-game series against the few NHL squads that would agree to play the Olympians. They posted wins against the Edmonton Oilers, the Winnipeg Jets and the Toronto Maple Leafs, a loss and a tie against the Washington Capitals and a loss to the New York Rangers. All the scores were close, except for their 5-0 and 7-3 thumpings of the Oilers and Jets respectively. The team was progressing swimmingly until they hit their first bump in the road, two mid-October games against the Americans in Minnesota, where they got pasted 7-2 and 6-0. This caused Jim Coleman, the lone member of the national media who followed the Olympians, to utter prophetically that goaltending would be the key to Canada's Lake Placid performance.

The Canadians rebounded from their first contact with the Americans to win four straight against their south-of-the-border rivals, establishing a demonstrable edge over the eventual gold medalists. Then they hit another rough spot in December, getting swept in all four games (USSR, USA, Sweden, Czechoslovakia) on the international ice surface at the pre-Olympic tournament in Lake Placid. Once again, they bounced back to win five and tie one against the Russians and the Czechs on the smaller ice surface at home in the Corral during late December and early January 1980. Twenty-six years later, as Kevin Primeau looks over his team's record during that rollercoaster pre-Olympic run, he stabs a finger at the point on the list that shows the strong December homestand and says, "That's when [goaltender] Bob Dupuis was at the top of his game."

By the time they got to Lake Placid in early February, the Canadians were still plagued by inconsistency and questions about goaltending. These questions were mostly self-directed, however, because few others in the True North Strong and Free were paying attention. Just days before the Olympic tournament opened, Terry Jones "introduced" these dedicated young men in his *Edmonton Journal* sports column. His opening read: "All year long, Canada has managed to ignore Father Bauer's Olympians. And you don't have to ask why. The simple truth is that this country doesn't get too worked up about a bunch of amateurs." Dolly Drake, who spent the winter living in a small Calgary apartment with her husband and took the team under her wing just as she had the Golden Bears, elaborates on Jones's point. "Canada never really embraced this Olympic Team, it was a very low profile team. I think management might have wanted that to keep the pressure off the players, but it's too bad in a way, because those kids sacrificed so much to play for their country and a little credit would have been nice for them."

The Americans were also flying under the radar. But even though their northern neighbors had gained the upper hand in the series between the two teams, the Americans had several distinct advantages as the Olympics began. Aside from the obvious one of being the home team, they'd played a better-planned, more consistent schedule that included a temporary slot in the highly competitive Central Hockey League, a pro circuit close to AHL caliber. The Canadians, on the other hand, traveled hither and yon in search of quality competition and ended up with a pre-Olympic season that Terry Jones called a "helter-skelter farce."

And there was another, more important difference – the Americans had one head coach, Herb Brooks, and everybody in the program knew exactly who was in charge. Contrast this with the Canadian setup, typically Canadian, with its three co-coaches: Tom Watt, the pre-eminent easterner; Clare

"Twenty gentlemen from Canada – a squad of grass green amateurs – scared the hell out of the Soviet Union." A pre-Olympic lineup of the young Canadian team Drake took to Lake Placid in 1980. (Top row L-R, Doug Buchanan, Dave Hindmarch, Shane Pearsall, Warren Anderson, John Devaney. Middle row, Paul MacLean, Tim Watters, Don Spring, Glenn Anderson, Kevin Primeau, Randy Gregg, Dan D'Alvise, Ron Davidson, Jim Nill, Brad Pirie. Bottom row, Ron Paterson, Roger Lamoureux, Stelio Zupancich, Joe Grant, Ken Berry, Kevin Maxwell, Carey Farelli, Bob Dupuis.)

Drake, the pre-eminent westerner; and Lorne Davis, the loyal old National Teamer. Factor Father Bauer into the mix, the former coach with the hands-on management style, and it made for a very complicated situation. This braintrust worked amazingly well together given the inherent potential for disaster, but the sheer weight of their intellects, egos and differing perspectives meant they couldn't possibly be on the same page all the time. There were conflicting views particularly on player personnel, which may have borne consequences for team consistency. Once the team arrived in Lake Placid, Father Bauer belatedly reduced the number of cooks stirring the broth by naming Drake as head coach, Davis as assistant, and asking Watt to "go upstairs to the booth." Watt ended up doing Olympic color commentary for CTV. The architect of the CIAU's great hockey dynasty says, "It was one of the biggest disappointments of my life."

Tom Watt recovered from this blow and the next year became the first CIAU coach to step into an NHL job, as an assistant with the Vancouver Canucks. The season after that, 1981-82, the Winnipeg Jets brought him over as head coach and he won the Jack Adams Award for engineering a stunning turnaround. Under his tutelage the Jets finished bang on .500 at 33-33-14, not so remarkable until you look at their previous season's record of 9-57-14. In the hired-to-be-fired world of the NHL, Watt served two more campaigns with the Jets before going back to the Canucks as their headman for two years. He also won a Stanley Cup as Terry Crisp's assistant with the Calgary Flames in 1989, and his last head coaching job was with his hometown Leafs in 1991-92. Hurt though he was about the 1980 Olympic tangle and the way his boss handled it, Watt's final word on the subject is simple and sincere: "Father Bauer was a great Canadian."

As for the young Canadian skaters, they found themselves on the tougher side of the draw for the Olympic tournament. They were pooled for the qualifying round in the Red Division with patsies Holland, Poland and Japan, but also up against the competitive Finns and the invincible Soviets, winners of four consecutive Olympic gold medals. This was virtually the same Soviet team that laid the 6-0 thrashing on the NHL's best the year before in the final game of the Challenge Cup, prompting their captain, Boris Mikhailov, to pronounce Canada number two in hockey.

The Americans drew into the Blue Division against weak sisters Norway, Romania and Germany, and their toughest rivals were Sweden and Czechoslovakia; both sound international teams, but not in the same league as the Soviets.

Canada dispatched their first two opponents easily, rolling to 10-1 and 5-1 scores against the Dutch and the Poles respectively. Next up came the Finns, a team they were quite capable of defeating with a solid effort. Everyone was conceding first place in the Red Division to the Soviets, so it would be between Canada and Finland for the pool's only other spot in the four-team medal round. Drake's squad went into the match confidently, but their goaltending and consistency hobgoblins jumped up and bit them right in the derrière.

They got off to a bad start, down 2-1 in the second period, by making mistakes that were, in Drake's post-game words, "uncharacteristic of this team." Goaltender Dupuis held the fort well during their shaky stretch but then disaster struck. With just under three minutes left in the second and the Canadian forwards exerting heavy pressure, the Finns dumped the puck in panic. The demonic black disc skittered down the ice and, with the hockey gods laughing at their own handiwork, eluded Dupuis's clearing swipe and found its way across the Canadian goal line. Our boys fought back gamely in the third period but too much damage had been done and they ended up on the wrong side of the 4-3 score in this must-win game. Jim Coleman, who knew the team well having followed it since October, said "they were capable of playing at least twenty-five percent better hockey… they discarded skill in favor of raw, uncoordinated emotion and the results were disastrous."

Disheartened though they were, the Canadians weren't about to give up on their hopes of reaching the medal round. They polished off Japan 6-0 and then steeled themselves to meet the daunting Soviets on February 20, 1980. If they were to advance, they had to beat the unbeatable. They knew their opponents well, having competed hard against various Soviet select squads seven times during their preparatory season, going 2-4-1 and never getting blown out. A handful of the Olympians had also joined a team of pros at Moscow's famous Izvestia Tournament in December '79, where they faced the full USSR Olympic unit. Of that team Dave Hindmarch says, still in awe a quarter-century later, "Oh my God, they were a machine! They were so strong on their home ice, we barely touched the puck the whole time."

But at Lake Placid, Hindmarch and his Rig 80 mates were not in awe of the Russians. They threw everything they had at the Big Red Machine and came oh so close to fashioning their own miracle on ice on February 20. With backup goalie Paul Pageau in net, and every last one of them playing like a man possessed, they worked their way to a 3-1 lead against the Soviets late in the second period. The famously unflappable Russians were visibly rattled by the intense Canadian forechecking, and Drake and Davis and their young charges could smell the scent of upset starting to waft in the air. As the momentum continued to build in Canada's favor, Ken Berry found himself at Tretiak's doorstep with the puck on his stick and the net yawning. Again the hockey gods laughed, and the biscuit bounced harmlessly wide; the score could have been, maybe should have been, 4-1 at the end of the second. Instead, as is so often the way of hockey, the Russians came steaming back down to the other end and with thirteen seconds left in the frame, future New Jersey Devil Alexei Kasatonov put the puck behind Pageau.

This helped the favorites regain their equilibrium and they potted two quick ones to open the third period. In two minutes and eighteen seconds at the end of the second and the beginning of the third, Canada's upset dreams went up in smoke. But the Canadians didn't quit, battling back to tie the game on a goal by Dan D'Alvise, one of Tom Watt's Toronto Blues. Soviet mastery proved to be too much from then on however, with the savvy old veterans of the Olympic wars scoring two more to consolidate a 6-4 win. To rub salt in the wound, the winner was tallied by none other than the hated Boris Mikhailov, whom Jim Coleman referred to as "that scowling rascal." In spite of his antipathy, the scribe generously accorded Mikhailov the honorific, "best all-round hockey player in the world." And Mikhailov's young foes? Coleman praised them unabashedly for never giving up, swarming the "enemy net… even in the dying minute of the game . . . causing near panic in the ranks of the World Champions." He surmised that dictatorial Russian coach Viktor Tikhonov, who dodged the post-game press conference, was "back in the Soviet dressing room changing his linen."

Coleman summed up the magnificent Canadian endeavor with stirring prose: "In one of the most emotionally gratifying performances ever given by a Canadian hockey team – let alone a squad of grass green amateurs – twenty gentlemen from Canada scared the hell out of the mighty Soviet Union last night before yielding grudgingly and courageously." He even told of a British journalist who stood nearby in the press box with tears rolling down his cheeks because he was so moved by the Canadians' valiant attempt. Terry Jones of the *Edmonton Journal* was just as inspired as Coleman. He evoked memories of September '72 as he described an effort that "gave Canada a summit series hockey thrill." Jones said that in spite of the loss, these kids "finally pulled off their impossible dream. They finally made Canada feel proud of them! Exceptionally proud."

The powerful, uplifting emotion expressed by Jones and Coleman was every bit as real, if not as grand, as the wave of feeling that rolled over Canada in September '72. But the events that followed caused it to evaporate quickly, too quickly for our Olympians to savor. They didn't get a chance to bask in the glow of Canada's appreciation for their achievement, because the Americans, the team our boys had bested before the Olympics, finished the job they had started. Canada's great effort was forgotten in all the ensuing frenzy. Just two days later on February 22, the USA, having seen Canada dent the Soviets' armor, bashed a hole right through it, beating them 4-3 in the medal round. Drake, reprising the clairvoyance he showed in Düsseldorf in 1955, predicted the Americans' improbable win on February 20 when he told the *Journal*, "I thought we were going to do it today and if I were to bet, I'd bet the Americans will do it."

The story of American coach Herb Brooks and his young bunch of miracle workers has been related many times over, through a variety of media. But the aftermath of the Canada-Russia game merits further discussion. On February 22, the morning of the historic USA victory, Hockey Canada president and CEO Lou Lefaive announced to the Canadian media assembled at Lake Placid that, "The players gave public credibility to the entire [Olympic] program with their fine game against the Russians" and therefore, "We'll continue with our plan to provide a team of amateurs to represent Canada in each year's world championships, beginning with Sweden in 1981." What Jim Coleman had labeled "The Great Experiment" the preceding August had been deemed a success. Father Bauer's vision, subscribed to by his dedicated group of coaches and young men, was that a cadre of well prepared, expertly coached and highly trained amateurs could compete with the Russians. It seemed that Hockey Canada had finally and truly bought into the vision, and that the good Father's dream would live on.

Terry Jones was enthused by the announcement and waxed rhapsodic about Canada's return to the Olympics, and about the upside of staying with Bauer's amateurs as our international hockey envoys. "Maybe we've finally got our heads screwed on straight," he argued. "Wouldn't you really rather have these kids – busting their butts on every shift – playing for Canada? Wouldn't you rather be represented by gung-ho kids in the world championships than by a scattered bunch of pros who missed the playoffs? Wouldn't you really rather be represented by a TEAM?" His acclaim for "these kids" included the American youngsters as well, who, as he so rightfully put it, were a "TEAM" just like our Canadian lads. Showing uncommon wisdom, Jones declared, "I say the American victory doesn't take away a thing from what the Canadian kids accomplished. I say it confirms we're on the right track."

Anatoly Tarasov didn't see it the same way. In a piece of revisionist analysis worthy of *Pravda*, he wrote in a March 1980 article for the *Globe and Mail* that "once again [Canada] sent a weak team to the Olympic forum." Conveniently forgetting the compliments he'd paid to Father Bauer the prior September in Prague, and ignoring Canada's respectable pre-Olympic record against the Soviets, Tarasov acknowledged our "fighting spirit" but was otherwise dismissive. He compared Canadian efforts to that of a bull charging a red flag and said that Canada "had only a superficial knowledge of [Soviet] tactical principles." His trivializing of the Canadian team contrasted starkly with the praise he heaped on Herb Brooks, whom he called "the trump card of the U.S. team." Brooks deserved every accolade that came to him, but Tarasov's comments smacked of bandwagon jumping.

The Americans got on a great roll at Lake Placid, one of the greatest ever; the Canadians just played hard, and at times very well, and did themselves and their country proud. The Americans grabbed the gold thanks pretty much to one well-timed, inspirational victory; the Canadians came within a whisker of pulling off the same win and ended up with nothing. In spite of the huge gulf between first place and sixth, where Canada ended up, these two squads were very close in talent and team play. Yes, there were differences like better pre-Olympic scheduling and a clearly demarcated American coaching and management hierarchy, but the ultimate distinction between the two teams was the one that can't really be explained – in 1980, for those few days in February, the Americans were simply a team of destiny.

And as the team of destiny, history has conferred immense glory upon them. Al Michaels's rhetorical question – "Do you believe in miracles?" – was a sound bite for the ages, just like Foster Hewitt's exultant cry on September 28, 1972. Jim McKay, Michaels's senior colleague at ABC Television, called the American win over the Russians "the greatest hockey game ever played on earth." Canadian journalist Terry Jones debunked this highly debatable claim, giving the game its due as "dramatic and thrilling" but reminding his readers that McKay obviously didn't know about Paul Henderson and September 28, or the Canadiens versus Central Red Army on New Year's Eve, 1975 or, he added, "a few Stanley Cups, too."

Jones's demurral aside, and even though the win was in an un-American sport, it was fashioned by an American team, on American soil, against America's greatest enemies, and on the world hockey stage. And so America embraced this team and the sport they played. Guys like Jim Craig, the goaltender, and captain Mike Eruzione played little or no pro hockey after 1980, yet to this day they remain household names and timeless heroes in the USA. Others such as Ken Morrow, Neal Broten, Mark Johnson and Mike Ramsey went on to long and distinguished NHL careers. And for Herb Brooks, their all-conquering coach, Lake Placid was a ticket from the NCAA's University of Minnesota to four NHL head coaching positions in seven seasons and, finally in 2006, to posthumous induction into the Hockey Hall of Fame.

As for the Canadians, most of them skated back into obscurity, whence they had come. Their country had pretty well ignored them before the Olympics, and once the Americans eclipsed their brilliant effort against the Russians, it was right back into the shadows again. And then, just a few months later, Hockey Canada delivered a final, crushing blow to these young men. Reneging on the commitment that Lou Lefaive announced in Lake Placid, the funding body pulled the plug on the National Team program and left many of the players twisting in the wind. The program would come back to life in 1983 under Dave King, building toward the '84 Olympics, but the cancellation deprived the 1980 bunch of any support base from which they could maintain their amateur status, still necessary in those days for Olympic play. So this tight-knit group, who'd spent the previous eight months sleeping two to a room on bunk beds in some old camp trailers, said good-bye to each other and wandered off in search of individual fulfillment.

Randy Gregg, perhaps the most fervent believer in Father Bauer's vision, went to Japan for two seasons. There, just as in Europe, he could get paid to play hockey and still be considered an amateur, while completing his medical internship at home in Edmonton during the summers. He finally got tired of waiting hopefully for the rebirth of the national program and signed with the Oilers in the spring of 1982; two years later, he won his first Stanley Cup. Glenn Anderson, the brightest of the Olympic lights, had already been an Oiler for two seasons by the time Gregg signed, and was marked as one of the fine young stars of Edmonton's dynasty in the making.

Don Spring, Dave Hindmarch, Paul MacLean, Tim Watters and Jim Nill all found their way into the NHL, some of them playing many years as solid journeymen. John Devaney, the team's leading scorer at Lake Placid, joined ex-U of A and Canada teammate Kevin Primeau for a season in Switzerland and then came home to begin a long, successful career as a chartered accountant. A couple more of the Olympians had brief cups of coffee in The Show and then bounced around the minors for a few years, and several others returned to university. Warren Anderson, an ex-Toronto Blue, came back to Dave King's program in '83 and competed in the '84 Olympics in Sarajevo. And Gregg and Watters both took leave of their NHL clubs for a few months in 1987-88 to play under King at the Calgary Olympic Games, when the IIHF finally decided to allow a limited number of NHLers to appear on Olympic rosters. For Gregg, the experience just wasn't the same as with that first group of young idealists under the inspiring leadership of Bauer, Drake, Watt and Davis. To this day, Randy Gregg counts his first Olympics – sixth-place finish and all – as the best hockey experience of his career, five Stanley Cup rings notwithstanding.

Canada's gut-wrenching defeat at Lake Placid wasn't tragic – that's a word you save for people dying of cancer – but it caused its own fair share of pain. Clare Drake calls the Russian game "one of the most heartbreaking losses I can remember" and to this day, has not been able to bring himself to watch the video. He was, however, masochistic enough to endure a viewing of the foul-up against Finland, a couple of hours he describes as "torturous." Unlike for Herb Brooks, no new doors opened for Drake coming off the Olympics. That was okay though. He hadn't taken the job as a stepping stone to something bigger; his intention all along was to return to the U of A after his year with the young Olympians. And so he did.

Who's to say how things might have been had Ken Berry popped in that open-net chance at the end of the second period in the Soviet game? Had our Canadian kids won that game and advanced to the medal round, they would have been on a roll similar to that of the Americans. Then, all bets would have been off. A medal of any color would have made national heroes of these young men and presented a much greater range of opportunities for players and coaches alike. Even with the discouraging sixth place, quite a few got their chance in The Show. Not the least of these was Clare Drake's colleague Tom Watt, who within two short years would parlay his international experience and remarkable U of T record into NHL success as the league's Jack Adams Award winner. But Drake quietly went home to Edmonton. While he probably would have said yes to the right offer, he wasn't actively searching out new prospects and, since nobody came knocking on his door, once again, as he had five years earlier, he returned to the familiar routines of university life and his beloved Golden Bears.

CHAPTER SIX

"The man's fingerprints are all over the game"

mentor • *noun 1 an experienced and trusted adviser. 2 an experienced person in an organization or institution who trains and counsels new employees or students.*
— ORIGIN from the name of Mentor, the adviser of the young Telemachus in Homer's Odyssey.
Compact Oxford English Dictionary

Counsel woven into the fabric of real life is wisdom.
Walter Benjamin, 1936

A mellower "Papa Bear" during the 1980s.

While Clare Drake spent the winter of 1979-80 in Calgary and globetrotting with the Olympic Team, Bill Moores was back in Edmonton performing much more than just a caretaking role with the Golden Bears. He'd been left with the remnants of the two-time National Champions, minus the five standouts who had departed for the Olympic Team. This left a gaping hole in his lineup but Moores, a superlative coach in his own right, shepherded the Bears to their sixth and perhaps least expected University Cup. His team suffered an unprecedented home loss to George Kingston's Calgary Dinosaurs in the Canada West conference final and only qualified for the nationals in Regina as a wild card entry. But showing the mental toughness of their coach, and with enough savvy veterans remaining, once they got to the big dance the Bears ran the table, downing the University of Regina 7-3 in the final.

The 1980 national championship marked the swan song for the core group Drake and Moores had started with back in the fall of 1976. There were just a handful of these fine players left when Drake returned for the 1980-81 season and, without the aggressive recruiting that typifies the CIS of the twenty-first century, the rebuilding effort would take several years. The Bears placed third in Canada West and missed the playoffs in both '80-81 and '81-82, the only two sub-.500 seasons in Drake's entire career at the U of A. There was one bright spot, however, an interesting diversion that provides further insight into the values that Drake had long since made a signature of Golden Bear hockey.

As defending National Champions, the Bears were chosen by the CIAU to represent Canada at the 1981 Winter Universiade in Jaca, Spain. That year there were no Iron Curtain hockey teams attending, nor had the Americans chosen to send a team. The Bears took an enhanced roster to the games, boosted with UBC players Jim McLaughlin, Bill Holowaty and Ron Paterson. For good measure, they also added two accomplished Alberta grads, defencemen Randy Gregg, whose season in Japan had just ended, and Larry Riggin, a former All Canadian then playing in Switzerland (Universiade eligibility rules allowed both onto the roster because they were within two years of graduating).

So the Golden Bears went into the tournament as gold medal favorites and met with few challenges on the ice. But there were still lessons to be learned. Forward Chris Helland, an All Canadian in 1979, had seen Japan with the Bears in '78 and now found himself and his teammates in a remote Pyrenees town in March 1981. Just like in Japan, he remembers his coach maintaining a balance, encouraging the players to experience the colorful local culture but still keeping them focused on hockey. The biggest lesson came at the small, smoke-filled arena in Jaca that hosted the hockey tournament. In spite of their generally weak opposition, actually because of it, the Bears faced a hockey challenge the likes of which they'd never encountered before. They played in one of the most lopsided games ever staged at the so-called competitive level, and it was so strange that it drew the attention of North America's leading sports magazine.

This game was the third of four the Bears played in Jaca. They started off with a 9-0 romp over the hapless Spanish and then played the plucky Japanese, who were outshot 73-15 but managed to keep the score semi-respectable at 7-3. Next came South Korea, beyond hapless, and for whom pluck would be totally irrelevant. The final score, with the Bears doing everything they could to keep it down, was 31-0. The temptation when looking at these numbers is to giggle, to call the game a "laugher." But as Drake avers, such an overwhelming mismatch is no good for either team, or for hockey itself. Having scouted the Koreans, Drake and Moores knew things would be bad and set up some ground rules for their team; for instance, once a player had scored twice, he would be ineligible to shoot from then on.

Chris Helland told the *Edmonton Journal*'s Cam Cole, who was along on the trip, "We really tried not to score. Coach Drake told us not to take slapshots. We didn't throw a bodycheck the whole game. We tried to get everyone on the ice to touch the puck inside their blueline before we could score." Helland's final words spoke volumes about his team's (and his coach's) highly developed sense of sportsmanship when he said, "It was sick – a sad, sad experience."

The debacle drew comment in *Sports Illustrated*, in an essay on the ethics of running up the score. The American periodical was criticizing certain Little League baseball and high school basketball coaches for pouring it on when they had an opponent at their mercy. The essay offered the Canada-Korea game at Jaca as evidence of a healthier attitude: "Mismatches are abhorrent, and people with true sporting instincts recoil from them." As an example of same, the magazine cited Helland's "sad, sad" remark in evidence of the Canadians' decency and their embarrassment about the fiasco. Helland reflects on the episode twenty-five years later, remembering the leadership Drake showed as he invented ways to keep his players engaged and yet minimize the damage on the scoreboard; as he found ways to rein in the assault on the dignity of their opponents. "It was all about respect," says Helland, "Respect for the other team, respect for the game."

In the final game of the Universiade tournament, Canada defeated Finland 6-1. This contest featured one of those little ironies that add piquancy to life. Outshot 68-13, Finland managed their only goal in the second period when they held a two-man advantage. Even then, they couldn't score themselves but needed Canadian goaltender Ron Paterson of UBC to sweep the puck into his own net. This gaffe – highly uncharacteristic of Paterson, who would earn CIAU All Canadian honors the next season – came chillingly close to the one by Canadian goaltender Bob Dupuis just twelve months earlier against the Finns at Lake Placid. This time, the results were different and Canada came away with gold.

The 1981 Winter Universiade gold medal was the highlight in two otherwise sub-standard seasons, but in 1982-83 the Bears got back into the Canada West playoffs, although they were quickly dispatched by Dave King's surging Saskatchewan Huskies. That same season the Huskies, who had lost national final heartbreakers to the University of Moncton in both the previous two years, would at last grab the brass ring with their first University Cup championship. The next season, in 1983-84, Drake was due for an academic sabbatical; his last had been in 1969-70, when he'd gone to the University of Oregon intending to complete his Ph.D. So again, as in the Olympic year, he left the team in the capable hands of Bill Moores. Moores won the Canada West title and got the Bears back to the nationals for the first time in four seasons, not really a long stretch, but an eon by Alberta standards. The Bears failed to make the final, which the Toronto Blues won under the direction of Mike Keenan for their tenth and last University Cup (as of 2006). As a minor recompense, Moores won his first Father George Kehoe Award as CIAU coach of the year. Meanwhile, Clare and Dolly were in San Diego, where at age fifty-five he was still learning, taking graduate courses in coaching and sports psychology at the state university.

When Clare Drake came back to Alberta to open training camp in the fall of 1984, he had coached the Golden Bears for twenty-three of the preceding twenty-nine seasons. He was advancing on his fifty-sixth birthday while working with players thirty-five years his junior. The game had changed dramatically since the 1950s, when he'd coached his Yorkton buddy Vern Pachal and other men who were within a few years of his own age. Tube skates had long since gone the way of the dinosaur (not the Calgary variety), equipment had mutated through many iterations, including the "Cooperall" long-pant experiment of the early 1980s. Game rosters had grown from twelve players to twenty, with even more "black aces" on the side waiting for their chance to get into the lineup. The University of Alberta no longer had the market cornered on western talent and Drake, because he'd spent so many years sharing his philosophies and tactics, was coaching against many of the very men he'd trained through his work in the National Coaching Certification Program. University hockey, in Canada West and throughout the CIAU, had become more competitive.

Granted, Drake had won fifteen conference titles during his twenty-three seasons, and five University Cups since 1963 when the CIAU held its first national championship. But his last Hardy Cup, the Canada West championship, had been in 1979; his last University Cup dated back to the same year – his protégé Moores had bagged the U of A's sixth in 1980. Drake's previous three years at the helm, before his sabbatical, had been disappointing. Why then, at his stage in life, having achieved so much already, did he return for yet another kick at the can? The answer to this question was the same as it had been in 1976, when he rebounded after his Edmonton Oilers setback, and then again in 1980 after the disappointment at Lake Placid. Drake kept coming back to the U of A for three basic reasons: he still found joy in working with highly-motivated, intelligent young athletes; as a tenured professor, he had a really good, secure job at a fine institution; and finally, because his passion for the great game of hockey was, and to this day remains, unquenchable.

Randy Gregg, who can go on at length about his old coach's technical brilliance and the high quality of his personal character, tells a small anecdote to illustrate what he thinks is the man's greatest trait. In 2006, he was watching Drake at a reunion of the '78, '79 and '80 Golden Bears at the CIS nationals in Edmonton. As his fellow alumni and their wives shared a few drinks and a lot of fond memories, with the coach at the center of the hubbub, he noticed Drake's eyes stray to the TV in the corner of the room. It was showing a crucial Oilers game in their late-season run for a playoff spot, and all of a sudden the coach was transfixed. The watcher observed the watcher, and was moved by the man's obvious love for, and fascination with, the game. "Even at his age!" marvels Gregg. "It was wonderful to see the excitement in his eyes, to see the joy he got out of watching the game played well." Another former defenceman named Randy makes a similar comment. Randy Carlyle, a Norris Trophy winner, was near the end of his playing career when Drake came to the Winnipeg Jets as Bob Murdoch's assistant in 1989. Drake had turned sixty by then, old from the perspective of even a veteran NHLer, yet what struck Carlyle most was his still-vigorous zest for the game, after all the years he'd spent in it.

Drake brought this unflagging passion with him on his return from San Diego in 1984 and, together, he and Moores took Alberta back to its familiar position near the top of the CIAU heap. He also led Canada to a new international triumph at Europe's most prestigious hockey tournament, the Spengler Cup, that only in recent years has gained a profile in Canada.

The Golden Bears' 1984-85 season was a strong one, their second 20-4 record in a row as they re-established their dominance of Canada West. They defeated Saskatchewan for Drake's sixteenth Hardy Cup and then traveled to Winnipeg for a regional playoff against the champions of the Great Plains Athletic conference, the Manitoba Bisons, to determine who would advance to the University Cup tournament. Manitoba had a tough, talented team led by Mike Ridley, that season's Sullivan Award winner as the CIAU's outstanding player and a future NHL trigger man, who registered close to 300 goals in twelve pro seasons. They were coached by Bison alumnus Wayne Fleming, the 1984-85 CIAU coach of the year, who would run Canada's National Team during the 1990s, serve as Olympic assistant and associate coach in 1992 and 2002 (winning silver and gold) and coach Canada at the world championships in 2001 and 2002. He also became an NHL assistant with Phoenix, the New York Islanders, Philadelphia (where he worked with Ken Hitchcock), and in 2006, the Calgary Flames.

Taking into account all their years in pro and international hockey, both Ridley and Fleming count that March weekend in 1985 among the greatest disappointments of their hockey lives. Alberta and Manitoba split the first two games of the best-of-three series and in the final game, the Bisons dominated the first two periods and were getting set to head to the nationals with a 4-2 lead late in the third. But with less than two minutes left, Bears' captain Tim Krug closed the gap to one, and then with only twelve seconds left and the goaltender pulled, Alberta forward Dennis Cranston tied it up during a frantic goalmouth scramble. Manitoba scored first in the non-sudden death overtime period, but the Bears wouldn't quit. They tied the game again and then popped the winner with fifty-one seconds left in the extra frame.

This was a crushing loss for Fleming – "It really hurt," he says. But his signal memory is of Drake's post-game knock on the door of the Bison dressing room. Fleming says he couldn't believe that as Drake's team celebrated the greatest comeback in Golden Bear history, their coach came looking for him. "Clare said, 'As happy as I am that we won, I feel really bad for you Wayne.' He told me that we'd pushed the Bears as far as anyone ever has," remembers Fleming, considering that a huge compliment. Fleming's admiration for Drake, which began when he took the head job at Manitoba in 1980 and Drake started giving him coaching tips, only increased after having suffered this devastating defeat. In spite of the cognitive dissonance Drake expressed to Fleming, the win remains one of the most meaningful for the old coach. Because he's a consummate sportsman, he places the highest value on such a hard-fought victory, over such an esteemed opponent.

The Golden Bears left Winnipeg in awe of their own good fortune and made the familiar trip east to another national finals tournament in Toronto. After knocking the Toronto Blues out in the elimination round they met York University in the championship game. The Yeomen were coached by Dave Chambers, with whom Drake collaborated in the National Coaching Certification Program, and their star was Don McLaren. Chasing right on the heels of the remarkable comeback in Winnipeg, Drake remembers this game as one where he made a crucial mistake. In terms of the play, the Bears almost annihilated York, outshooting them 52-16, but they lost 3-2. Drake and Moores have never been big believers in matching lines, which is consistent with their philosophy of "rolling four," sticking to their game plan and letting the other team worry about what they were doing. Drake allows there are certain instances, however, where line-matching offers a tactical advantage and, in hindsight, he acknowledges that this was one of them. Don McLaren had one of those landmark games against the Bears in 1985, carrying York to their first University Cup on the strength of his first-period hat trick. The Bears came at Yeomen goaltender Mark Applewhaite in waves, as evidenced by the shot total, but his acrobatic performance preserved McLaren's handiwork. The York sniper had obviously merited special attention, having inflicted such single-handed damage.

In one of those striking coincidences we find so often in the world of sport, Chambers and McLaren each played their part in a career highlight for Drake earlier that same season. The Spengler Cup is the oldest international tournament for club teams in the world, founded in 1923 and staged in the beautiful Swiss resort town of Davos. Originally a competition for club teams from traditionally weaker hockey nations like Great Britain, France, Italy and Switzerland, over the years its entry qualifications were relaxed to include national or select squads. In the 1950s and 1960s, clubs and select squads from Czechoslovakia and the Soviet Union began participating, with the result that from 1965 to 1983, Iron Curtain teams ruled the tourney. Famous Russian and Czech names like Spartak Moscow and Dukla Jihlava were part of a nineteen-year run that saw western Europe completely shut out of the gold at Davos. In 1984, Hockey Canada decided to send its first team to the Spengler Cup and offered the head coaching job to Clare Drake. His assistants were Dave Chambers of York, and Andy Murray, who had coached at Brandon University and at the time was running a Swiss A division club.

Canada's entry was a grab bag assortment: top CIAU players, a few pros from the American Hockey League, and the rest chosen from Canadians playing professionally in Europe. Drake and Chambers met ten of the players in Toronto just before Christmas '84, whence they headed to Switzerland to meet up with Murray and ten more who had gathered there from various parts of Europe. On the roster were four Golden Bears – defenceman Parie Proft, forward Dennis Cranston and two All Canadians, goaltender Ken Hodge and defenceman Tim Krug – and All Canadians Bill Holowaty from UBC and McLaren, who would become the Bears' assassin later that year. This motley bunch had no training camp and little time to come together as a team. Their first match-up in the single round robin affair was against the favorite and champion from two years earlier, Dukla Jihlava of Czechoslovakia, who boasted future NHLers Frank Musil and Petr Klima in their lineup. The Canadian arrivistes were serious underdogs in this game, as they were for the whole tournament, but they had a balanced group of intelligent, talented amateurs and pros who were open to Drake's team-first concept. Moreover, they had a canny coaching triumvirate who helped them coalesce into a disciplined, hard-skating unit.

In spite of losing their opener to the Czechs on Boxing Day, they grew in confidence and cohesiveness through the next two games, beating the German entry, Schwenningen of the *Bundesliga*, and the host team, HC Davos. Meanwhile, the Czechs had suffered a loss and a tie, which meant that Canada could win gold if it defeated the Russian club, Chimik Woskresensk, in its last round robin game on December 30. Dennis Cranston recalls how big, strong and fast the Russians were. A smooth-skating little guy who finished his checks like a man thirty pounds heavier (much in the fashion of Bill Moores), Cranston shakes his head and laughs, "I couldn't get close enough to the Russians in that game to hit the way I normally did." Cranston also remembers watching Drake, Chambers and Murray work together, and he was impressed with the respect the senior man accorded his two assistants, giving them every opportunity to add their own input as the staff addressed the players.

Canada had to overcome 2-0 and 3-1 deficits against the Russians, and Don McLaren was a big contributor with two markers, including the tying goal with 1:48 remaining (Drake should have remembered this in March!). Then, team captain Rob Plumb, a former Red Wing draft choice playing in the Swiss B division, scored his second of the game on a breakaway with only forty-eight seconds left to clinch Canada's first gold at the Spengler Cup. The wildly pro-Canadian crowd, tired of nineteen years of Czech and Soviet domination, was ecstatic.

Decades before TSN discovered the Spengler Cup and introduced it to Canadian audiences after the turn of the millennium, the tourney held a huge reputation in the rest of the hockey world. It en-

Dazzling debut in Davos! Canada's first Spengler Cup representatives, the 1984 gold medalists. (Drake, bottom row, fourth from left, with a youthful Andy Murray two seats to his left [Dave Chambers not in picture]; Golden Bears Ken Hodge, bottom row, far left, Tim Krug, middle row, fourth from right, Dennis Cranston and Parie Proft, top row, far left and second from left, respectively.)

joyed this status, and still does, not just because of its grand tradition, but also because of the beautiful wood-and-glass arena where the games are played in Davos, the rabid enthusiasm of the fans and the magical ambience of the Swiss Alps at Christmas time. Davos is an international ski destination and the rich and famous flock there during the festive season for the snow and the hockey. The victorious Canadians discovered this at a chi-chi party after their gold-medal win, when Bill Holowaty was able to schmooze and get his picture taken with Susan Lucci, the American soap opera star.

Andy Murray himself became a Spengler celebrity, winning another five gold medals in Davos as Canada's head coach after his first as Drake's assistant – an all-time tournament record. Canada has won three more without Murray, for a total of nine since Drake started it all in 1984. Andy Murray went on to NHL assistant coaching positions with Philadelphia, the Minnesota North Stars and the Winnipeg Jets. Then he took over Canada's National Team for two years in the mid-nineties. He also became the first Canadian head coach to win world championship gold twice (in 1997 and 2003), and in 2006 completed a successful seven-year run as head coach of the L.A. Kings, where he established the Kings' record for wins. The St. Louis Blues hired him as their head coach in early 2007. Of his love for the Spengler Cup he says, "It's the best tournament in the world, even better than the Olympics." He was sitting in his office when he told a caller, "I don't have any [NHL] team pictures on my wall… but I'm looking at my Team Canada and Spengler pictures right now."

"I never saw him have a bad day." Andy Murray, here running the L.A. Kings circa 2005, on Drake's ever-positive, always-respectful commitment to "making a difference."

And of working with Clare Drake, Murray says the same things so many others have. He speaks of the old master's intensity, attention to detail and continuous drive for excellence. He talks about how much he's learned from the man, having seen every presentation of Drake's he could attend and read every NCCP paper Drake has submitted. But it's the values Drake has modeled that made the biggest impression on him. An understated man himself, Murray talks quietly, matter-of-factly, about not-so-matter-of-fact matters as he describes the uplifting aura Drake projects. "I never saw him have a bad day, he's always positive, always teaching and he's so respected because he treats people right." Then he paraphrases a speech Drake gave to the U of A convocation when he received his honorary doctorate; Murray wasn't in the audience, but he read the text and it stuck with him. "Clare told them that their responsibility in life is to make a difference," he says. "I use that all the time with my players. I used to say to the National Team guys, 'Some of you may end up in the NHL and become millionaires, but when you get to the end of your life, the most important thing will be that you played for your country, and that you made a difference'."

The Spengler Cup victory is one of the achievements that Drake prizes most, partly because it was a first for Canada, partly because it came at such a great tournament, and not least for Drake, because he so enjoyed collaborating with fine coaches like Dave Chambers and Andy Murray. As for the loss to Chambers a few months later, he and his Golden Bears would recover from that to win another University Cup – Drake's sixth, the team's seventh – the very next year.

The 1985-86 season was momentous for Drake for more than one reason. On October 8, in a pre-season exhibition game against Red Deer College (of the Alberta Colleges Athletic Association) that would have little significance otherwise, he collected his 556th victory to become the "winningest college hockey coach" in North America. This epithet was conferred on him by *Sports Illustrated*, the nonpareil American publication that included him in its time-honored "Faces in the Crowd" feature for the December 2 edition of that year. In Canada, Drake was a "university coach," but that made him small potatoes in our NHL-dominated culture. Had he been an American "college coach," his exploits and his influence on the game – even in hockey, decidedly lesser fare on the U.S. sports menu – would have garnered him attention more like that given to John Wooden, the man with whom so many have compared him. He would more likely have been an *SI* cover story than a "face in the crowd."

Drake's win, which coincidentally came the day before his fifty-seventh birthday, broke the existing record held by John MacInnes, who coached in the NCAA at Michigan Tech from 1956 to 1982. And the head Golden Bear would extend his mark to 697 victories by the time he retired in 1989. This record stood until 1993, when it was surpassed by another Michigander, Ron Mason, who coached Edmonton Oiler Shawn Horcoff, son of Golden Bear John Horcoff, at Michigan State. The twenty-first century Oiler center has proclaimed his respect for Drake, and at the time the old coach set the record, a contemporary Oiler center chipped in his own two bits' worth. Number 99 sent the professor a warm note of congratulations on embossed Wayne Gretzky stationery and included a personally autographed photo – nowadays this memento carries much more than intrinsic value, although for Drake its market price is of small relevance.

Otherwise, there was little fuss over the event, and Drake took the team to another first-place finish in Canada West. This one was a bit different, because it was the first time since 1976 that Drake stood behind the Bears' bench without his good friend Bill Moores. Moores, looking for a new challenge, had taken the head coaching position of the Regina Pats of the Western Hockey League, where his mentor started his brief junior stint back in 1947. To fill Moores's Bunyanesque shoes, Drake recruited two more former players, Kevin Primeau and Jack Cummings, goaltender for the '78 National Champions.

Primeau, who spent a total of four seasons playing for Drake (including the '75 and '78 National Champions and the '80 Olympic Team) has fashioned his own successful coaching career, serving on the Edmonton Oilers staff from 1991 to 1996 and as a headman in the German, Swiss and Austrian elite divisions. He remembers coming back to his home turf after his travels as a player – with brief stops in the NHL, the Central and American Hockey Leagues, and the Swiss A division – and having to learn a new lexicon as a Drake assistant. "In seven years, since I graduated in '78, he'd created totally new terminology for everything the Bears were doing on the ice." Primeau realized then that Drake would never stop growing and changing, regardless of his station in life; and of course, he was struck once again by the man's tremendous inventiveness. In the same conversation Primeau adds his own variations on the theme that Andy Murray and all the rest talk about – the way Clare Drake cares about people: "I didn't have an agent when I went to negotiate my first pro contract [with Oilers coach and GM Glen Sather] and Coach came along to help me out. He even asked Slats to give me a decent number, because they'd assigned me some goalie's number for training camp."

As Drake's sidemen, both Primeau and Cummings were astonished at how much input they were given by the old master:

Even in the University Cup final against UQTR, I came down from the press box at the end of the second period and Coach says, 'Cec [Primeau's nickname], what did you see from up top?' Then he turned to Jack and asked for his comments. Even at the most crucial time in the whole season, he was making sure he involved everybody.

The Bears took a somewhat rocky road to get to the final Primeau referenced, even though they'd finished first that year. Drake, Primeau and Cummings, with Dolly's invaluable assistance, took the team on a nine-game, thirteen-day tour of Switzerland over Christmas and New Year's. They played a grueling schedule primarily against Swiss A division teams, losing their opener to Andy Murray's Zurich club and then winning seven in a row before an 8-2 New Year's Day lesson at the hands of the powerful Soviet unit, Moscow Spartak. While the trip was a wonderful bonding and educational experience, the Bears came home exhausted and injured. Not completely recovered by playoffs, they lost to Saskatchewan in the Canada West semi-finals and only gained a berth in the nationals because they were the host team. But some of their key producers healed in time for the tournament and the team that came in the back door defeated the University of Quebec at Trois-Rivières to win Drake's sixth, and Alberta's seventh, University Cup.

There were two rookie defencemen who cherish the memories of 1985-86, the travel, the championship and the lessons learned. Howie Draper and Eric Thurston, who both carried on the Drake legacy as head coaches of the U of A Pandas and Golden Bears respectively, first met their mentor that season. Thurston will never forget the hockey epiphany he experienced when he arrived at the U of A, after logging three years of major junior in the WHL and one year of pro in the Netherlands. "It was like I'd come home, after being away all my life," he says of first encountering the fine balance between the sophistication and simplicity of the Drake way, "I had the feeling I'd never really played hockey before until I got to Alberta… then it all made sense." He only stayed for that one campaign with the Bears, but it imprinted deeply, bringing him back to work as an assistant under Rob Daum, another ex-Bear who rang up ten stellar years at the Alberta helm. During that decade Daum won six Canada West titles and three University Cups with Thurston at his side, and then the assistant became the boss and won his own national championship in 2006, the Golden Bears' twelfth overall.

In 1986-87, the Bears hosted the nationals again, and again they got in through the tradesmen's entrance, but this time it wasn't because they lost in the Canada West playoffs. George Kingston's Calgary Dinosaurs romped to their best conference record ever but didn't get a chance to beat the Bears in the playoffs because they weren't around. As defending CIAU Champions, Alberta had been given another invitation to represent Canada at the Winter Universiade, staged in Strbske Pleso, Czechoslovakia, in 1987. To attend these games, they had to withdraw from the Canada West post-season, leaving UBC, Calgary, Saskatchewan and Manitoba to battle for the Hardy Cup. The Huskies upset the Dinosaurs in Calgary in the final and took the conference slot at the nationals. As hosts, the Bears were already guaranteed their spot, so they chose to return to Europe for a second straight season, this time to attempt to reclaim the Universiade gold they'd won in Spain.

But it was a far different tournament than the one they'd cruised through in 1981. Instead of steamrolling the Spanish, Koreans and Japanese, the Bears now had to face opponents made of sterner stuff, like Czechoslovakia and the Soviet Union. And this time, they didn't have extra help from grads like Randy Gregg and Larry Riggin, or pickups from other conference teams. They were on their own, although they did have sound leadership and guidance. Bill Moores was back from the WHL, now co-coach with Clare Drake, and former Golden Bear, Olympian and Winnipeg Jet Don Spring rounded out the staff. And the *chef de mission* for the Canadians was none other than Clare's old chum and coaching colleague, Dr. Murray Smith.

The Koreans had come back to the games after their debacle seven years earlier in Spain and were much improved. The Bears only beat them 14-1 this time before facing the Russians. They gave a good account of themselves against a typical Soviet "student" team, comprised of a bunch of older pros who might have been registered at the Academy of Motorcycle Maintenance, or some such institute of higher learning. The Bears actually created more offensive chances than the Soviets but couldn't finish and wound up on the short end of a very tight 4-3 contest. Then they defeated a surprisingly competitive team from the People's Republic of China, which set them up to play Czechoslovakia in the first game of the medal round. The hosts were determined to win the whole shebang on their home turf and so loaded their roster with at least fifteen players from the Czech first division. The wheels came off for the Bears and they suffered a crushing 12-4 defeat to the eventual gold medalists — one of the most lopsided losses in their storied history. They rebounded to beat the Finns 6-2 for the bronze medal.

Given the opposition, the Universiade bronze in 1987 was a bigger achievement than the gold in 1981. And once more, the lessons learned off the ice were equally, if not more, important. Dennis Cranston, who added this hard-won bronze to his 1984 Spengler Cup gold and 1986 University Cup, was now the captain of the Bears. In addition to appreciating the warm reception the fans gave the Canadians, he had the opportunity to touch the life of a young Slovak hockey player. After a qualifying round game, the ten-year-old had shyly sidled up to Cranston and asked him how much his hi-tech Canadian skates cost. The captain's answer left the youngster in tears at the realization he'd never own anything so fine. So the team set the lad up with a new pair of skates and Cranston had the heart-warming pleasure of giving him the news and presenting him with a Golden Bears jersey.

The Bears came back to the nationals in 1987 as favorites to repeat, but as is so often the case, the game has to be played on the ice before the results can be posted. Their upset loss to UQTR that year, on home ice, still holds a bitter taste for Howie Draper. But one of his outstanding memories has nothing to do with the defeat. At the end of a practice early in tournament week, as the team completed a full-ice, high-speed breakout drill, Coach Drake took his customary turn up the ice with the puck, following the last group of players. The drill always ended with the players taking a shot on goal, and Drake skated in slowly on his fifty-eight-year-old legs to take his own shot; this was a fun little ritual he had with the players, all done with a laugh and plenty of friendly trash talking. The coach's hands were still working just the way they had thirty years earlier when the *Denver Clarion* had called him "the punch in the [UBC] attack," and he roofed one on netminder John Krill. When he raised his arms in celebration, his skate caught a rut and he pitched face-first into the goalpost. All the laughter and cheering turned to shocked silence as the coach lay bleeding on the ice from a horrendous cut to the forehead. Bill Moores got to him first, bending over him in concern to ask if he was okay. In response, Drake scrambled to his feet, blood gushing from the wound, and chirped "Yeah! Wasn't that a helluva goal?" For Draper, this episode tells much about the character of the man, his toughness, his intensity and focus on the task at hand, and his irrepressible enthusiasm.

Clare Drake's last two seasons at the University of Alberta were rather anticlimactic compared to most of the twenty-six that had come before. He earned his second Father George Kehoe Award as CIAU coach of the year in 1987-88, the first having come thirteen years earlier when he led the Bears to their 1975 University Cup. But there was to be no such result in '88, as George Kingston defeated Drake for the Hardy Cup in his final season at the Dinosaurs' helm before departing for the NHL. Then, in 1988-89 Drake won his seventeenth and last Hardy Cup on his way to one more appearance at the nationals in Toronto. His final game behind the Golden Bears' bench was another stinging loss to York University, this time in the semi-final. As they had in 1985, the Bears outshot the Yeomen dramatically and were again robbed by goaltender Mark Applewhaite (the tournament MVP, now in his final year), losing in overtime on one of those horrid, bad-angle shots that bounced in off a skate. York then defeated Wilfrid Laurier University for their second consecutive University Cup and third in five years.

Drake came home to Edmonton and spent a couple of months reflecting on twenty-eight Golden Bear seasons stretched over thirty-four years. While he pondered his past and his future, the news came that he would be inducted into the Canadian Sports Hall of Fame along with iconic hockey broadcaster Danny Gallivan, Phil Esposito of the Boston Bruins and '72 Summit Series fame, and alpine skier Gerry Sorenson. His official induction date was also his thirty-eighth wedding anniversary, May 12, 1989. Typically, he told the *Edmonton Journal*'s Mark Spector, "You must recognize all the things that have to be in effect before these awards can happen" and then, in reference to Dolly, his daughters and son-in-law, and all his colleagues and players over the years, he added, "as a coach, you have to have the big support system." Bill Moores, one of the pillars in that system, gave his own take on the honor: "What's happened is he's built a tradition, and that tradition says that you don't do anything less than your best. Then what has happened is his veteran players lead so well that Clare doesn't have to say very much."

It was Drake's love for that very tradition that had him wrestling with the prospect of retirement and yet made it possible for him to finally let go. It wasn't the tough loss at the '89 nationals, but rather an awareness that it was time for him to pack up his 1,030 games as head coach of the Golden Bears, his .695 winning percentage and 697 wins, his seventeen Canada West championships and six University Cups, and move on. Just like his father thirty-three years earlier in Yorkton, Drake knew he needed to make room for somebody else. In a letter to team alumni, he explained how tough it was to leave the U of A, but he told them the "blow is softened for me [because] the change will elevate Bill Moores to the role of head coach and I know he will do a great job . . . and that the traditions and commitments of the team will continue as we all know them." It was not only easier for Drake to step aside knowing the program would be in good hands, he felt it was imperative, for the sake of the very hands into which he was passing the torch. Moores understood the tradition better than anyone and was more than ready to ensure it lived on.

When Drake officially announced his retirement in early July at a U of A news conference, he did it with his trademark humility and lack of fanfare. While there was a healthy turnout of local media, with many university colleagues and alumni also in attendance, Clare kept the occasion low-key, just as he had most everything else he's ever done. He was quiet, even somber, but not overtly emotional as he explained his decision. Part of his statement included the news that he'd been offered a job by Bob Murdoch of the Winnipeg Jets, a two-year contract as an assistant on Murdoch's staff. But for Drake, this was almost an aside, the final particle that tipped the scales in favor of vacating the position he'd defined for more than three decades. The old coach spoke mostly about the U of A tradition, and his strong confidence that his trusted sidekick would maintain it. When lauded for his role in building that tradition, in fact chiseling it into time-proof marble, Drake demurred. "I don't know if it was Clare Drake," he said to Cam Cole of the *Edmonton Journal*, "I'd like to think it was the Golden Bear team, the tradition, that made [young men] want to play here." Cole's rejoinder was "But of course, they are one and the same, aren't they?"

The columnist, who had been fascinated with Drake since his student days of the mid-1970s, echoed Moores's May comments in his heartfelt discourse about how the man influenced his players and set the standards that became the tradition:

> Clare Drake changed people's lives. I have seen it happen; seen wayward rookies who became better human beings because of the experience of playing on Drake's team. I've seen goons go straight, and slackers develop good work habits, and hundreds of kids learn all about discipline and team play and character – by osmosis, almost. After three or four years with Drake, the veterans had it, and they taught it to the kids. And so on, and so on. That's how a tradition of excellence was built on the campus by the river. And that, more than merely a great hockey coach, is what the U of A lost when Drake [announced] his retirement.

One "goon gone straight" – Ted Olson, the fighter-turned-lawyer – paid his own tribute to the retiring legend with another perspective on the tradition. Insightfully, he told Cole: "Over the years, there's a pattern there that's way beyond coincidence. There's a calmness about Golden Bear teams I'm sure comes from him; an ability to deal with pressure and to be aware of your resources and how to produce them."

Cam Cole was off the mark on one count. The U of A indeed lost a great hockey coach when Drake retired, but his "construction work" on the campus by the river was by no means lost as well; it has stood the test of time. In perhaps the greatest testament to all that Drake achieved at Alberta, the tradition he seemingly injected into the very DNA of the place and its people has not just survived but flourished in the decades since his departure. The continuing excellence of Golden Bear hockey and the young men who play it – not to mention the flowering of U of A women's hockey under Drake's former player Howie Draper – is almost without parallel in the ranks of North American sport.

Hockey's greatest professional tradition, the Montreal Canadiens, started their modern ascendancy around the same time Drake's Bears began theirs, in the mid-1950s. They enjoyed several great runs in the sixties and seventies but haven't been a serious Stanley Cup contender since their last championship in 1993. John Wooden won ten NCAA titles from 1964 through 1975 with his invincible UCLA Bruin teams. But after his 1975 retirement the program has struggled, winning only one more national championship (in 1995) in the years since. The Bruins returned to the NCAA final in 2006, when they lost to the University of Florida, but have had many seasons over the past thirty where they labored to contend even for their conference championship.

Choose your sport, choose the amateur or professional ranks, and you're hard pressed to find a record to match that of Alberta's hockey Golden Bears. They're more than a dynasty; they're an institution. Bill Moores picked up right where Drake left off, winning three Canada West titles and a national championship in his five seasons following Drake. His totals, including the two years he covered for Drake, gave him a .717 winning percentage, four Hardy Cups and two University Cups, plus two

CIAU coach of the year awards in his seven campaigns as the boss of the Bears.

A year after Moores departed for Japan in 1994, Rob Daum, who played for Moores and Drake in 1980 and '81, moved behind the bench and, almost inconceivably, managed to raise the bar. In his ten seasons from 1995-96 to 2004-05, Daum was CIS coach of the year twice, and claimed six Hardy Cups and three University Cups. Along the way, he posted a jaw-dropping .792 winning percentage. Daum's successor Eric Thurston, a member of the 1986 National Champions, kept the ball rolling in his rookie year of 2006, winning the U of A's forty-fourth conference championship out of the sixty-nine that Canada's western university teams have sought since the 1930s. Thurston also carried off Alberta's CIS-record twelfth University Cup.

From 1963, when the CIAU held its first national championship, to 2006, the teams of Drake, Moores, Daum and Thurston have qualified for thirty-one out of forty-four national championship tournaments and made fifteen final game appearances, winning twelve times. For five decades, the Alberta Golden Bears have remained at the top of the CIAU/CIS, winning at least two University Cups in each of those decades and contending for the big old silver bowl in almost every season during that span.

This kind of enduring excellence doesn't happen by accident. It's the product of deeply rooted values that have weathered dramatic societal changes over the half-century since Clare Drake arrived in the bustling city on the North Saskatchewan River. Impressive though the winning percentages,

Number 99 with number 1 (in victories among North American college hockey coaches, 1985). Wayne Gretzky congratulates Clare on his record-setting career mark.

"Coming home." Eric Thurston, coach of the Bears' twelfth national championship squad in 2006, describes how it felt to learn the game from Clare Drake.

championship tallies and silverware may be, Drake and those in the hockey community he established are prouder of other, less noticeable achievements. For instance, it's no fluke that since the CIAU/CIS instituted its Academic All Canadian Awards in 1991, Golden Bear hockey players have earned more than 100 selections – the most in the CIS hockey. (By the way, as of 2006 the Bears also lead in All Canadian selections, with forty-nine since their inception in 1971.)

So the Drake tradition has not only produced great teams and great players, but also fine students who then go on to apply the principles they learned from the old hockey professor to their careers and in their communities. Drake himself put it best in his retirement letter to his former players when he said, "Your individual successes as people and as graduates of the university are truly the most important measure of the Golden Bear hockey program." This is indeed the crowning glory of the tradition that Drake established, and while the coach would only count himself as one part of it, Cam Cole's rhetorical question asserts the whole truth – the man and the tradition really are one and the same.

The Golden Bear tradition of excellence on and off the ice – Clare Drake's legacy at the University of Alberta and in the community of players whose lives he touched – is a profoundly important body of work. But it doesn't make him a revolutionary, the seminal influence on Canada's game that men like Ken Hitchcock, Dave King and George Kingston proclaim him to be. To understand that aspect of his career, we must turn our attention back to the NHL where, after thirty-four years as a professional coach, Drake finally arrived.

At Bob Murdoch's invitation, Clare and Dolly Drake moved to Winnipeg in the summer of 1989, renting an apartment that would be their in-season home for the next two years. Murdoch's contract offer meant a lot to Drake for several reasons. Most significantly, it was the first offer to come from pro hockey since the ill-fated Oilers deal of 1975. When Wayne Gretzky congratulated Drake on setting the record for most North American collegiate victories in 1985, his sincere good wishes held an unintended irony. Number 99's letter mentioned the "increasing number of excellent coaches who have left the university ranks to work successfully in the National Hockey League" and commented on how fortunate the U of A was to be able to keep Drake. While both Gretzky's points were accurate – CIAU men like Tom Watt and Bob Boucher (of St. Mary's) had broken the NHL's "brainiac barrier" by then, and the U of A was indeed fortunate to still have Drake – the irony was that though Drake had pioneered the method movement and set its first foot into the entrenched world of pro hockey, he'd been left behind. The U of A's good fortune came to some extent at Drake's expense. When Ed Willes of the *Winnipeg Sun* inquired of the old professor why he hadn't made the jump to pro earlier, he replied simply and honestly, "Basically, no one asked me."

But now Bob Murdoch had asked, and Drake considered the source of the invitation. That was the other reason why the offer carried meaning for its recipient. Murdoch had played his amateur hockey in the mid-1960s for the University of Waterloo Warriors. After graduation he logged two seasons with Father Bauer's National Team, based in Winnipeg, and then was signed as a free agent, along with his National Team buddy Ken Dryden, by the Montreal Canadiens. Murdoch might have been the first CIAU player ever to win a Stanley Cup, as a roster player with the Canadiens in 1971 and then a solid blue line contributor on their 1973 championship team. He played a heady, positional game that served him well through eleven solid seasons in the NHL with Montreal, Los Angeles and the Flames of Atlanta and Calgary. His smarts opened coaching doors and he stepped directly off the ice into an assistant's position on Bob Johnson's staff with the Calgary Flames in 1982-83.

Calgary was a coaching hotbed during the early eighties: "Badger Bob" headed the Flames; the intellectual George Kingston ran the university Dinosaurs and assisted part-time with the NHL club; and the fast-rising Dave King was based there while coaching the twice-reborn National Team. Murdoch soaked up everything he could in this expert environment. He had his own mentor in his boss Johnson and he heard many stories about another influential mentor through Kingston and King. So when he took the head coaching position at Winnipeg in 1989, and met the man Kingston and King respected so much at a May coaching seminar, he jumped at the chance to offer Clare Drake a job.

Drake was excited about the opportunity because he trusted Murdoch's integrity and intelligence, and Murdoch, who was about to gain access to a brilliant hockey mind, says, "I was thrilled when he agreed to work with us." What Murdoch hadn't bargained for was the impact both Clare and Dolly Drake would have on his own life, and on the team community. Ask him about Drake's contribution during those two years and the first words out of Murdoch's mouth are, "What a wonderful man!" Then comes a stirring tribute, first detailing the old coach's hockey expertise, his passion and thorough commitment to excellence, and his innovations – key introductions like the controlled change (that Drake adapted from the Russians for Golden Bear use in the early seventies); an aggressive penalty killing system; and strict use of a stopwatch to time shifts, holding players accountable for regulating their ice time to forty-five second bursts.

But soon Murdoch expands to broader, more human issues. For all that Drake did for the Jets, says Murdoch, "He helped me more as a person. A number of people affected my life; he was one of them, so was Bob Johnson." Murdoch is referring to the example Drake has set through the values he lives by and the relationships he's built with his fellow coaches, his players, his wife and his children. And speaking of Drake's spouse, Murdoch's wife Bev chips in that Dolly Drake "taught me most of what I know about hockey." This included not just the game as it unfolded on the ice – Bev was new to hockey when she married Bob – but how to help her husband deal with the heavy pressure of being an NHL coach.

Dennis McDonald, the former technical director of the CAHA who helped start the NCCP, weighs in on the same subject. He was the Jets' assistant general manager in '89, and cites the important role Clare and Dolly both played in building a sense of community among management, the coaches, the players and their wives and families. "They included people," says McDonald. "They made everyone feel welcome and like they belonged."

For Murdoch, it also counted a lot that Drake showed such strong allegiance as he made the difficult transition from legendary head honcho at the U of A to assisting a younger and less experienced boss in Winnipeg: "I never felt he came to Winnipeg as a stepping stone toward an NHL head coaching position. Clare accepted his role with us very respectfully and was extremely loyal to everyone in the organization."

And finally, Murdoch remarks on a Drake trait that countless others have noted over the years, one that provides a balance so sadly lacking in so many other professional coaches: "I knew from George Kingston about Clare's ritual at Alberta where, on Thursday, after a week of practice and just before the weekend games, he'd say to his assistants, 'The hay's in the barn, let's go and have a little nip together.' Well, at Winnipeg we'd sort of say the same thing when the schedule allowed for it. He was a steadying

"Sense of community." (Drake, standing, far right), Bob Murdoch (squatting in front of Drake), Alpo Suhonen (squatting, second from left) and their close-knit, young Winnipeg Jets squad of 1989-90.

influence."

Most coaches who have ever iced a team against Drake, or shared the bench with him, or schmoozed with him at an NCCP clinic, have been invited for a post-game or post-seminar libation. Drake's favorite tipple is light rum and Coke (now the diet variety as he continues to work on his septuagenarian form), and he's poured literally thousands of them for friends and acquaintances over the years as he's hosted or participated in what he calls "board meetings," where hockey strategies and stories provide the fodder for hours of amicable discussion.

This is the strange contradiction in this man who's been characterized by his wife as a bit of a loner, but who loves the fraternal aspects of the game. Drake, for all his contributions through the NCCP, found no better forum for the maven side of his personality than his board meetings. His fondness for socializing also included his teams, and his players appreciated that, strict disciplinarian though he was at the rink, he encouraged them to have fun off the ice, especially as a team unit. He was a great believer in parties as powerful team-building mechanisms; that's why he and Dolly hosted or attended so many of them over the years. And while these parties were by no means dry, alcohol was never their central feature. Rather, they were constructed around old-fashioned kinds of fun, stuff that university students did in the 1950s – singing old songs, staging goofy skits – but that in Golden Bear culture lived on

"The hay's in the barn." George Kingston (left), Drake and Bob Murdoch (right), reunited at the Nagano Winter Olympics, 1998 (Drake was there as mentor coach to the Canadian Women's Team).

decade after decade thanks to the strong team traditions Drake and his veterans maintained.

This same culture extended to road trips. Rick Carriere, a big, tough defenceman during the mid-eighties, was one of many team captains who can remember being dragooned by Drake into making up song sheets and organizing guitar accompaniment for the long bus rides to Saskatoon. Of course, there were always a couple of cases of beer for the homeward leg of the journey, and that always sat fine with the coach as long as moderation governed consumption. Drake had few rules for his teams. He preferred "guidelines" (common understandings around behavior that afford more flexibility than rules), and his guidelines emphasized values like respect and personal responsibility. He expected his veterans to model these values in the classroom and the community, as well as in the dressing room and on the ice, and by and large over the years, this system succeeded in keeping many hundreds of young men out of trouble. This was also the healthy by-product of a team environment where fun, enjoyment and camaraderie were explicitly named as team values.

Chris Helland, the All Canadian whose quote on the 1981 Korean disaster in Spain ended up in *Sports Illustrated*, recalls one of his favorite Drake moments from a time years after both men had left

The Pioneers' Panel, NCCP, Toronto, 2006. (From left, Drake, Tom Watt and George Kingston.)

the Bears. Helland hosted a pre-nuptial gathering for his younger brother Jeff, also a Bear alumnus and stalwart on the 1986 University Cup Champions, at his place near Sundre, Alberta, just a stone's throw from the eastern slopes of the Rocky Mountains.

By then in his seventies, Drake attended and, as is his wont, was the life of a party that ran well into the night, nourished somewhat by a few beverages but more by great fellowship and a lot of hearty singing around the campfire. As the guitarists in the group began to tire, Drake whipped out his kazoo and kept the music going. The guys, almost all of them ex-Bears, were touched by the authenticity and vulnerability shown by their sometimes-stern old coach, and in equal parts impressed by his ability to carry a tune. The *pièce de résistance* came the next morning, when Helland got up early to make breakfast for the boys. As he worked in the quiet kitchen, all of a sudden Drake appeared at his side to help mix the pancake batter. Before long, the old coach had Frank Sinatra booming on the stereo (he has an abiding love for traditional swing, jazz and blues), and he and Helland belted out the lyrics along with the Chairman of the Board while they got the flapjacks on the grill and the rest of the gang wandered in for breakfast. Helland treasures the comradeship that these men, by then mostly in their forties, experienced that night and morning. He lays most of it at Drake's feet, not just for having brought them together as Golden Bears in the first place, but for having taught them the enduring importance of what they were sharing as members of a community years later in the western foothills of Alberta.

Clare Drake's balanced commitment to these values is the steadying influence Bob Murdoch talks about, and it has sustained his zest for life over the years, whether he's teambuilding or just enjoying the company of old friends. Drake's brilliance as a hockey strategist, innovator and maker of teams was enhanced to the tenth power because of his unique persona, the one that in the same instance allowed him to be occasionally distant from his players and yet forge such strong bonds with them, the one that combined the maven-connector-salesman archetypes that Malcom Gladwell defined as the agents of social change, the one that caused Bob Murdoch to call him a wonderful man.

There were more practical and immediate consequences to Murdoch's decision to bring the maven to Winnipeg. With the help of Drake and Alpo Suhonen, the Finnish master coach who would later become the first European to hold an NHL head coaching job, Murdoch turned the Jets' fortunes around in a single season. In 1988-89 they'd finished in fifth and last place in what was then the Smythe Division, which also included Edmonton, Calgary, Los Angeles and Vancouver. Their record was 26-42-12. But the next year Murdoch, Drake and Suhonen showed up to engineer a complete about-face for the Jets, making the most out of an exceptional defence – featuring standouts like Randy Carlyle, Phil Housley, Dave Ellett, Moe Mantha and Teppo Numminen – to raise them to a third-place division finish and an improved 37-32-11 record. The twenty-one-point jump was enough to earn Murdoch the Jack Adams Award for NHL coach of the year, an honor he adamantly credits also to Drake and Suhonen. They capped the season with an outstanding seven-game playoff series against the eventual Stanley Cup Champion Edmonton Oilers, who pulled off one of the greatest comebacks in their history to eliminate the pesky Jets.

However, the good times weren't to last in Winnipeg. The next season, 1990-91, general manager Mike Smith attempted to boost the Jets' offensive output and raided the defence for trade bait in his quest to acquire better forwards. The trades left the team splintered and ineffective and they stumbled back to last place in the Smythe Division and a dismal 20-43-11 record. As George Kingston points out, winning the Jack Adams Award carries a special cachet that can almost guarantee job loss for its recipient. Murdoch wasn't immune to the "Adams syndrome" – many coaches have contracted this debilitating disease (including Red Berenson, Tom Watt, Ted Nolan, Pat Burns, Bob Francis and Bill Barber, all of whom were fired two seasons or less after having won the Adams) – and he and his staff were dismissed at the end of the '90-91 season.

The Drakes went back home to Edmonton, and this time Clare, now sixty-two, figured full retirement was his only option. He'd enjoyed the two years with the Jets immensely (he has especially fond memories of the devoted Winnipeg fans, who bade a sad farewell to their team only five years later) but the numbers – his age and the long years spent in university hockey – added up to no new offers of full-time NHL positions. The phone kept ringing, however, with all kinds of opportunities to stay connected to the game he loves. Invitations to present at NCCP national seminars and at other clinics and conferences for coaches at all levels just kept coming in.

And there was another NHL call, too, in 1992. George Kingston and the fledgling San Jose Sharks were in their second year together, and as their inaugural head coach he was looking for extra help in

"The boutique expert." At seventy-seven (summer 2006), Clare was still teaching, presenting and sharing, more often than not on powerplay and penalty killing, specialties he's become renowned for within his profession.

whipping this recently assembled crew into a competitive team. Kingston had snapped up Bob Murdoch after his firing and made him associate coach, and in season two of his expansion odyssey he added Drake to his staff, giving him the title of "special assignments coach." Effectively, Kingston invented a new role for his old mentor; at Kingston's behest, Clare Drake became one of the game's first consultants.

Drake maintained his home base in Edmonton, but spent training camp with the Sharks and then flew to San Jose or met the team on the road roughly once a month through the season, for a few games or practices at a time. His job was primarily to help develop individual players, identifying the parts of their game that needed work and making suggestions, usually directly to the players themselves, about how they could improve their performance. Kingston and Murdoch saw him as an invaluable resource, and as Kingston says, he "wanted this man's mind available to the players." The coaches themselves also took advantage of Drake's always-percolating brain. Kingston puts it in his own philosophical way: "We needed Clare to come in and look at the forest occasionally, when we were caught up in the trees, or sometimes if we couldn't see past the forest, he would focus in on the trees for us."

By the time he signed on with San Jose, Kingston had been in and around the NHL for long enough to know that the five-year plan he built when he took the job wasn't likely to see fruition. And sure enough, after the 1992-93 season, he, Murdoch, Drake and the rest of his staff went the way of all expansion coaches… out the door. But Drake's one-season fling with San Jose as a pioneer consulting coach started him on a second career, one that's kept him active and still influencing the game he loves late into his seventies.

It should come as no surprise that the maven-connector-salesman has enjoyed the same success in this second career that he did in his first. The respect and status he holds within the coaching fraternity continued to grow because of new adherents that kept joining the movement, many of whom reached the upper levels of their profession after Drake's "retirement." One such is Tom Renney, who began calling on Drake for help when he was coaching the Kamloops Blazers of the Western Hockey League. Renney picked the master's mind on crucial tactical issues such as penalty killing and cites Drake's savvy as a factor in the Blazers' 1992 Memorial Cup championship. With that feather in his cap, Renney moved up to take over Canada's National Team from Dave King, and went back to the well for more hockey sustenance.

He asked Drake to serve as an ongoing mentor for him and his staff, and so the latter would travel to Calgary, where the Nats were based, to observe practices, answer questions and offer advice. Renney says it was "like opening up an encyclopedia" and in 1994, when he coached Canada's last amateur Olympic Team to their shining silver medal in Norway (earned in a shootout loss to the Swedes in the final), he used Drake extensively in preparing the squad for the Olympic tournament. "He would give us pages and pages of notes," recalls Renney, "and he taught us good work habits and how to pay attention to detail. He had a lot to do with our success in Lillehammer." Among the tactical benefits Drake brought to that courageous, talented group led by Paul Kariya was the ability to generate intense pressure on the attack, and to support that with a sound defensive system that would help them regain the puck when they'd lost possession. Also, notes Renney, Drake's concept of team was "second to none" and he helped them build "a team culture that could withstand any kind of adversity." Renney still considers the 1994 Olympics to be one of the highlights of his life and is grateful to the man he calls "a pretty special guy."

Proponent of "rolling four" and "Psychology Today's 'coach of the year'" for 2006. Tom Renney, head coach, New York Rangers, 2006.

The remarkable thing about the Drake-Renney connection is that the younger coach never played for his mentor, nor did he work as his assistant, nor even ice a team against him. At least one generation removed from Drake, Renney got to know him mainly through the NCCP's summer coaching seminars. He was smart enough to simply walk up to the old professor after his presentations and ask him questions. He found, as so many others have, that Drake was humble, affable and willing to take all the time necessary to discuss any topic of Renney's interest. Thus grew a relationship that has survived more than fifteen years, and that has succored Renney in his professional journey to a revitalized NHL career with the New York Rangers.

When Tom Renney left the National Team in 1996 for his first foray into the NHL as head coach of the Vancouver Canucks, Andy Murray took over his position in Calgary. Drake's former Spengler Cup assistant knew a good thing when he saw it and continued to use Drake in much the same fashion as Renney had. Hockey Canada had also perceived value in this consulting role and had hired Drake to work as mentor coach with the National Women's Team the year before.

He stayed with the women's program through the 1998 Olympics, supporting their gold medal efforts at the 1995 Pacific Rim Tournament, the 1996 Three Nations' Cup and the 1997 world championships. He also accompanied them to Nagano for their Olympic silver in 1998 – his seventieth year. Fittingly, this man who'd started coaching in the 1950s and been an agent of change ever since, was enthusiastic about one of the biggest new developments to arise in his half century in the game – the dramatic growth of women's hockey. Glynis Peters, the manager of the national women's program in 1995, told Drake in a thank you letter following the Pacific Rim Tournament that while the coaching staff valued his technical assistance, she wanted to specially acknowledge his "very sincere acceptance of the game of female hockey on its merits and [his] complete commitment to the event and the team."

As Drake continued to consult through the nineties and into the new millennium, he also continued to be in demand at NCCP seminars and other clinics staged by various provincial hockey associations and amateur organizations. And as he kept on participating and contributing, his influence continued to spread. His technical wizardry remains just as sharp as ever, partly because he's never stopped learning himself. At every seminar or conference where he presented, he also made sure to attend as many other presentations on the agenda as he could. Ken Hitchcock recounts his amazement at seeing Drake at clinics in his mid-seventies, sitting near the front, paying avid attention and taking copious notes as someone decades his junior spoke to a topic on which Drake had long been considered an expert: "There's a certain stage you reach in your coaching career where you don't think there's a lot new comin' on, but then you spend a weekend with this guy and you realize you're on a constant learning curve." And Bill Moores shares an "I-should-have-known-better" laugh as he talks about his old friend's attendance at the NCCP national seminar in Toronto in July 2006. Drake, George Kingston and Tom Watt had been invited by the NCCP to sit on a "Pioneers' Panel" and were also honored with a dinner. Moores asked Drake if he'd been able to get to any of the other presentations and chuckles as he reports Drake's almost indignant response: "Of course, Bill, I went to all of them." "That's Clare," Moores says, "Never miss a chance to learn something new."

Drake kept his hand, and his head, in the game simply because of his passion for it. But his ongoing contributions at coaching seminars of all types meant the consulting work kept coming in. In the late nineties, Hitchcock hired Drake to evaluate players for improvement purposes at his Dallas Stars

These people really like each other! Clare and Dolly and family, 2005. (From left, daughter Jami, Clare, Dolly, son-in-law Ron, daughter Debbie, grandson Mike, granddaughter Jacqueline and grandson Matthew [inset].)

training camps and to pre-scout the opposition during his five consecutive playoff appearances with Dallas. He says of the Stars' 1999 championship drive, "We pretty much ran on his information. Here we're battling and clawing for the Stanley Cup and we're counting on Clare." Hitchcock's winning formula prompted others to follow suit.

Mike Johnston, co-author with Ryan Walter of *Simply the Best*, knew Drake from his coaching days in the early eighties at Camrose Lutheran College (now the U of A – Augustana Campus) just an hour outside of Edmonton. Like his buddy Hitchcock, Johnston would drive to the arena at U of A to watch Drake's practices; he also soaked up everything he could learn from him at seminars. After spending most of the nineties as assistant and then head coach of the National Team, Johnston joined Marc Crawford with the Vancouver Canucks and remained his associate coach as the latter hired on with Los Angeles in 2006. When the Canucks woeful penalty killing was hurting them during the 2000-01 season, Johnston suggested to his boss they bring in the man whom he calls "the best guy in North America on the PK." Johnston and Crawford met with Drake in September 2001 to learn his penalty-killing system and, armed with his diagrams and their notes on his teachings, retooled the Canucks PK unit. Did Drake's help make a difference? Johnston says the Canucks' penalty killing went from near the bottom of the league in 2000 to third overall by the 2003-04 season.

Drake has become a boutique expert on special teams, both penalty killing and powerplay, in the

"Jut-jawed intensity" and gratitude to "the grandfather." Mike Babcock, head coach, Detroit Red Wings, 2006.

minds of many professional coaches. In almost any conversation with men like Perry Pearn, Wayne Fleming or Andy Murray, sooner or later they'll mention that "great presentation Clare did" on penalty killing or powerplay. And they all say they've still got the notes on it and pull them out every year. Crawford and Johnston kept reusing Drake's material with the Canucks and will assuredly do so with the Kings. So too, does Hitchcock with the Blue Jackets and Renney with the Rangers. But the old professor also remains relevant on a broader range of hockey strategies and tactics. Hitchcock and Fleming met with Drake prior to the 2002 Olympics in Salt Lake City, gleaning his wisdom from his 1980 Lake Placid experience and reviewing some of his theories on puck movement and defensive zone coverage as they prepared for their spellbinding run to the gold.

Whether consulting directly with national and NHL teams, or through his ongoing contributions to the NCCP, Clare Drake's keen mind and humble, open personality have continued to pervade hockey at all levels of the game. In 2006, as he advances toward his eightieth birthday, he's still going strong, still true to the "guidelines" he's worked and played by over the decades, still leaving his fingerprints all over the place. His drive to teach, to share, for continuous improvement, rolls on unabated and so, in collaboration with his old buddy Murray Smith, he did some consulting for the Kelowna Rockets of the Western Hockey League during the 2005-06 season. Imagine this seventy-eight-year-old riding the team bus from Vancouver back to Kelowna, surrounded by young men sixty years his junior, as he reported to their coaches on his evaluations. The youthful context didn't phase him at all. In early 2007, Drake was once again hanging out with youngsters, serving as mentor coach for Alberta's under-seventeen team at the Canada Winter Games in Whitehorse. When teased about the incredible age gap, he ripostes with a favorite old chestnut: "Age is about mind over matter, and if you don't mind, it doesn't matter!"

Drake is also delighted to support his treasured Golden Bears – cut him and to this day he bleeds green and gold – and their latest head coach. He advised Eric Thurston, his former player, as the Bears charged to their twelfth University Cup in 2006, and continued to help during the 2006-07 season. And he spoke with his old friend and protégé Bill Moores frequently during the Edmonton Oilers' gripping 2006 playoff run, respectfully, even diffidently, offering up the occasional strategic observation or suggestion for assistant coach Moores's welcoming ears.

Finally, in Drake's mind, and perhaps that of another very special client, he continues to work the best consulting gig he's ever had. One of his grandsons, Mike Gabinet, is a twenty-five-year-old defenceman playing for the Idaho Steelheads of the East Coast Hockey League in 2006-07. Mike is the son of Clare and Dolly's oldest daughter Debbie and her husband Ron. Drafted by Andy Murray's L.A. Kings in 2001, Gabinet completed his four years at the University of Nebraska-Omaha and played pro in Finland during the NHL lockout season before returning to North America. Drake has been closely involved in Mike's life – as he has been in the lives of Mike's older sister Jacqueline and his teenaged cousin Matthew, son of the Drakes' younger daughter Jami – since he was a tyke.

Gabinet has fond memories of Clare taking him to the rink on campus early on weekday mornings before school, where the two would skate together and the grandfather would help the kid with his fundamentals. His reminiscences also include post-game visits in the Golden Bears dressing room, where he got to shake hands with the players who were his boyhood heroes. Now, Gabinet is fashioning his own yeoman career as a pro, with the warm, caring support of one of the game's greatest coaches who just happens to be his "Gramps." "I call him all the time, whenever I have a problem, whenever I have a question, when I need advice on how to approach my coach, or talk to a teammate. He's always got time for me," says Gabinet, "he's always positive, he's always got a good read on what I should be doing."

For Mike Gabinet, "Gramps" would be great even if he weren't a Canadian hockey revolutionary. He loves being part of the close-knit family headed by Clare and Dolly; he loves the times they have together at family dinners, and on family vacations, as they share in the same quality of laughter and interesting conversation that characterize Drake's "board meetings."

As Wayne Fleming likes to point out, Drake's greatest body of work lies in the people he's taught, inspired and supported; they're the ones who have worked the major changes in Canadian hockey. Men like Kingston, Moores, Pearn, King, Renney, Murray, Fleming, Johnston and Hitchcock – the first a co-founder of Canada's university "method movement," the others, ongoing contributors to its accumulated knowledge and values – have set their own standards and exerted their own influence to keep Canada, and the elite league it used to "own," growing in the game apace with the hockey world's other practitioners.

The latest, but probably not the last, disciple to make his mark is Mike Babcock, an ascending NHL coaching star of the new millennium. Babcock is another member of the new breed, a graduate of the McGill University hockey program who also put in a year with Dave King's Saskatchewan Huskies. He didn't make it to The Show as a player and so set out to reach it as a coach. One of his first jobs was with Red Deer College of the Alberta Colleges Athletic conference, where he competed against Perry

Pearn's NAIT Ookpiks and got overwhelmed by the Golden Bears in pre-season exhibition games. He moved between head coaching jobs with Moose Jaw and Spokane of the Western Hockey League and, sandwiched between them, took one year (1993-94) to guide the University of Lethbridge Pronghorns to their sole CIAU national championship. His six-year run at the helm of the Spokane Chiefs twice garnered him the WHL's coach of the year award and earned him the opportunity to coach Canada's National Junior Team to gold at the 1997 tournament in Switzerland.

Thereafter, two successful seasons with Cincinnati in the American Hockey League propelled him to the big time with Anaheim, where he instantly drew the spotlight by taking the Ducks to the 2003 Stanley Cup final as a rookie head coach. While the Ducks failed to meet expectations the following season, Babcock and Tom Renney assisted Joel Quenneville with Canada's team at the 2004 world hockey championships in Prague, winning gold. During the 2004-05 lockout Babcock moved to take over the coveted head coaching job of the Detroit Red Wings.

Mike Babcock has a reputation for his commitment to team discipline, his studied approach to the game and a jut-jawed intensity that vibrates right through the phone as he voices his thoughts. He is voluble and yet somehow pointed as he expounds on Clare Drake, a lot of his statements punctuated by exclamation marks. He starts like others, by comparing Drake to John Wooden – "U of A hockey is all about principles, work ethic, enthusiasm!" – and builds from there. He talks about the man's class, about the footsteps Drake laid out for others to follow as he studied and developed the game and, like Ken Hitchcock, Babcock calls him "the grandfather." It's as if all these guys got together and agreed on a common vocabulary for describing Drake, but you get the idea they've talked about him at their seminars and conferences, and as they've expressed their mutual gratitude for his legacy the words have been repeated and taken hold.

Babcock's a guy who doesn't pull his punches, and he makes no exceptions for this topic. Now that he's really on a roll, he hits his listener with a declaration that has bells on it. "The reason I'm a head coach in the NHL is because of Clare Drake." How can this be, you wonder? Babcock's only direct exposure to Drake was on the losing end of an exhibition game when he was at Red Deer College. He didn't play for him, wasn't one of his assistants, didn't collaborate on any international teams with him; he's of a much younger generation and his career was barely underway as Drake's came to an end.

But Mike Babcock isn't done yet. By way of explanation, he moves on to another comparison, this time with Scotty Bowman. "Scotty Bowman's the greatest coach in hockey… well, Clare Drake's gotta be right there." Once he's established the parallel, Babcock starts to explain the differences between the two masters. First, there's the profile: Bowman's is huge, known to the most casual fan of the game; Drake's is much lower because of where he spent his career but, as Babcock says, the people inside the profession sure know what's he done. And next comes the truly telling distinction. Babcock talks about how much Bowman has shared with him, but says that's because, as coach of the Detroit Red Wings, he's been able to develop a relationship with the all-time Stanley Cup winner. With Clare Drake, explains Babcock, access to the same quality of precious knowledge is available to "any minor hockey coach who wants to pick up the phone and call him."

And there Mike Babcock has it… in a nutshell. That's how this man – who built his own hockey laboratory at the University of Alberta, who started the method movement among fellow university coaches to study and grow the game, who helped create and build Canada's National Coaching Certification Program, who worked tirelessly not just to help himself but all coaches improve continuously, whose fingerprints are all over the game – ended up starting a virus that spread through hockey to invade and mutate even that most change-resistant bastion, the NHL.

As we see from Babcock's experience, you didn't have to know the man personally to benefit from his wisdom. You didn't have to be one of his former players, or an assistant coach or even an opposing coach. Like Ken Hitchcock and Tom Renney and so many others have, you could just call him, or walk up to him at an NCCP seminar and ask him whatever you wanted, and he'd take all the time in the world to talk to you, to trade stories and information, to share notes and papers and diagrams.

Ken Dryden adds his own weighty imprimatur to Babcock's testimonial. The former National Teamer, Summit Series hero, Stanley Cup winner and lawyer-turned-politician has also served as a federal cabinet minister. In June 2006 he took time out from the busy-ness of his campaign for the leadership of the federal Liberal Party to talk about Clare Drake, a man who by his own admission he doesn't really know. While Dryden has met Drake briefly at the odd NCCP seminar, he claims no relationship with him, and so offers a most objective assessment of the old coach's contribution to the Canadian game. In another of his past roles, as president of the Toronto Maple Leafs, Dryden was one of the leaders of the Open Ice Summit, a three-day conference held in Toronto in August 1999. Using TV and web technology, this grand event provided an interactive opportunity for Canadians from all across the land to voice their opinions, in concert with experts like Dryden, Wayne Gretzky, Bob Gainey, Scotty Bowman and Hockey Canada president Bob Nicholson, on the state of hockey in our nation. Dryden says that during those three days he and his colleagues interviewed or listened to hundreds of people talk about the roots of our game, its current status, and how it should grow in the future. As the dialogue progressed and the input mounted, three names kept coming up, over and over again. Dryden explains, in his quiet, pensive way, that it became obvious these were "the mentors . . . the reference points of Canadian hockey, men who'd laid the foundations." Then he reveals the names . . . George Kingston, Dave King and Clare Drake. We already know whom Kingston and King identify as the inspiration for their careers and the stimulus for much of their own hockey learning. They stand, along with so many other giants in their profession, pointing back at the grandfather, the first mentor.

His measured tones in stark contrast to Babcock's impassioned speech, Dryden makes the same point as the Red Wings' coach: "For many years, when people wanted additional answers for their game, in their minds there would be those three people, and almost anybody could connect with them." Warming to his theme, Dryden makes one of those profound hockey statements for which he's famous: "Coaches are coaches. The atom coach in Shaunavon, Saskatchewan, and Scotty Bowman inhabit the same world. Clare Drake always knew that; he knew he inhabited that same world." As Dryden concludes, his words take on a semi-religious tenor, only fitting given how so many of us feel about our beloved game. His words should be the final ones on Clare Drake, because he pays him the ultimate compliment, especially to a man who's always cared more about what can be accomplished than who gets the credit. Ken Dryden sums up Clare Drake's body of work as "a quiet act of faith…the achievement of helping so many, of supporting anyone who believes in improvement and wants things to be different."

CHAPTER SEVEN

Clare Drake on Coaching

Failures in sport are the things that educate us. Winning is the healthy outcome of the ongoing process of hard work and character development.
Clare Drake

Introduction

It would be a mistake to tell the story of Clare Drake's contribution to our great game of hockey without hearing from the man himself. This chapter barely scratches the surface of his remarkable body of knowledge, but it does offer some of the Coach's thoughts in his own words. Gleaned from the collection of his personal notes, seminar presentations and articles written for various publications, what follows are some of Coach Drake's views on the philosophical aspects of coaching. He has much else to say on other, more technical aspects of hockey (some of which can be found in Hockey Canada's coaching manuals, and a lot of which we hope will appear in a future publication) but we've chosen here to stay with ideas for broader application. We've organized this section into four parts:
 1. On Being a Coach.
 2. Building a Positive Team Environment.
 3. Helping Your Athletes Achieve Their Potential.
 4. Practice – The Agony of Repetition.

In keeping with Clare's lifelong mission to help coaches improve, these sections are aimed primarily at the developing coach, but will hopefully be of interest to all who coach in sports or other pursuits.

"The man's fingerprints are all over the game."

Coach Drake's Introduction

I'm excited and challenged by the opportunity to record for posterity some of my coaching philosophies and strategies. I believe that many of the conclusions I've reached will prove interesting to a wide range of readers.

My hope is that people interested in coaching and teaching, with a primary emphasis on hockey, will find something of value here. I also strongly believe there are some generic principles of coaching that apply not only to other team sports, but also to business and other walks of life that rely on a team approach to achieve success. I know in my own personal development as a teacher and coach, I often made it a point to study ideas and concepts from other sports and disciplines.

I believe that many of the principles I've included below apply to coaches and players at all levels – from beginners with little or no experience right through to the most experienced elite players and coaches. I've always believed that the beginning coach with a sincere interest in the game should not feel intimidated by all the technical information out there. Just start slowly, don't try to do too much and build your knowledge and experience gradually.

1– On Being a Coach

Beliefs and values

I believe that if you're going to be a coach, you need to develop a philosophy of coaching based on your beliefs and values. We often don't spend enough time thinking about our beliefs and values and organizing them into a framework that could become our philosophical approach to coaching. Any discussion about building your coaching philosophy should begin with beliefs and values.

I use the term "belief" quite often so I would like to make it clear exactly what it represents to me. A *belief* that you hold lets you *trust* something; it gives you a conviction that something is right, a feeling of certainty. But it's important to remember that a *belief is not a truth*, although it may become a truth after lots of verification. A *value* is a standard or principle that is regarded as desirable or worthwhile (i.e., honesty).

All of our beliefs represent limits (not truths). We examine them, we test them and then we may find ways to go beyond them and set new limits. As we mature and gain new experiences, we often find ourselves questioning our earlier belief systems and values. This is as it should be! It sets the stage for the potential to change. Hopefully, when and if change is necessary, it will be positive.

Our beliefs and values do not appear out of thin air. They are created and directed by ourselves (they are *our* responsibility) from the things we have accepted from our environment and from others whom we respect. They come from three major sources:

1. The primary source for most of us is our parents and family. They demonstrate and teach values in what to say and do. The parents' responsibility is to provide a set of rational expectations (values) for their children.

2. The second source is the peer group an individual wants to be part of, and in so joining, accepts the values of that group. Large or small, one person or many, these reference groups change throughout a person's lifespan, affected by age and environment.

3. The third source is that of personal experience, things we go through or observe happening to others. We come to view certain values as core and integrate some of them into our own set of values.

Our beliefs and values become the guiding principles that provide meaning and direction to our lives. They determine our actions – the ways we behave as we try to do the right thing at the right time. Our beliefs and our values are our own conscious choice. We can choose values that are positively supportive or negatively limiting.

As a coach, one of my major beliefs is that the example I set by my actions is the most powerful and positive influence I have. As coaches we are role models for our athletes. Our treatment of them, our planning, our reaction to adversity, to victory or defeat, will to a large measure be copied by our athletes. As coaches we enjoy a privileged position in the lives of our athletes. We have an entry point into the lives of our players that offers the potential to affect them profoundly. Therefore we have an obligation to use our influence in a positive, ethical manner.

We know that sport is rich with learning about oneself and one's values, but it's also characterized by the pursuit of performance goals, a drive for excellence and personal achievement. All of these are good things. However, we have to be aware that sometimes the values related to the development of the athlete as a whole person can get lost under the pressure to win at any cost. In minor hockey, the pressure usually comes from parents or athletic organizations. In professional hockey it comes from ownership, management, media and fans. So the reality of coaching is that we must strive for balance, and sometimes we may have to adjust our approach to problems, but we must try never to compromise the ethical values we believe in.

Coaching is a combination of intuitive art (motivation, communication, etc.) and factual science (technical skills, tactics, etc.); therefore, a coach must prepare as completely as possible in both areas. As you develop your expertise in these two areas, you will increasingly become more able to give your athletes a rare gift – the opportunity to grow and develop their skills relative to their interests, abilities and potential. Ideally then, as a coach you should work toward becoming:

a) a skills teacher – developing skill, tactics and strategies related to your sport; and

b) a values teacher – helping athletes develop respect for themselves and others.

Why coach?

As part of developing your own personal philosophy of coaching, you should ask yourself why you would like to become a coach. There are many positive, valid reasons to make this choice, and some reasons that may not be so positive. In North America most coaching and administration at all levels of sport is carried out by lay volunteers, almost all of whom are sincere, well meaning and dedicated (usually parents of the young athletes involved). Some reasons for coaching you may identify with: you enjoy providing leadership to others; you enjoy the potential of passing on life skills and values to others; you have a strong interest (purpose, passion) in a particular sport; you enjoy seeing skill and behavioral development in athletes; you like to be part of a group committed to common goals; you enjoy working in a positive, caring teaching environment; or, you like the idea of "putting something back" into a game that was good to you.

You should not be involved in coaching young people if you are doing it solely for external rewards (financial, personal recognition) or if you feel a need to exercise authority over people. A personal comment on the issue of financial reward for the coach working with amateur players: I believe it is a positive step forward in coaching development that many associations and sports clubs are hiring paid professionals to oversee the *mentoring and development* of coaches in their organization. This can provide consistency and guidance for developing coaches. The idea of a mentoring network for less experienced coaches is an idea whose time has come and I believe will prove to be a very positive development for hockey in general. This is very common in Europe and is one reason the skill level of European players progresses quite quickly.

You should not only examine your own motives for coaching, you should also understand why players play. Some common reasons:

Younger players (5 – 10)
It is an exciting and fun game.
I like to learn new things.
It feels good to do something well.
It makes my parents proud of me.
I like to be with my friends and make new friends.

Older players (11 – 15)
It is an exciting and fun game.
I like to learn new and improve old skills.
I want to be good at sports.
I like to be with friends.
I like to compete against my peers.
I like to earn recognition from my peers.

Whatever your motivation for coaching, here are some basic understandings you should start with. All those involved in team sports – coaches, support personnel and players – are unique individuals with diverse background experiences. This diversity affects coaching and playing styles, beliefs and values. Coaches have to reach agreement on the philosophical, technical and tactical approaches they want to implement. Your main philosophical goal is to unite a group of individuals, helping them coalesce into a strong team with a personal commitment to a common purpose.

Six key traits of successful coaches

1. They have solid leadership qualities.
2. They plan and organize very well.
3. They are excellent communicators and teachers. (They develop a deep knowledge of the game. They provide positive correction and guidance. Their feedback is consistent, relevant and understandable.)
4. They develop good motivational techniques.
5. They create a positive, disciplined learning environment.
6. They have a sincere interest in their players as individual people.

All of these traits must work in combination with each other to be effective. Individually, their importance depends on the age level, the situation and the ability level of the athletes.

The coach as leader

A special word on leadership, the first trait on the list of six: for your team (or organization) to become and remain successful it must develop effective leaders. The challenge of leadership is to help others care about who they are and what they do. There are no set formulas. Leadership is an unselfish, ongoing journey of personal discovery and learning. Leadership begins at the top and then spreads. Coaches show good leadership by encouraging leaders to grow from within the team. They also delegate meaningful responsibility for their assistants, allowing them to run drills, explain a tactic or simply "change the voice" the team hears. Here are some more characteristics of good leadership:

- The coach-leader must be able to define a "vision" for the team and then gradually encourage input from players so they share "ownership" for that vision. The team vision becomes the baseline reference for keeping the team "on course."
- The coach-leader is a democratic thinker and appreciates the freshness of new ideas.

- Coach-leaders are not extreme in personality, but model good balance.
- Coach-leaders have a high degree of physical, mental and spiritual energy.
- They can show compassion, empathy and are genuinely interested in people.
- They possess a shared sense of humor (free of ridicule or sarcasm).
- They are philosophical, with clearly expressed values and beliefs; yet they have the ability to face reality and can adjust to it without compromising beliefs and values.
- They are considerate, honest and fair with people. This behavior in turn generates respect from coaching colleagues, players and parents.
- Coach-leaders realize that every one has something to offer and are ready to work with all kinds of people. They understand that we all have our weaknesses, and know the wisdom of the old saying: "You often have to close one eye to make a friend. And then sometimes you have to close both eyes to keep a friend."

Building your own coaching philosophy

We've discussed beliefs and values, and where they come from, and looked at some key traits of successful coaches. Now you should be ready to identify, using your own words, a coaching philosophy that you (and your coaching staff) can be comfortable with. Following are some examples of beliefs and behaviors that can comprise a coaching philosophy, but it's up to you to amend these and put your own personal stamp on them. Your coaching philosophy might include:

- Showing a genuine interest in the athlete as an individual person, apart from your expectations and concerns for he or she as an athlete.
- Being more interested in replacing poor behavior with good behavior (attitude and skill acquisition) than in being critical of athletes (who can't avoid making mistakes if they're going to learn).
- Developing the communication skills that will allow you to give your athletes the knowledge, abilities and experiences necessary to maximize their potential.
- Creating environments and situations that require athletes to make decisions and then take appropriate action to implement those decisions.
- Teaching the concept that a person's best effort is acceptable – miracles are not required, mistakes are necessary for growth.
- Understanding that if you create the proper environment, positive growth will take place.
- Being organized, planning well and communicating plans to all involved.
- Being consistent in your actions and reactions (to the challenges your sport and your athletes present).
- Being honest and fair with all players: building trust and "walking the talk."
- Always acting in a manner consistent with your beliefs and values.
- Always stressing the importance of hard work, talking about and modeling perseverance at the difficult things that many people like to avoid (the "little things").

A note to beginning coaches or those working with younger or less competitive players: this is a long and comprehensive list. You can start by choosing two or three items off it that best apply to your situation and working on those. As your understanding and confidence improves, you can add to your philosophy. It's important for both you and your athletes to keep things simple and suitable for their age level.

On winning and losing

Your coaching philosophy should include well-thought-out ideas about winning and losing. To believe that winning in competitive sport is not important would be unrealistic and naïve. Winning is an important goal because it helps us measure progress; however, it may not be the primary objective. The importance of winning versus losing can vary with the competitive environment.

In the professional sport environment, winning is vital. It boosts the psyche of the fan (fans are the consumer-participants who provide the money to sustain the product) and enhances their feelings of direct association with the team they support. Winning also provides a degree of entertainment value.

In the sport excellence and competitive, non-professional environments, winning is not absolutely necessary, but it is preferable. It indicates achievement of or progress toward a predetermined goal, and it may affect financial support from amateur sport organizations and sponsors.

In amateur and recreational youth hockey, a strong emphasis on winning may not always be appropriate because it doesn't necessarily measure the athlete's personal enjoyment or satisfaction.

There are positives to both winning and losing. Winning against an evenly matched opponent indicates that a team is progressing in skills, tactics and strategies. It can help athletes learn to enjoy victory without having it breed arrogance, helping them to develop the positive quality of humility.

Losing must be kept in perspective. It can be used to provide information on what phases of the game need more work. A loss in which a team puts forth a fine effort is nothing to be ashamed of. Coaches must never allow one or two individuals to carry the major responsibility for a loss (or win). Winning and losing should be shared experiences.

Failures in sport (temporary setbacks, mistakes, disappointments – not all of which are synonymous with losses) are the things that educate us. Every mature person has to learn to adjust to failure. We all fail at something sooner or later. The caliber and quality of a person is best shown in his or her ability to meet disappointment, learn from it and bounce back. If coaches and athletes are continually trying to avoid failure by always staying within their personal "comfort zones," they may never find out what they are capable of achieving.

Thus, loss and failure are best viewed in balance against winning. An overemphasis on winning can often result in:
- Decreased enjoyment on the part of the players (from striving to meet unattainable goals and unrealistic expectations).
- Restricted participation (a "shortened" bench eliminates lesser-skilled players and encourages early drop out from the sport).
- Undesirable behavior from players (arguing, blaming, complaining).
- Poor performance (due to high anxiety levels).
- Restricted development of the athlete (fear of failure can inhibit initiative and experimentation).

Since an overemphasis on winning can generate these negative results, I'd like to suggest another perspective on it. I prefer to see winning as the healthy outcome of the ongoing process of hard work and character development. It's about what your athletes do on a day-to-day basis; it's about them getting a little better today then they were yesterday.

Winning is about process; the actual process the individual engages in to better him or herself. It is about personal growth and self-development. The real value in competition is the process you undergo when you participate. This process involves just plain having fun; it involves relating to people and seeing how they relate to you; and it involves the continual testing of your abilities so that you can better judge yourself as an individual.

Teaching players to learn how to win isn't teaching them to expect to win. It's teaching them to believe that if they perform to the level of their capabilities – the level they've built for themselves by making small steps of improvement each day – and that if their teammates do the same, then they are capable of winning. Teach them not to have doubts (i.e., "are we good enough?"), but to understand that no matter how much talent a team has (yours or your opponents'), only a strong collective team effort will offer the best opportunity for success. If you help your players stay positive about their prospects, stay in the present and focus on the overall process, then winning will eventually follow. This must include the understanding that between two evenly matched teams (or individuals), sometimes one or two lucky bounces will determine the outcome.

As for adversity (such as bad bounces), when you and your players face it they will be prepared if they've been persistent and positive in working hard to maximize their strengths. Hopefully this will give them a solid foundation to lean on.

A final thought on winning. Teach your players to become "want-to-win" athletes, not "have-to-win" athletes. If they feel they "have to" win, they become vulnerable to nervousness, nervousness creates tension, and tension inhibits performance. If they feel they "have to" win, their focus can switch from the game plan, and from the skills they've developed, to the outcome – the win or the loss. This will also inhibit performance. I'll leave the last word on this subject to a great competitor, Joe Sakic, whose response to a question from a TV sports reporter said it all. Joe was asked: "You're the team captain, your team's down a goal, don't you feel you **have** to get a goal to start a comeback?" Joe's response: "No! I *want* to get a goal."

2 – Building a Positive Team Environment

Once you've thought through your beliefs and values and established your coaching philosophy, you can begin to build a positive environment for your players, assistant coaches, managers and the team you all comprise together. Here are some general characteristics of a positive team environment. It should be:

- Consistently reflective (in both words and actions) of the beliefs and values held by you, as coach, and other team leaders.
- Well structured, with efficient planning and organization for all participants.
- Warm, supportive and respectful, with honesty and fairness in all interpersonal dealings, resulting in a high degree of trust and loyalty among players and coaches.
- Encouraging of shared values and expectations, in turn creating a sense of ownership for all participants.
- Challenging and innovative.
- A fun place to be, but also a place where cooperation and individual responsibility (to work hard and smart) are expected of everyone.

Components of a positive team environment

To achieve the kind of environment we just described, the following processes and components are necessary:

- Your team needs a "blueprint for excellence," in other words, a well-defined vision and purpose. This includes identifying the physical and mental attributes necessary to be successful at the level of competition expected. Both players and coaches need to have input into the team mission and

vision statement.
- This blueprint should include clear and relevant team goals (set with input from the entire group), with strategies and time lines for achieving those goals.
- You must have a well-defined and efficient system of communication that includes processes where players can take some personal responsibility for decision making.
- Everyone on your team (coaches, players and support staff) should have clearly defined roles.
- You must have a few (just a few, mind you) organizational rules.
- You should gradually develop, with player input, a set of team guidelines (see below for the difference between guidelines and rules).

Team goals

Developing team goals is a process that should involve the players and thus develop their sense of ownership of those goals. One way of beginning this process is for the coaches to suggest some possible "value" words, like those listed below. The players can work from this list to help choose the values most important to them, which the coaches can then work into team goal statements (see examples listed on facing page). This process should be done over a period of time and depends a lot on the maturity of the players, their level of commitment and the level of competition your team is involved in. Team goals, like the team identity statement and team guidelines, can be modified over time.

Here are some "value" words you might use in developing your goal statements:

outwork	sustained pressure	initiate
pro-active	supporting	sharing
consistent	involvement	practice intensity
commitment	physical/mental toughness	excellence
enjoyment	responsibility	accountability

And here are some team goal statements you might develop (with player input) from the "value" words.

1. To never be outworked by an opposing team: for twenty minutes at a time, over sixty consecutive playing minutes, to play at a "work intensity" level that puts sustained (shift after shift) pressure on our opponents.

2. To play as individuals and as a team, so we initiate, challenge, create and sustain a level of enthusiasm that forces our opponents to play to the intensity level that we establish.

3. To support each other in all aspects of the game so that we achieve close and unselfish cooperation between everyone connected to the team. As a result, all our combined efforts are directed toward a common set of goals.

4. To play with physical and mental toughness so we earn the respect of our opponents and make them aware, by our persistent effort, that we will be consistently involved in the game both mentally and physically.

5. To practice as a team with the intensity, enthusiasm, enjoyment and commitment to effort that provides the environment for each player to realize his or her potential.

6. To have all players accept total personal responsibility for their actions; to know that an individual's responsibility is to themselves, their teammates and the team; and, to be fully accountable for that responsibility.

7. To overlay our commitment to excellence with a clear sense of fun, enjoyment and camaraderie.

Team identity

Team goals help a team establish its identity. What are the traits you want your team to be known for? Here are some possible characteristics of a team identity:
- Hard working, intensely competitive.
- Pro-active, not reactive.
- Cooperative, sharing, supportive and unselfish.
- Players who are positive, upbeat, enthusiastic and persistent.
- Good mental and emotional control.
- Players who accept responsibility for their performance and behavior both on and off the ice.
- A team that earns the respect of others through their behavior and performance and in turn displays respect for the integrity of the game of hockey and all those connected with it.

Team rules

Rules are designed to control behavior and are more rigid than guidelines. A ***few*** of them are necessary and appropriate so a team or organization can function effectively. Be careful with rules, though; taken to extremes, they may have the effect of inhibiting some of the unique strengths and talents of players. In my opinion, you should ***not*** have too many rules. Let the team guidelines cover most areas of concern.

Unlike with team guidelines, there should be no player input on rules. Coaches make the decisions about team rules based on what they feel is fair. Here are four basic rules we've used over the years:

1. Be on time for all activities, both on and off the ice (a suggested rule of thumb – be five minutes early).
2. Team goals will take priority over individual goals, but they should not be contrary to one another.
3. Coaches are the control center for instruction and information. When players are called in they should hustle and when coaches speak, players should listen and observe "actively" (with ears and eyes).
4. Players must practice hard! If they don't invest their full effort as a matter of habit in practice, it can become too easy to quit in tough situations. Players must learn to enjoy the "agony of repetition."

Team guidelines

Guidelines can set the tone for a team of very different individuals who share a commitment to achieving high goals. They allow you to make the most of the unique strengths of all concerned. In many cases, too many rigid rules may have a negative effect. Guidelines are more flexible than rules and are intended to guide behavior, encouraging the development of mature behavior and self-discipline. A clear set of guidelines that everyone understands and supports is a positive and necessary factor in team success.

Guidelines are necessary because players joining a new team often come from a wide variety of backgrounds where different behaviors were either expected or allowed. For example, the same action by a player under Coach A might receive criticism, while under Coach B it might receive praise. Some teams and coaches send out mixed messages; they treat different players on the same team in a different manner for the same action and therefore lack consistency or fairness. To help your team perform to its full potential, you need to adopt a team concept that everyone understands and accepts.

The following guidelines illustrate how you can communicate clearly what you expect of assistant coaches, support staff and players; and what they can expect of you in return. These have been adapted from guidelines originally developed for a university basketball team by Dr. Murray Smith of the University of Alberta. I consider my use of team guidelines for every team I've been associated with to be one of the most positive additions to my coaching repertoire.

1. Positive attitude: Don't sulk or dwell on your own or your teammates' errors in a negative way. Learn from errors and setbacks. Expect a lot of yourself, but at the same time, always settle for the best you can be today!

2. Unselfishness: Cooperation and sharing is the key to success. In a team environment no one can achieve success on his or her own. Envy, jealousy or personal rivalries are not acceptable.

3. Responsibility: Personal responsibility is the basis of all individual action. You are responsible for all things within your control and other people connected to you are equally responsible. Accept responsibility for errors and eliminate excuses! Focus on improvement and changing negatives into positives.

4. Respect: Treat your teammates, coaches, management, support staff, officials and opponents with equal respect. Show respect to all people you come in contact with, unless they do something to cause you to lose your respect for them.

5. Coachability: Accept coaching instructions and other directions, including lineup and role assignments, in a positive, cooperative manner. You are entitled to question coaching decisions that affect you, but make sure you do so at the right time and place.

6. Intensity: You are responsible for developing and maintaining a high level of intensity relating to your performance. To improve your control of your emotions, focus on attention and personal motivation.

7. Discipline and consistency: Successful people develop a strong sense of purpose that helps them form the habit of doing the things (often uncomfortable) that must be done to reach their goals. We are creatures of habit and habits are a function of consistency. Every single qualification for success is acquired through habit.

8. Leadership: Every person connected to the team can be a leader in his or her own way. You can be a leader by doing your share, by showing enthusiasm, by supporting your teammates, by never letting up or getting down in tough situations, by persevering until the job is done.

9. Excuses: Accept responsibility for your own mistakes or errors without making excuses. Learn from your mistakes; they show what you must do to improve.

10. Work Ethic: Hard work is the cornerstone to any successful endeavor and is defined by prolonged, difficult effort (if it doesn't meet this definition, it's not hard work!). Hard work builds its own momentum.

A final note on team guidelines: they apply to everyone who is part of the team. Being a team member requires a commitment to live by the principles set out in the team guidelines while the team is together.

Team roles and how they support success

The importance of specific roles within a team varies, as do many of the concepts we're discussing, with the age level, the competitive level and the experience level.

In youth hockey the athletes are being introduced to the game and its various component parts. Ideally, they should become reasonably proficient in all aspects of the game. That's why with younger players and in less competitive environments, all the players should be given equal opportunities to improve and equal exposure to a variety of roles.

As players move up the performance ladder specific roles become more important. Player roles represent a set of responsibilities within the team and are usually linked to the design of the team's offensive and defensive systems. Sometimes, they're determined by an individual's strengths or weaknesses.

Roles may be taken into account in determining lineup combinations. For example, you might have a defence pair combining one player with good offensive skills with a more conservative, stay-at-home type of player with strong defensive abilities.

Similar considerations apply to forward units. You may want to build a team that has two lines with a little more scoring potential, one line with strong defensive capabilities (your checking or "stopper" line), and one line you call on as your "energy line." This breakdown of role units is common in the NHL.

The most important point about roles is that to be effective, they must be clearly understood (no role ambiguity). Ideally, the individual player or unit should not just understand their role, but accept it willingly. Also, players should understand roles on the team other than their own, in case they have to step into another role due to injury or changes in personnel. Players who have a clear understanding of their role are more confident, more satisfied and perform better. Coaches must make players feel that all roles (big or small) are vital to the team's success. And everyone who has a role to play on the team – coaches, players, managers, trainers – must be able to evaluate how well they perform their role and contribute to the team's success.

Defining success

The ability to evaluate role performance depends on a common team understanding of success, of what it means to succeed. Here are the definitions of success we used within the Golden Bear environment:

Team success – continuous movement toward a previously determined, worthwhile goal.

Individual success – the peace of mind which is a direct result of self-satisfaction in knowing you did your best to become the best that you are capable of becoming (quoted from John Wooden's Pyramid of Success).

Evaluating role performance

With an understanding of what success means, you can measure the performance of all team members in their roles against this standard. Here are some evaluation criteria that apply to different roles within the team.

Coaches

Every member of the coaching staff has the responsibility to provide players with:
- The best knowledge of the game available.
- The best learning environment possible, enabling players to improve their skills and knowledge.
- Honest, objective, accurate and continual feedback relating to their strengths and weaknesses.

How do you and the rest of your coaching staff rate on these criteria?

Players

Using the criteria listed below, each player should assess his or her abilities and attitude realistically. Then, working in cooperation with coaches, the player should determine specific steps to best accomplish team and individual goals. With this approach, all team members have the opportunity to establish themselves in a positive, contributing role. Individual roles may change or be modified from week to week, or over the course of the season, as the abilities and attitudes of individual players improve. But the important thing is that role responsibilities remain realistic and attainable and that each person is enthusiastic and positive about the importance of his or her contribution. Here are some descriptions and evaluation criteria for player roles. Note that several of these roles can be performed by any member of the team, while others require more specific skills:

Attitude players:
- Show spirit, enthusiasm and hustle.
- Continually drive to keep teammates "up."
- Are dependable, with a positive attitude toward teammates and coaches.
- Play with heart, character, and extra effort.

Player Rating: _____

Practice players:
- Work consistently at honing skills in practice.
- Demonstrate enthusiasm and fire, especially during practice.
- Continually push and challenge teammates to become better.

Player Rating: _____

Hitters:
- Demonstrate toughness and aggressiveness within the rules.
- Finish body checks consistently.
- Give determined second effort.

Player Rating: _____

Bumpers and grinders:
- Are strong on the puck in corners, along boards, in front of the net.
- Don't give up the puck easily when being checked.

Player Rating: _____

Playmakers:
- Are unselfish, and share the puck.
- Are always aware of where their teammates are on the ice, set teammates up.
- Will take a hit to make a play.
- Control the puck and play with poise and patience.

Player Rating: _____

Scorers:
- Show determination and drive around the net.
- Are strong on the puck, tough in front of the net.
- Work hard on goal scoring techniques.

Player Rating: _____

The leadership role for players

Regardless of the specific role a player fits into, every player has the responsibility to show leadership in that role, and players can also be "active followers" in other aspects of team performance. Player-leaders demonstrate the following characteristics: staying positive, encouraging others, playing hard and following the rules, and helping with equipment and other team chores. Player-leaders help create a sense of ownership among other players. They also define, encourage and promote good "follower-ship."

Players who aren't yet ready to lead can be effective, or active, followers. Active followers demonstrate enthusiasm without expecting star billing; are committed to a purpose or person outside themselves; and manage themselves well, showing good self control and judgement. Active followers are not mindlessly obedient, servile or unquestioning; rather, they're honest, credible and stand up for what they believe in. Most active followers progress to become good leaders, the way rookies grow into veterans.

3 – Helping Your Athletes Achieve Their Potential

Communication

When it comes to communicating with your athletes, teaching them and helping them reach their potential as players and as individuals, I always keep in mind a famous Chinese proverb someone once told me: *I hear, and I forget. I hear and I see, and I remember. I hear and I see and I do, and I understand.* Over the years, I tacked on my own addendum to this proverb: *And after I understand, I repeat and repeat and repeat until it becomes habit.*

In all communication, the spoken words are a minor part of the message! The more important part of the message is transmitted through your personal conduct – the way you model your enthusiasm, your intensity, your organization, your concentration. Much of this is accomplished through your body language, so be conscious and careful about how you use your eyes (e.g., eye-rolling) and your gestures (tossing of hands and arms in frustration). Also you should attempt to use "other voices" to give players a break from your own. Audio and videotapes, newspaper articles, players (current and former), guest presenters and consultants can all communicate with your team in your stead.

Here are some behavioral principles that will promote effective communication:
- Be positive and enthusiastic; enthusiasm is caught, not taught.
- Be demanding but considerate; your expectations should be clear, fair and based on your players' current abilities and experiences.
- Be consistent in the way you treat everyone (e.g., learn and use all your players' names as soon as possible).
- Make your non-verbal behavior consistent with what you say – walk the talk! In all our communicating as coaches, whether verbal or written, whether one-on-one or in group discussions or in formal meetings, we must work to strengthen relationships by consistently following these principles:
- Use mistakes and disappointments to guide improvement. Learn from the past without dwelling on it negatively. The past cannot be changed!
- All communications (verbal and non-verbal) should preserve the respect of all parties, present or not. This rules out personal attacks, sarcasm and ridicule.
- Listen actively without interruption, to ensure clear understanding of each speaker's message, without showing emotional reactions either for or against.

- Strive for inclusion; we should hear from everyone. Share airtime, ideas have an integrity of their own.
- In a creative atmosphere, innovation and novel ideas must be given a chance to flower and either prove or disprove themselves.
- Encourage shared humor that is free of ridicule or sarcasm.
- Take responsibility for yourself and be as open to constructive change as you expect others to be.
- Mistakes are a natural result of trying to improve, the natural outcome of calculated risk taking. Admit mistakes without making excuses. The biggest mistake you can make is to refuse to acknowledge a mistake.
- Be rationally and respectfully assertive in challenging others if they are negative or become personal with their criticism. Any legitimate criticism or correction can be stated in positive terms.

Your responsibility as a coach is to translate your knowledge and the concepts and skills that you want your players to learn so they understand you clearly. Remember! It's not about what *you* know, but about what *they* understand. You and your assistants must translate your knowledge and ideas into actions that players can take. You can do this on a one-on-one basis, in small groups and with the full team.

About learning

To be a successful coach-communicator, you have to understand that people learn in different ways and at different rates. So you must be patient. People learn in a variety of ways, some by seeing, some by doing. Some learners know their world best through music, others may know it best through their physicality – playing sports – or through drama. Some don't learn well through words while others do. Everyone can learn in one way or another.

All learning takes time and patience, from both the teacher and the student. And learning can't happen without good two-way communication. Communication builds relationships, mutual respect and trust. The most important building block in getting people to do what you want them to do is good relationships, and these are based on trust! There are three basic principles to learning that all coaches should understand:

Relaxed confidence is the essence of learning –
- All learning requires risk taking. Encourage this by expressing confidence in your players' ability to acquire necessary knowledge and skill if they apply consistent effort.

Positive instruction optimizes learning –
- Identify the knowledge or skill you're teaching with a clear, simple statement of the idea or concept.
- Good definitions clarify both what is important and what is not.
- Show (demonstrate) and tell; do this with patience and repetition.
- Make sure the "tell" (or talking) part of your teaching comes in brief phases, so your players can internalize the concept and incorporate it as part of their "self-instruction," or self-talk.
- Try to use a positive description of "what to do" (rather than framing things in the negative – "what not to do").
- Paraphrase your instructions: "another way of saying that is…"

Feedback fuels learning –
- Feedback provides information about the effectiveness of efforts to learn. As such, it can often be rewarding; it also guides correction and the process of deciding what to learn next.

- Positive feedback is more than just making rewarding statements; more importantly, it is information that can improve effectiveness.
- In providing earned praise, make it specific rather than general (e.g. "The effort you put out in that period was really good – keep it up" is better than "Good job out there").
- Listening to and observing players carefully are the keys to providing effective, specific feedback.
- Use open-ended questions to elicit feedback from the learner that will help you determine his or her level of understanding (e.g. "Tell me what that means" or "When would you apply that?").

Active listening

Active listening is another crucial element in two-way communication. You might have to teach your players to be active listeners, and the best way to do this is model the behavior yourself. Your players, with you modeling for them, ***must*** learn to listen, because ***opportunity sometimes knocks softly!***

The distinction between "hearing" and "listening" is fundamentally important to worthwhile communication. *Webster's Dictionary* points out that while hearing is the ability to "perceive sounds," listening means "to attend closely with a view to understanding." Thus, implicit in the activity of listening is the concept of understanding and then taking action based on new or reinforced insights.

As far back as the 1920s, author William Keefe explained that listening takes courage. It is a skill that is learned, not inherited, and as with any learned activity, proficiency has a price. One of the most difficult parts of becoming a good listener is developing disciplined control of our emotions. Emotions like fear, boredom, anger or extreme excitement act as blocks and filters that either stop or distort the process of understanding. Active listening requires a mind that is focused in the here and now.

But the biggest hurdle to overcome in learning to be an effective listener is laziness. Listening is hard work. It is a three-step process wherein you, the listener, must:

1. **Establish the context**. You can do this quickly by answering these questions: Why is the speaker talking about this now? Why is it important now? How does it relate to what I am doing now?

2. **Suspend judgement**. Avoid hasty approval or disapproval. It's very difficult to keep your own preconceived thoughts from interfering with the speaker's complete message, but work hard at keeping your mind open and listening for complete ideas. The mind is a lot like a parachute – it works much better when it's open! Don't jump to conclusions, don't be defensive.

3. **Reflect**. You need to reflect on the information presented in order to have it stick. New information needs time to work itself into your frame of mind. Thus you have to work actively to take the speaker's ideas with you. Then slowly, all your mental powers (many of which are subconscious) can be used to really make these new ideas useful to you, or you many eventually reject them. In the context of hockey practice, players should repeat to themselves the key points just made by the coach as they move off to begin the next drill.

Active listening embodies these three actions– establish context, suspend judgement, reflect. Clues that active listeners present are things like asking for clarification, but not repetition. They don't interject their own ideas unless these are requested and they have an alert posture aided by eye contact. But most of all, active listeners are people who demonstrate immediate signs of understanding by exhibiting appropriate actions. Active listening leads to purposeful, relevant actions.

Finally, active, effective listeners understand the advice of the ancient proverb, which observes "we are all given two ears and only one mouth – perhaps so we can listen twice as much as we talk." Hearing is inherited, listening is learned!

Discipline

In hockey, as in life, the very best kind of discipline is that which is self-imposed, that which one exercises over oneself, rather than that which is imposed from an external source. Of course, self-imposed discipline is a product of what you have been taught, what lessons you have learned from your experiences and decided to live by. It's very important to understand that self-discipline is learned, and like any learning, it can be extended and improved if we decide to do that.

Disciplined behavior is essential for success in any highly complex and competitive situation, and high performance hockey is both. Good discipline, together with good techniques, good tactics and hard work, give your team an opportunity to be successful.

While we may value an attitude that, in turn, values discipline, we can never look into a person's head to confirm what attitudes are there. All we can do is observe a person's behavior, to see if their behavior is disciplined. Coaches and players alike should be able to identify behavior that indicates disciplined play, and likewise, behavior that shows a lack of discipline. The consequences of poor discipline should be reduced playing time!

Behavioral indicators of disciplined play
Players on competitive teams demonstrate discipline by:
- Being on time for all practices, games and team functions.
- Getting into and maintaining their best possible physical condition.
- Consistent hustle and effort (first shift, last shift and everything in between).
- Showing enthusiasm, spirit and cooperation with teammates and coaches.
- Consistently improving individual techniques and responsibilities.
- Sticking to the game plan with patience and poise (emotional control).
- Consistently playing "smart-tough" (e.g., being the first to the puck, taking a hit to make a play, making hard, legal shoulder checks, being strong along the boards and in the corners).
- Unselfish play away from the puck that fully supports teammates.
- Helping in all possible ways to chip away at an opponent's lead, fighting back from a deficit right to the final whistle.

Behavioral indicators of poor discipline
Poorly disciplined players:
- Lack hustle and fail to be aggressive within the rules.
- Forget the team concept and play solo.
- Lack consistent technique (e.g., losing races to the puck, avoiding checks, etc.).
- Show poor judgment and anticipation (e.g., careless offsides).
- Gamble unnecessarily, taking bad chances at the wrong time.
- Complain about teammates and coaches.
- Retaliate against opponents for real or imagined causes (playing "dumb-tough").
- Get distracted by an official's call instead of focusing on their own responsibilities.

Playing tough

The Golden Bear approach to hockey has always included toughness. We call it playing "smart-tough" instead of "dumb-tough." Here are the Golden Bear principles of "smart-tough" hockey:

- Focus on your opponent's body, not the puck. Block out your opponent consistently and legally, at each opportunity. Win the one-on-one challenges in all areas of the ice.
- Always try to be first to a loose puck and then maintain strong control when you have possession.
- Never pull up to avoid legal contact if it will help make the play, offensively or defensively.
- Develop the ability and desire to give and take a good legal check.
- Fight away from checks and through screens; do not accept being checked and screened.
- Drive hard to the net with or without the puck; be strong in traffic.
- Hold a strong screening and deflecting position in front of the net; compete hard for rebounds.
- Be ready, willing and able to block shots when necessary.
- Maintain your concentration and intensity through sixty minutes. Stay mentally tough and determined and reach down for second effort when it is needed.
- Stay cool and poised under pressure; don't retaliate.
- Never let your opponent intimidate you; support each other in all aspects of the game in good times and in bad.
- Always be a sacrificing, unselfish defensive team player.
- Make your opponent aware – by your determined play – that you are going to be physically involved in all aspects of the game.
- Strive for the consistency of playing as hard in your first shift as you do in your last, and all those in between.
- Always compete hard in contact areas (i.e. along the boards, in the corners, behind or in front of the net). Offensively, this will help you control the puck and move it (with stick or feet) or pass it to a teammate. Defensively, this will help you to block out, neutralize or pin opponents (on the defensive side) and never let them beat you back to a dangerous scoring position.
- Maintain sustained and consistent pressure on your opponents.
- Never give up! Never concede anything! Never quit!

4 – Practice – The Agony of Repetition

Organizational planning

An important part of building a successful team or organization is to develop a plan that will help lead you (and your team or organization) to your desired goals. I like the old adage that says: "If success is a journey, your plan will become the map, compass and vehicle for completing that journey."

As you build your plan you need to consider three major elements: scope, sequence and evaluation. The first two, scope and sequence, can vary considerably depending on your team goals and the age and competition level of your team.

The scope of your plan might be quite simple for a beginning hockey club of young players, aged eight to ten, for example. It could cover a period of eight to twelve weeks. On the other end of the spectrum, the planning scope for a national team preparing for an upcoming Olympics could cover a period of up to three years.

The sequence aspect of your plan sets priorities and chronological order for training and competitive activities according to your athletes' current abilities. It takes into account what skills and techniques you as coach feel are important for the players and the team to achieve their goals. It answers the question: what needs to be practiced at what stage of the season?

And you must evaluate continually, and accurately, as you progress through the scope and sequence of your plan. You evaluate to identify your players' strengths and weaknesses and make appropriate adjustments. Divide the season into four parts – pre-season, early season, late season and post season – and plan and evaluate on this cycle. Start with your master plan, then evaluate and plan some more, and repeat the process throughout the parts of the season. Throughout the process, be flexible; be ready to make changes to your plan!

Plan to start your season with your first team meeting. Schedule it separately from your first tryout or training camp session. Use the first meeting to discuss the expectations you have of the players and to give them an opportunity for input on expectations they have as team members. The meeting should be positive and end on a note of encouragement and anticipation. You should also address the tryout or team selection process and practices. This includes covering housekeeping details like the timing and location of on-ice sessions, equipment needs, etc. You must explain your practice philosophy and explain why practices have value: they improve individual skills; they improve team performance; and they improve individual and team discipline.

A practice philosophy

Players and coaches alike must consistently maintain a positive attitude toward practice and have a true appreciation for its value. This means being excited about practice, being excited about the opportunity to get better. You, your coaches and your players should all understand that practice holds tremendous value as an organized system that helps direct training. It serves as a guide to enable coaches to check progress; an opportunity for athletes to set and meet a series of goals; an opportunity for skill development, for team systems improvement, for conditioning and in the bigger picture, for teaching your players values. It is also plays a large part in motivating your team and last but not least, it's a chance for your players to have fun.

Your team should practice with intensity, enthusiasm and enjoyment. It should have a commitment to effort that provides the environment for each player to reach his or her potential. Your players' goal for practice should be to make their effort and work ethic identical to what they bring to a game.

Perhaps the most important concept to grasp about practice and its value is summed up by a phrase that's been part of Golden Bear hockey talk for decades – "the agony of repetition." It is the agony of repetition that creates good habits and better skills in athletes. You as a coach, and your players, must believe in the agony of repetition! The will to win is common, but the will to **prepare** to win requires effort and commitment.

Some principles of practice planning

In planning and organizing your practice, remember that the coach's responsibility is to create an environment in which players can become the best they are capable of being. Create a simple, easy-to-do process for your practice planning and preparation by making a template or form that you can fill out for every practice. Keep it on file for reference and make sure it provides space for drill sequences and key coaching points that you want to cover in each practice. Make sure all the coaches helping with the practice have a reference card they can take on the ice showing the same information that's in your plan.

There are several factors you should consider as you plan your practices. First, you must plan practice activities appropriate to the age and ability of your athletes. Identify the skills they need to work on – skating, shooting, passing, etc. – and plan your practice accordingly. The same applies to team systems that need work – breakouts, defensive zone coverage, etc. Also take into account recent game results and performances and address issues in a timely fashion. The time of the season is another factor to consider, and also be sensitive to the physical and mental condition of your team.

There are five basic principles that I believe provide the foundation for practice planning:

Maximum use of ice time available
- Make sure players are paying attention and focused at all times.
- Cover some aspects of the practice (agenda, goals) in the dressing room before the players take the ice.
- Create an efficient flow from one drill to the next.
- Make sure specialized practice equipment (e.g., cones) is readily available.
- Do warm-up stretching or conditioning off the ice.

Maximum use of ice surface
- Plan to use the entire ice surface.
- Have your assistants (or parent volunteers) supervise other areas on the ice where you can't be.
- Create "work stations" to use as much of the ice surface as possible.

Maximum activity for all players on ice
- Select drills that encourage maximum activity – avoid players standing in lines waiting.
- Use "work stations" effectively to allow players maximum repetitions of skills in smaller areas of the ice surface.
- Avoid excessive use of scrimmage; balance the time you spend between individual skills and team play.

Maximum application of practice to game situations
- Drills should contain game-like situations.
- Analyze your team during games and design your practice accordingly. Work from a checklist of the skills, concepts and attitudes that you want to teach.
- Explain to the players how the drill they're doing in practice applies to the game situation.
- Drills should be appropriate to age and skill level.

Maximum application of the principles of learning
- "Positive instruction" optimizes learning, although excessive use of superlatives (e.g. "great job") can dilute the message. Be honest and respectful with constructive criticism (e.g. "you can do better").
- Relaxed confidence is essential to learning and continuous relevant feedback drives learning (the number one reason for below-average performance is a lack of positive correction).
- Encouragement and approval are powerful influences on learning. Every player should experience both on a regular basis. Withholding approval when performance is not up to par helps maintain the effectiveness of approval.
- At times, appropriate disciplinary consequences are useful and should be applied.
- Research also shows that more learning takes place if success is possible but not certain. If tasks and challenges are either too easy or too hard, it diminishes the individual's potential to learn.
- Individuals will improve their own skills more quickly if you give them the means to recognize their own progress; teach them to measure their progress against themselves, not in comparison to others.
- Introduce "self-challenge" and competitive drills gradually.
- And remember, learning basic skills and tactics requires "the agony of repetition!"

Some principles for running practices

Your practice really begins before your players hit the ice. Make sure you take time before they leave the dressing room to discuss the specific objectives you have for that day's session and to go over the drills you will be doing. This is also the time for warm up stretching, so you can make the best use of your time on the ice together.

Once you're on the ice, explain what you want from the players quickly, clearly and concisely. Make sure that you and your assistants really know the material you're going to cover. You should all be carrying your plans on cards and have a rink diagram board handy, so you can draw drill patterns for your players.

Tell them the purpose of the drill you're setting up and how it relates to a game situation and, if you can, use "cue words" to make the connection for them. Some of your drills can run concurrently from stations at opposite ends of the ice, with one assistant coach explaining the drill and working with one group (say, defencemen) while another works with the forwards. Keep the goalies informed about the drills and what their role will be in them, and make sure they're involved in some aspects of each drill.

It's important to consider how you time drills and when you work them into the day's agenda. Finesse drills, (i.e. passing, timing, power play, etc.) require good ice and should be done early in practice. Also, if you're doing a drill to teach a major concept, run this early in the practice to allow adequate time for it and to eliminate fatigue being a factor in your players' ability to concentrate. Unless you're working at the early learning stage of a skill or concept, make most of your drills competitive; set them up so you have player versus player or player versus the clock. Plan for variety in the type and duration of your drills, and have occasional breaks between them when players can grab a quick drink from their individual water bottles or skate some relaxing laps. These breaks should be carefully timed and controlled by a coach.

Keep the atmosphere positive and upbeat, and try to include one fun drill in most practices; a relaxed, fun atmosphere encourages learning. And try consistently to end on an "up" note, leaving your players looking forward to your next session. Always observe, evaluate and provide relevant feedback, and encourage your assistant coaches do the same, especially through their station work. Never be satisfied with mediocrity! Consistently challenge your players to do the drills the right way and to build their own, self-imposed level of intensity into the way they practice. Your team leaders should be setting the example here. Finally, try to make time to have a quick debriefing session with assistant coaches (and your captains at appropriate times), to evaluate the just-completed practice and plan for the next one.

Conclusion

I'd like to conclude with a few words about how to improve oneself as a coach, something I've worked at throughout my career. While there is no secret to coaching success, there are some common denominators. The main ingredient in most success stories is hard work, but work ethic must be accompanied by a strong sense of purpose and belief in what you're doing.

Just as players do, we coaches must have a sense of purpose (or passion) that drives us to form the habits necessary to succeed. We are all creatures of habit and good habits are a function of consistency.

Every single qualification for success is acquired through habit. If you don't deliberately form good habits, you will unconsciously form bad habits. Often, the things you have to do to be successful are difficult, time consuming and unpleasant. But you have to do these things consistently, day in and day out, year in and year out, if you want to accomplish your goals and fulfil your passion. So create a positive, optimistic learning environment and then gradually begin to build championship habits. Continue to reinforce those success-forming habits and keep linking them to your overall goals or purpose.

Now, some specifics about how to do that. First, get into the habit of continually preparing and studying. Build up your base knowledge of the game gradually and thoroughly. As you work at this, improve your communication skills, so that the more you learn about the game, the better you can communicate your knowledge and understanding to your players. This is the key to winning your players' respect. Your knowledge and understanding, and your ability to communicate it, will inspire them to listen to you. And if they actively listen to you, you will be able to influence them and get them to believe in what you are teaching them.

So, how do you study the game of hockey? Nowadays, there are a lot of resources available to help coaches. As far as I can see, the process breaks down into three basic steps:

1. **Read** – There are many books and articles about coaching and leading in sport and business (i.e. management and organizational theory). Read the ones that seem appropriate and make notes of the ideas that appeal to you.

2. **Listen** – Active listening is a difficult skill to master but it's one you must work at. Listen at clinics and seminars (including those on subjects other than hockey) and pick up ideas from your colleagues, peers and mentors in all areas of your life.

3. **Observe** – Watch other successful coaches who are worthy of being role models. Watch their practices and see if they are well organized, if their drills might work for you, if their players are energetic and enthusiastic, and if they give and receive good feedback. Watch their games and see if they exhibit good control of their own behavior and of what happens on the bench. Watch how they run their shifts (forty to fifty seconds long, changing smoothly on the fly), how they allot ice time to players, and how they react to adversity and success.

As you work on these steps to improvement, always keep in mind that your relationships – with your players, your assistant coaches and trainers, your opponents, the officials – are built on integrity, and your integrity will be defined by your actions. If you act with integrity, you will win the trust of others, especially your players, and you will be able to trust them in turn. This mutual trust is fundamental to all forms of learning and will enhance your own ability to improve, as well as the ability of those you seek to teach, to guide and to coach.

If you develop the habits of learning and improving continually, and if you earn the trust and respect of others as you share yours, you will experience success as a coach; you will come to know its true meaning. John Wooden's definition of success works best for me. I wish you the self-satisfaction and peace of mind he talks about, as you become the best that you can be. There are many young people depending on you!

Acknowledgements

Coach Drake's Acknowledgements

I'd like to acknowledge some of the many people who have helped me develop as a coach, or who have played significant roles in whatever success I've enjoyed in my life. I believe very strongly in mentoring. I've had the honor to be a mentor to some people, and I've had the great fortune to be mentored in turn by many. I'd like to express my gratitude to these people: first, to Dolly, for her love, patience and guidance of our two daughters, and her sharing and understanding of the complexities of a coach's life. Also, my thanks to my daughters Debbie and Jami, my son-in-law Ron Gabinet, my grandchildren Jackie and Michael Gabinet and Matthew Drake, for their consistent support and encouragement. And of course, I'm very grateful to my father, Clarence "the Admiral" Drake, and my mother Grace. They introduced me to the sporting life and gave me the opportunity and the encouragement to challenge myself in the directions I chose.

My early influences all came from a healthy childhood and adolescence spent in Yorkton, Saskatchewan. It was a close, supportive community that presented a lot of good opportunities in sport, including everything from hockey, baseball, football and basketball to cricket and curling. I was lucky to have school chums and teammates who kept all of us interested and enthusiastic. It was a great beginning for me.

As a junior and university hockey player, I learned a great deal from two influential coaches, Murray Armstrong of the Regina Pats and Frank Frederickson of the UBC Thunderbirds. As I progressed and became a university coach, I had the good fortune to learn and collaborate with many good people. Some of these included: George Kingston, a great student and teacher of the game; Dave King, an always-tough coaching competitor and a great innovator, tactician and teacher; and other university colleagues such as Ed Zemrau, Ron Watson, Peter Esdale, Dick Wintermute, Brian McDonald, Jack Cummings, Don Spring, John Devaney, Kevin Primeau, Tom Watt, Wayne Fleming, Paul Arsenault, Andy Murray, Bob Hindmarch, Pierre Pagé, Bill Liskowich, Perry Pearn, Bert Halliwell, Mike Coflin, Mike Johnston, Dave Adolph, Barry Trotz, Dave Chambers, Graham Wise, Jean Perron, Reg Higgs and Bob Boucher.

In my shorter career as a football coach, I learned much and received great support from Steve Mendryk, Gino Fracas, Frank Morris, Don Barry, Arnie Enger, Roy Stephenson, Jim Donlevy and Leigh McMillan.

During my work with Canada's Olympic Team in 1979-80, it was a privilege to associate with Father David Bauer, Tom Watt, Lorne Davis and Rick Noonan. This was a Hockey Canada project, and my relationships with the people in that organization go back a long way and have been very positive. I particularly appreciate the confidence shown in me by Bob Nicholson, Johnny Misley, Paul Carson and Dean McIntosh, who were instrumental in my receiving the Geoff Gowan Award. Hockey Alberta is another organization with which I've enjoyed a long and happy relationship – thanks to Scott Robinson and the staff there.

After I left the CIS, I was privileged to work with a number of fine men in the NHL: Bob Murdoch, Alpo Suhonen, Dave Prior, Dennis McDonald, George Kingston, Ken Hitchcock, Doug Jarvis, Rick Wilson, Bob Gainey, Marc Crawford, Mike Johnston, Jack McIlhargey, Rob Cookson, Greg Gilbert, Brad McCrimmon, Brian Skrudland, Tom Renney, Perry Pearn, Mike Babcock, Craig MacTavish, Bill Moores, Charlie Huddy, Craig Simpson, Pete Peeters and Brian Ross.

I also want to acknowledge the many wonderful young men who comprised the teams I was connected with. As coaches we can lead – and teach skills, tactics and values – but major credit for any successful program must go to the athletes themselves. They must be willing to learn, to commit to being a little better each day, and to unselfishly work toward team goals. They start out as rookies, and grow and mature as players, students and, most importantly, as people. Their individual successes as people and as graduates are truly the most important measure of the Golden Bear hockey program. Some of their names are scattered through the preceding pages, most of the rest must go unmentioned simply for lack of space; they all made their mark.

My special thanks go to a small faction within this group who are often overlooked, the student managers and trainers. These young men worked long, hard hours and made huge contributions to the success of our teams, and unlike their on-ice teammates, they received little or no acclaim. Some of their names include: Morris Boyer, Jim Donlevy, Derek Drager, TD Forss, Peter Friesen, "Gus" Gushaty, Ian Hallworth, Jim Halterman, Art Hooks, Ken Irving, Steve Knowles, Doug Merrill, Dave Sande, Marty Schmidt, Arvid Stensland and Gord Tucker. Our first athletic therapist, Ray Kelly, taught many of them.

Continuing in this context, there was one man who went above and beyond with his many years of devotion and service to the Golden Bears. Rink manager Ron Urness, known to generations of our players as "Ron Rink," ran a fine facility, mentored our managers and even drove the team bus. Flo Macapagal and his staff continue that tradition to this day. Thanks for everything guys!

And finally, I must make special mention of two individuals: Murray Smith, who has been a personal friend, coaching colleague and my most influential mentor for over fifty years; and Bill Moores, an equally great friend and colleague with whom I continue to enjoy a strong personal and professional relationship. I feel a deep sense of gratitude to these two.

Author's Sources and Acknowledgements

This is a memoir. NJ Linfoot, a fellow writer in Edmonton, explained memoir writing adroitly with the help of a quote from Joseph Kertes, of Humber College, Toronto. Kertes said: "Memoir writers must manufacture a text, imposing narrative order on a half-remembered jumble of events." Ms. Linfoot also cited Marshall McLuhan (among the most quotable of Canadians ever): "Anyone can tell the truth with facts. It's when you don't have the facts and tell the truth that you're special."

I make no claim to be special, and I actually had access to plenty of facts while writing this memoir. But there was also the matter of quite a few "half-remembered jumbles." I had to strive for the truth while not always being able to ascertain established fact. This was only natural given that my subject's relationship with our sport extends back about half way to its primordial beginnings. I was continually asking a man to remember details about things that happened half a century earlier. Parts of his story are also culled from my own memory banks, which are fogging up only thirty years after the "fact." Ditto for the other people I spoke to – most struggled to recall some of the precise details around events that transpired many years ago. Collectively though, I believe that we've managed to perceive and remember the truth. That was certainly the motivation of everyone I talked to during this project, and it was my highest intention in writing this story – telling some important truths about our game and its foundations. I've done my best to check the memories of the observers and participants, these individual perspectives, against each other and against the facts where they apply; to verify accounts and provide as clear a picture as possible. If I've represented things in this memoir as fact, or truth, and they appear to the reader to be otherwise, I apologize. Any errors within these pages are entirely my own.

As to the sources I've consulted, well of course there were Clare and Dolly Drake themselves. But because of their reticence and profound humility, I had to speak to many others to get descriptions and evaluations of Clare's activities, attitudes, and ultimately, his contributions. The claims made herein on his behalf don't originate with him; they come from a wide-ranging group who have known him for greater or lesser portions of his career. Most of these people are named in the narrative, but a few stand out for the extent of their experience with Clare, or for their outspokenness and eloquence regarding his contributions. Bill Moores, George Kingston and Ken Hitchcock were leaders; Murray Smith also pitched in here, and provided much insight and information on the early years of Clare's career at U of A. Source materials for this period included Steve Knowles's fine assemblage of WCIAU and CWUAA records.

I was able to cover Clare's crucial time in Germany through his own memories supported by clippings and other memorabilia he'd saved. The compelling story of the Penticton Vees came mostly from Dick and Bill Warwick. My thanks to Bill for his gift of Sid Godber's quirky, inspiring little book on the subject, *Go Vees Go*; it filled in many of the blanks and added a lot of color. Dennis McDonald was key to helping figure out the origins of the National Coaching Certification Program. Dozens and dozens of Clare's ex-players and coaching colleagues told me the stories and particulars of his career at the U of A, the Olympics and in the NHL. I double-checked facts wherever possible through data repositories such as the CIAU/CIS *Almanac*, NHL.com and Hockey Canada's website. These sources and numerous other websites were my verification points for the information you'll find on the broader context of Canadian hockey history. And then there's the "newspaperology" that also provided a lot of the fact and opinion woven into this story. I spent hours poring through microfilm of the *Edmonton Journal* sports pages, and David Bandla and Jeremy Derksen gave valuable help by unearthing a lot more from the old broadsheet and other print media.

I was influenced by, and included, quotes, views and treatments from a number of books, prominent among them: *A Bright Shining Lie*, by Neil Sheehan (Random House, 1988); *Canada on Ice*, edited by Michael Benedict and D'Arcy Jenish (Maclean Hunter Publishing Ltd., 1998); *Simply the Best*, by Mike Johnston and Ryan Walter (Heritage House Publishing, 2004); *More! All Star Poet*, by Stephen Scriver (Coteau Books, 1989); *Ice Level*, edited by Cam Cole (CanWest Books, 2005); *The Best of Jim Coleman*, edited by Jim Taylor (Harbour Publishing Co. Ltd., 2005); *They Call Me Coach*, by John Wooden (The McGraw-Hill Companies, Inc., 2004); *Why I Hate Canadians*, by Will Ferguson (Douglas & McIntyre Ltd., 1997); *The Tipping Point*, by Malcolm Gladwell (Back Bay Books/Little, Brown and Company, 2000); *The Game*, by Ken Dryden (Macmillan, 1983); and, *Tropic of Hockey*, by Dave Bidini (McLelland & Stewart Ltd., 2000).

Now to the fun part... expressing the enormous sense of gratitude I feel to the all people who supported this project. I mentioned many of them in the narrative, but some went above and beyond in their efforts to help. First and foremost are Clare and Dolly, who opened their home and their lives to me for several years. Through countless meetings around their breakfast table, and literally hundreds of phone calls, they were unfailingly patient and good-humored. Coach...Dolly...thank you!

Murray Smith was more than a source for this book, he became my friend and mentor along the way – with editorial input, encouragement, teasing, and either a pat on the back or a friendly kick in the ass whenever I needed it. To you Murray, my deepest gratitude.

My thanks to George and Wendy Kingston, who were also ardent supporters. They graciously took my many phone calls and always made time to answer my incessant questions. The Ultra Hockey Man has fashioned his own remarkable career, yet he praised his mentor's selflessly and fulsomely.

Likewise to Bill Moores and Ken Hitchcock who, with their unequivocal affirmations of the thesis for this book, helped get the project rolling. And to my buddy and writing colleague Steve Scriver, for his astute insights, and for his generosity in sharing his research (especially in regard to photos) and his passion.

More thank yous:

To editor Katherine Koller for her support, diligence and critical eye; and to second editor Peter Midgley for his guidance on story arc.

To Cam Cole, Linda Cameron and Michael Luski for their editorial feedback and encouragement.

To Rick Pape, for his stylish design and his empathy.

To the *Edmonton Journal*, for many of the photos that grace these pages.

To Bill Dowbiggin, for managing publishing and marketing.

And to Bob Kinasewich, for believing in this vision and driving the project.

Finally, I'm grateful for the love of my dear family and friends, all of whom, in their own way, helped me meet the challenges of starting and finishing this book.

INDEX

Academic All Canadian Awards 155
Adolph, Dave 23, 76, 128
Ahearne Cup 5, 79, 99
American Hockey League (AHL) 26, 63, 66, 131
Anderson, Glenn 120, 126, 132, 138
Apps, Syl 26, 27, 71
Armstrong, Murray 29, 30, 36
Arsenault, Paul 76, 92, 95
Babcock, Mike: 22, 116, coaching career 167-168, 169
Barros, Ross 100, 108, 109, 123
Bauer, Father David 9, 33, 48, 69, 76-78, 92, 109, 119, 126, 129-135, 137, 138, 155
Beddoes, Dick 47, 48-49
Bentley, Roy 29
Bidini, Dave "Tropic of Hockey" 118
Bobrov, Vsevolod 5, 53, 55, 56, 57
Boucher, Bob 76, 93, 94, 95, 109, 155
Bouwmeester, Dan 124
Bowman, Scotty 95, 129, 168, 169
Brooks, Herb 134, 136-139
Brooks, Wilf (United Cycle) 19, 123
Brown, Kenneth "Life After Hockey" 6
Burke School, Yorkton (SK) 25-27, 63
Campbell, Clarence 8
Canada Cup, 1976 10, 12
Canada Cup, 1981 12
Canada-Soviet Summit Series, 1972 4-7, 10, 16, 19, 42, 53, 74, 81, 92, 94, 96, 99, 103, 111, 117, 132, 152
Canadian Intercollegiate Athletic Union (CIAU) 4, 8, 13, 16, 23, 24, 67, 69, 93, 95-99, 109, 117, 126, 134, 142, 144, 154, 155
Canadian Interuniversity Sport (CIS) 4, 16, 24, 69, 112, 154, 155
Canadian National Women's Hockey Team 158
Canadian Sports Hall of Fame 24, 152
Canadian University and College Coaches Association (CUCCA) 92 93
Carlyle, Randy 144, 160
Carlyle, Steve 89, 90, 98, 99, 110, 119, 123
Carriere, Rick 158
Challenge Cup, 1979 12

Clarke, Bobby 6, 97
Cole, Cam 107, 118, 143, 153, 155
Coleman, Jim 107, 132, 133, 135, 136, 137
Conacher, Brian 7
Costello, Murray 78, 92
Cranston, Dennis 145, 146, 147, 151
Cummings, Jack 149, 150
Daum, Rob 76, 150, coaching career 154
Davis, Lorne 129, 131, 134
Deacon, James 7
Devaney, John 116, 130, 132, 134, 138
Devaney, Tom 85, 90
Drake, Clare
 "back-post, skates up-ice" 128, "grandfather of sharing information" 23, 95, 166, 168; "head-on-a-swivel" 31, 128; "On Coaching" 170-191, "stay-up 119, "the agony of repetition" 104, 123; 2-1-2 forechecking system 99, 117, 119, 125, 127; at UBC 31-33, attended first coaching clinic 60, coaching in Düsseldorf, Germany 39-42, 46, 57; coaching record and honours 7, 24, 34, 71, 152; controlled change 99, creative practices 78, drive-skating progression 126, Edmonton Oilers (WHA) 109-113, first year coaching Bears 58-60, Golden Bears player 35-38, hired at U of A 61-62, influence of Frank Frederickson 31, physical appearance and personality 21, player on-ice communication 128, positive, rational atmosphere 71, rolling four lines 111. 112; sabbatical at U of Oregon (1969-70) 98, San Jose Sharks 160-161, scouting Russians (1955) 4-5, 54-57; Winnipeg Jets (NHL) 152, 155-157
Drake, Clarence "CJ" 22, 25
Drake, Dolly (nee Carlson) 23, 28, 34, 35, 39, 43, 44, 57, 60, 61, team role 90; 98, 116, 133, 143, 150, 152, 155, 156, 157, 165, 167
Drake Grace 25
Draper, Howie 88, 89, 150, 151, 153
Dryden, Dave 95, 110, 111
Dryden, Ken 3, 6, 122, 155, 169

Dzurko, Vic 66, 71, 79, 123
Eagleson, Alan 5, 12, 132
Eaves, Cec 93, 94
Edmonton (JR) Oil Kings 59, 62, 65, 102, 103, 110
Edmonton (Sr) Flyers 15, 61
Edmonton Oilers (NHL) 36, 119, 126, 130, 133, 138, 149, 160, 167
Edmonton Oilers (WHA) 8, 59, 116, 122, 144, 155
Esaw, Johnny 7
Ferguson, Will "Why I Hate Canadians" 5
Fleming, Wayne 15, 127, coaching career 145, 166, 167
Frederickson, Frank, 22, career overview 30-31, 36, 39, 43, 128
Gabinet, Mike 165, 167
Gladwell, Malcolm "The Tipping Point" 22, 23, 29, 62, 103, 160
Golden Bears (U of A) 1964 University Cup 67, 71; 1968 University Cup 83-85, 87; 1975 University Cup 100, 1978 Pacific Rim Tournament 115, 117-120; 1978 University Cup 120, 1979 University Cup 129, 1980 University Cup 104, 120, 142; 1985-86 Swiss Tour 150, 1986 University Cup 148-150
Gregg, Randy 115, 116, 119, 126, 130, 132, 138, 142, 144, 150
Gretzky, Wayne 9, 12, 15, 19, 149, 154, 155, 169
Hamber Cup 33, 36, 58, 60, 70
Hamilton, Al 88, 110, 111, 112
Hardy Cup 36, 58, 60, 69, 70, 144, 150, 152, 153, 154
Hardy, Dr. W.G. 36, 39
Helland, Chris 142, 143, 158, 159
Helland, Jeff 159
Henderson, Paul 4, 7, 10, 53, 138
Henwood, Dale 23, 24, 75, 83, 85, 89, 95, 96, 105, 108
Hewitt, Foster 4, 7, 53, 56, 137
Hindmarch, Bob 4, 5, 69, 70, 76, 77, 85, 93, 95, 102, 103
Hindmarch, Dave 116, 126, 130, 135, 138
Hitchcock, Ken 14, 19, 22-25, 38, 43, 70, 75, 95, 96, 107, 123, 124, 126, 127, 128, 145, 155, 164-169
Hockey Canada 10, 19, 23, 92, 93,

94, 98, 103, 104, 109, 126, 128, 129, 130, 137, 138, 146, 164
Hockey Development Council 93, 94, 103
Horcoff, John 100, 108, 109, 149
Hughes, Thomas "Tom Brown's School Days 27
Hunter, Bill 109, 110
Irvin, Dick, Sr. 49
Jack Adams Award 61, 74, 127, 134, 139, 160
Johnson, "Badger" Bob 156
Johnston, Mike 22, 67, 68, 166, 167
Johnston, Mike (with Ryan Walter) "Simply the Best" 38, 66, 75, 94, 116, 165
Jones, Terry 110, 132, 133, 136, 137
Kamsack Cyclones 32, 34
Keenan, Mike 75, 107, 117, 129, 143
King, Dave 22, 43, 75, 94, 95, 123, 125-127, coaching career 128-129; 138, 143, 155, 156, 162, 167, 169
Kingston, George 4, 5, 6, 13, 22, 64, 65, 66, coaching career 67; 69, 75, 76, 78, 93, 94, 95, 102, 103, 108, 122, 126, 128, 132, 142, 150, 152, 155, 156, 158-161, 164, 167, 169
Kokudo Bunnies 104, 119-120
Kulagin, Boris "Chuckles" 5, 99
Lacombe (Sr) Rockets 59, 79, 81, 98
Lariviere, George 76, 95
Lindsay, Bob 33, 34-35
Liskowich, Bill 105
Litzenberger, Eddie 25
Lowe, Kevin 15
Ludwig, Jack 6, 8, 93
Martin, Jacques 15, 107
McDonald, Brian 68, 69, 83
McDonald, Dennis 93-97, 156
McKnight, Steve 100, 102, 109, 112
McLaren, Don 145, 146
MacTavish, Craig 104, 112
McMaster Marlins 70
Medicine Hat Tigers 29, 47, 54, 107
Messier, Doug 79
Middleton, Brian 100, 102, 108, 109, 123-124
Mikhailov, Boris 12, 135, 136
Molstad, Ed 82, 83, 90, 122
Montgomery, Wes and Val 116
Montreal Canadiens vs. Central Red Army, 1975 10, 138
Moores, Bill 16, 19, 22, 26, 69, 75, 76, 88, 97, 103, coaching career 104; 105, 107, 116, 119, 120, 122, 123, 126, 127, 142-146, 149, 151-154, 164, 167
Murdock, Bob 127, 144, 152, 155, 157, 158, 160, 162
Murray, Andy 22, 75, 112, 146-150, 164, 166, 167
National Coaching Certification Program (NCCP) 76, 78, 93-96, 98, 104, 105, 107, 126, 128, 148, 156, 157, 158, 159, 160, 164, 166
Newbolt, Sir Henry 18, 27, 28
Olson, Ted 121-122, 153
Overland, Wayne 8, 86, 111
Pachal, Vern 25, 26, 30, 63, 65, 66, 67, 68, 69, 71, 123, 124, 143
Pearn, Perry 16, 22, 75, 105, 106, coaching career 107; 108, 112, 127, 166, 167, 168
Penticton Vees 5, 29, 34, path to world championship (1955) 46-57, 79, 120, 129
Pioneers' Panel 159, 164
Poplawski, Ted 104
Posner, Michael 12
Primeau, Kevin 100, 116, 117, 121, 133, 134, 138, coaching career 149, 150
Prystai, Metro 25, 26, 28, 61
Quinn, Hal 12
Quinn, Pat 15, 75
Renney, Tom 22, 75, 96, 112, 124, 128, 162-164, 166, 167, 168, 169
Rupp, Adolph 60
Sabetzki, Dr. Gunther 39, 42, 57
Schmitter, Fritz 42, 43, 46, 47
Schneider, Val 82, 83
Scriver, Stephen "All Star Poet!" 2, 86, 88
Severin, George 124
Shero, Fred 61, 69, 74, 95
Shore, Eddie 26, 63, 65, 66, 68
Smith, Austin 58, 62-63, 65, 67, 69, 71, 79, 96, 124
Smith, Dr. Donald 35, 36, 39, 58, 60, 61,
Smith, Dr. Murray 21, 23, 36-38, 58, 60, 61, 62, 65, 67, 68, 81, 110, 151, 166
Spengler Cup 24, 67, 129, 144, 145 148, 151
Spring, Don 116, 134, 138, 151
Springfield Indians (AHL) 26, 47, 63
Strathcona High School (Scona Comp, Edmonton) 36, 58
Tarasov, Anatoly 5, 7, 77, 97, 124, 132, 137, 167
Thurston, Eric 76, 150, 154
Tikhonov, Viktor 12, 13, 136
University Arena 36, 46, 58, 108
Van Vliet, Maury 35, 61, 62, 81, 82
Vanier Cup 36, 82, 83, 85
Varsity Arena 8, 108, 112, 116, 123, 124, 126
Warwick, Bill 29, 47, 48, 50-57
Warwick, Dick 29, 30, 33, 47, 48, 51, 54-57
Warwick, Grant 29, 40, 47, 48, 54, 56, 57
Waterloo (Sr) Mercurys (Edmonton) 9, 15
Watson, Ron 68-70, 71, 81, 83, 92, 96, 98, 122
Watt, Tom 4, 5, 69, 76, 78, 80, 82, 90, 98, 101, 102, 108, 117, 126, 127, 129, 131, 133, 134, 135, 136, 138, 139, 155, 159, 160, 164
Western Canada Intercollegiate Athletic Association (WCIAU) 33, 36, 38, 58, 69, 70, 83
Winnipeg Jets (NHL) 36, 99, 107, 127, 133, 134, 152, 155-157
Winnipeg Jets (WHA) 9, 118
Winter Olympics, 1980 24, 129-137
Winter Olympics, 1968 5, 90
Winter Olympics, 2006 52
Winter Universiade, 1972 5, 98,
Winter Universiade, 1975 109
Winter Universiade, 1981 24, 142 143
Winter Universiade, 1987 24, 150 151
Wintermute, Dick 67, 68, 69, 71, 100, 105
Wooden, John 24, 86, 114, 149
World ice hockey championship, 1955 49-56
World junior hockey championship 13, 15, 105, 107, 128
Yorkton (SK) Collegiate 34
Zemrau, Ed 79, 98